THE BLOUDY TENENT

OF PERSECUTION FOR CAUSE OF

CONSCIENCE

CLASSICS OF RELIGIOUS LIBERTY 2

BAPTISTS

HISTORY, LITERATURE, THEOLOGY, HYMNS

WALTER B. SHURDEN
GENERAL EDITOR

This series explores Baptists in all facets of Baptist life and thought. Open-ended and inclusive, this series seeks to publish works that advance understanding of where Baptists have been, where they are, and where they are tending. It will promote the exploration and investigation of Baptist history; publish classics of Baptist literature including letters, diaries, and other writings; offer analyses of Baptist theologies; and examine the role of Baptists in societies and cultures both in the US and abroad.

Walter B. Shurden is the Callaway Professor of Christianity in the Roberts Department of Christianity and Executive Director of the Center for Baptist Studies, Mercer University, Macon, GA.

Of related interest

Thomas Helwys, *A Short Declaration of the Mystery of Iniquity* (1611/1612); edited by Richard Groves
    Classics of Religious Liberty 1

John Taylor, *Baptists on the American Frontier: A History of Ten Baptist Churches of Which the Author Has Been Alternately a Member* 1823/1827 [2nd]; Edited and Introduced by Chester Raymond Young

THE BLOUDY TENENT

OF PERSECUTION FOR CAUSE OF

CONSCIENCE

discussed in
A Conference between
TRUTH and PEACE.
Who,
In all tender Affection, present to the High
Court of Parliament, (as the result of
their Discourse) these, (among other
Passages) of highest consideration.

CLASSICS OF RELIGIOUS LIBERTY 2

ROGER WILLIAMS

Edited by
Richard Groves
Introduced by
Edwin Gaustad

Mercer University Press
2001

(Originally, printed in 1644 in London)

ISBN 0-86554-766-1
MUP/H578

© 2001 Mercer University Press
6316 Peake Road
Macon, Georgia 31210-3960

First Edition.

∞The paper used in this publication meets the minimum requirements of American National Standard for Information Sciences—Permanence of Paper for Printed Library Materials, ANSI Z39.48-1992.

Library of Congress Cataloging-in-Publication Data

CIP data are available from the Library of Congress

TABLE OF CONTENTS

To Edwin Gaustad,
Whose devotion to religious liberty
is unsurpassed

PREFACE

hen Roger Williams landed in London in the summer of 1643, in hopes of securing a charter for the struggling colony he had founded, England was deep in the throes of civil war. Archbishop Laud was imprisoned in the Tower. King Charles had fled London. That very summer the Westminster Assembly held the first of twelve hundred meetings to reform religion in England. Edwin Gaustad describes the political and social scene: "Nothing stable, nothing certain, nothing beyond question or challenge—Roger Williams' very own element."[1]

In pursuit of his political aims, Williams spent much of his time lobbying members of Parliament, especially the eighteen members of the commission who had the responsibility of making the final decision, and attending sessions of the Westminster Assembly.

When he was not attending to matters related to his effort to obtain a charter for the Providence Plantation, Williams busied himself performing pastoral duties among the poor. He later wrote that while in London, his time was "eaten up in attendance upon the service of Parliament or city, for the supply of the poor of the city with wood (during the stop of coal from Newcastle, and the mutiny of the poor for firing)."[2]

He also used spare moments to write. During his fifteen-month stay in London, he published: a twenty page pamphlet, *Queries of Highest Consideration*, addressed to Five Dissenting Brethren and beyond them to Parliament; *A Key Into the Language of America*, a book about Native Americans, which brought Williams instant notoriety in England; *Mr. Cotton's Letter Examined and Answered*, a response to a letter written by John Cotton; and *The Bloudy Tenent of Persecution*, his most well-known book.

---

[1] Edwin Gaustad, *Liberty of Conscience: Roger Williams in America* (Grand Rapids, Michigan: William B. Eerdman's Publishing Company, 1991) 59.

[2] *The Bloudy Tenent Yet More Bloudy.* Cited by Caldwell in his 1867 introduction to *The Bloudy Tenent of Persecution*, iii.

Commenting on the conditions under which *The Bloudy Tenent* was written, Williams later wrote, "God is a most holy witness that these mediations were fitted for public view in change of rooms and corners, yea, sometimes (upon occasion of travel in the country concerning that business of fuel) in variety of strange houses, sometimes in the fields, in the midst of travel; where he has been forced to gather and scatter his loose thoughts and papers."[3]

Small wonder that in Edward Underhill's estimate, "(the book) bears evident tokens of haste, and occasional obscurities show that he had found no time to amend his work."[4] Edwin Gaustad is more blunt in his appraisal. He said that the book is "messy....Under the best of circumstances, Williams was not a great stylist. Under these far from ideal circumstances, style suffered even more."[5]

The Bloudy Tenent went through two printings in its first year of publication, probably because copies of the first printing were burned. Writing just three years later, Samuel Richardson asked "whether the priests were not the cause of the burning of the book entitled, *The Bloudy Tenent*, because it was against persecution?"[6] Williams claimed that it was burned "by the Presbyterian party (then prevailing)."[7] The two printings were almost identical. One difference was that the first printing included a table of errata; in the second printing the errata were corrected. There was also a slight title change from the first printing to the second. In the first printing the title was *The Bloudy Tenent of Persecution, tenent* being the plural of the Latin *teneo*, meaning an opinion held by more than one person. In the second printing the title was *The Bloudy Tenet of Persecution, tenet* being the singular of *teneo*. Caldwell was of the opinion that the change was likely the choice of the printer, since Williams continued to use *tenent* eight years later in *The Bloudy Tenent Yet More Bloudy*. He also points out that *tenent* was used as late as 1726 by Wollaston in his *Religion of Nature*.

Williams began his book with several customary introductory pieces. The first piece consists of a listing of twelve theses that Williams intended

<hr/>

[3] Ibid.

[4] Edward Bean Underhill, in the introduction to his 1848 edition of *The Bloudy Tenent of Persecution.* xxxiii.

[5] Edwin Gaustad, 69.

[6] *Tracts on Liberty of Conscience*, 270. Cited by Caldwell, xiii.

[7] "Letter of John Cotton, March 26, 1671." Cited by Caldwell, xiii.

to develop in the book. The theses included bold statements in opposition to persecution for cause of conscience and in support of liberty of conscience and the separation of church and state. Underhill titled it "Syllabus of the Work" in his 1848 edition, though it was untitled in the first edition. I have followed Underhill in this regard.

The second introductory piece was addressed "To the Right Honourable, Both Houses of the High Court of Parliament." Williams pleaded with the members of Parliament to break the cycle of religious persecution that had taken the lives of thousands of Protestants and Catholics in the preceding century in England, saying, "Whatever way of worshipping God your own consciences are persuaded to walk in, yet, from any bloody act of violence to the consciences of others, it may never be told at Rome nor Oxford that the parliament of England has committed a greater rape than if they had forced or ravished the bodies of all women in the world."

In the third introductory piece, addressed "To Every Courteous Reader," Williams claimed that "two mountains of crying guilt lie heavy upon the backs of all men that name the name of Christ, in the eyes of Jews, Turks, and pagans:…the blasphemies of their idolatrous inventions, superstitions, and most unchristian conversations…(and) the bloody, irreligious, and inhuman oppressions and destructions under the mask or veil of the name of Christ."

The body of the book begins with an excerpt from a book titled *An Humble Supplication to the King's Majesty, as it was presented, 1620,* though Williams titled the book *Scriptures and Reasons Written Long Since by a Witness of Jesus Christ, Close Prisoner in Newgate, Against Persecution in Cause of Conscience, and Sent Some While Since to Mr. Cotton.* The anonymous author (Williams claims that it was written in milk by John Murton, who was a prisoner for sake of conscience in Newgate Prison in London) made a cogent case for liberty of conscience (religious liberty) citing scriptures; the works of "famous princes," including King James; and "ancient and later writers," from Hilary, Tertullian and Jerome, to Martin Luther.

William's inclusion of the next piece, "The Answer of John Cotton of Boston, in New England, to the Aforesaid Arguments Against Persecution for Cause of Conscience," was controversial in his own time. John Cotton said that Williams had sent the excerpt from the *Humble Supplication* to him around 1635, and that he (Cotton) had written his response in a personal letter to Williams. He claimed that Williams, "against the law of the love of the Gospel, and without my knowledge, published it, with his reply, adding thereto a refutation." Williams' version of events was that he had never corresponded with Cotton on this subject. Rather, Cotton had received the *Humble Supplication* from a minister in Roxbury, to whom Cotton's response was addressed. The minister sent the papers to Williams already printed. Williams concluded that the papers were not private, and included them in his book. This was not the first or last time Williams and Cotton found themselves at cross purposes.

Williams' response to Cotton's reply to *An Humble Supplication*, in the form of a dialogue between Truth and Peace, occupies a major portion of *The Bloudy Tenent.*

The last section of the book, "A Model of Church and Civil Power," was also a source of conflict between Williams and Cotton. Williams claimed that Cotton "and the ministers of New England" were the authors of the work, and that they sent it to the church in Salem. He said that the work was a "further confirmation of the bloody doctrine of persecution for cause of conscience." Cotton said Williams' claim was a "double falsehood:" He did not write it, and the ministers who wrote it did not sent it to the church in Salem. Cotton was certainly aware of the piece. At the conclusion of his reply to the *Humble Supplication,* he referred to "a treatise sent to some of the brethren late of Salem, who doubted as you do."

Two hundred years after the first printing of *The Bloudy Tenent,* the Hanserd Knollys Society in England published a new edition, under the direction of Edward Bean Underhill, one of two honorary secretaries of the society. In 1867 the Narragansett Club published Samuel L. Caldwell's edition of *The Bloudy Tenent.* Caldwell's edition was included in the publication of *The Complete Works of Roger Williams* (1963).

Both editions are excellent. Their differences are mainly in style. Caldwell followed Williams' first edition "literally," even to the point of including the original table of contents with the page references to the first edition rather than to his own edition. Underhill adjusted the page numbers to his work. Underhill included four items at the end of the table of contents that do not appear in either Caldwell or the first edition. Caldwell's literal approach also preserved archaic spellings as well as verb and pronominal endings, e.g. "Sathan useth excellent arrowes to bad markes...." Underhill modernized, by mid-nineteenth standards, spellings and verb and pronoun endings. Caldwell even reproduced the symbol that stood for both "s" and "f," and used it consistently throughout his work. Underhill did not. Both editions retained Williams' extensive use of marginalia—comments printed in the margins of the text, in some cases expanding the content of the text. Caldwell and Underhill tracked down many references that Williams, in his haste, had not bothered to include in his work. These references were included in footnotes in the two editions, along with extensive commentary. Underhill appended to his edition another piece, *Mr. Cotton's Letter, Lately Printed, Examined and Answered*, which was published in 1644 when Williams was in London. This piece, a response to a letter to Williams from John Cotton, was not attached to the first edition, and it is not appended to Caldwell's edition. It is included in volume I of Williams' *Collected Words (1963)*. It is not included in this edition.

My procedure was to work from a printed copy of the first edition that is available on microfilm, with continual reference to Underhill's edition and Caldwell's. Stylistically, this edition is more similar to Underhill's edition than to Caldwell's. Following Underhill, I chose to substitute modern spellings, verb and pronominal endings for archaic seventeenth century spellings and endings. I did not, however, substitute currently used words for obscure words. Obscure language is explained in footnotes. Scripture references that were inserted by Underhill, were retained, set off by brackets; it was necessary to make corrections in the few instances in which he made a mistake in tracking down a text.

In most (but not all) instances I was able to replace the references cited by Underhill and Caldwell—often sixteenth and seventeenth century editions that would be difficult or impossible for the reader to locate—with more recent editions.

I chose not to include Williams' marginalia, for two reasons: first, they rarely add significant information to the text; second, by causing the text to be narrowed on every page, they add significantly to the length of the book. Where a marginal note added significantly to the content of the text, I placed it in a footnote. I omitted marginal notes that in my opinion do not make a substantive addition to the text.

I have included Williams' original table of contents as an appendix to this work, with page references to this edition. A word needs to be said about the original table of contents. Whereas readers are accustomed to expecting a table of contents to outline the basic elements of the book,

Williams' original table of contents outlined, sequentially, ideas that were set forward in the text. Consequently, the items in the table of contents do not correspond to chapters in the book. The value of the original table of contents is not its usefulness in helping the reader make his or her way through the book, but in the pithiness in which the various entries sometimes capture an idea in the text.

It has been noted that, due to the circumstances under which it was written and published, *The Bloudy Tenent* shows the marks of haste. Chapters are sometimes misnumbered. Listings can become confusing, especially when Williams changes forms in mid-stream, e.g., "First," "2," etc. Often there are listings within listings, and Williams was not careful to alter the forms to make it easier for the reader to follow his thought. In order to be as literal as possible, while still making the book more "reader friendly," I have reproduced the text as it was originally printed, even when specific details are out of order, mistaken, or unnecessarily con-fusing. I have attempted to explain the disorder, mistake, or con-fusion in footnotes.

I would not have been able to complete this work without the aid of scholars who offered their expertise. I would like to thank Stephen Boyd, department of religion, Wake Forest University, for tracking down sometimes obscure bibliographic references in the original text; John Woodard, curator of the Baptist Collection at the Z. Smith Reynolds Library, Wake Forest University, for making the resources of his outstanding archives available to me; Richard Barnett, department of history, retired, Wake Forest University, for his assistance in searching out sometimes minute details of seventeenth century English history; Rebecca Wall, department of English, Winston-Salem State University, for invaluable assistance in converting seventeenth and nineteenth century grammar into forms that are more familiar to modern readers; Edwin Gaustad, professor emeritus of history at the University of California, Riverside, for lending his support of this project in the form of an excellent historical introduction; James Powell, department of classical languages, Wake Forest University, for assistance with Latin translations; and numerous friends and colleagues who offered their support and encouragement.

Richard Groves
Winston-Salem, North Carolina

SERIES FOREWORD

As Baptists enter a new millennium, they number approximately 43 million members in over 200 countries in every continent of the world. Almost 400 hundred years ago English refugees, seeking to breathe the heady air of freedom, established the first little Baptist congregation in 1609 in Amsterdam, Holland. About thirty years later, Baptists founded their first church in North America at Providence, Rhode Island. Both in the old world and the new, they struggled valiantly to survive and to witness to their faith. Hassled, heckled, and persecuted both in England and America in the seventeenth century, Baptists of the twenty-first century now have evolved to become the largest Protestant denominational family in North America. It is, therefore, an appropriate time for Mercer University Press to launch a publishing venture called *Baptists*.

Characterized by diversity from their very beginning, Baptists express themselves today in such a variety of ways that many who claim the Baptist name will not claim others who claim the exact same name! Baptists differ today—and they did from their beginning—in what they believe, how they worship, their attitudes toward other Christians, and their understanding of what is most important in Christian discipleship. Baptist pluralism, however, reaches far beyond their understanding of the gospel. Their diversity is social, economic, racial, and geographical. A history of four centuries of fragmentation and controversy has only compounded the complex appearance of the Baptist family. To speak of Baptists, therefore, as a monolithic group is impossible. No single tradition or group of Baptists captures the enormous variety in Baptist life.

Despite the pluralism of Baptists, one can still identify some prominent and universal "convictional genes" of Baptists. These several Baptist convictions are all rooted in a singular, common principle. It is called *the voluntary principle in religion*, and it is the core value of Baptist life. The voluntary principle means

that for faith to be valid, it must be free;
that coercion of any kind and all kinds is excluded from the realm of
*   religion;*
that the only conversion that counts is conversion by conviction;
that cramming a creed down a person's throat is rape of the soul;
that where there is no autonomy, there is no authenticity;
that God alone is Lord of the conscience.

The *voluntary principle in religion* impacts three basic Baptist convictions. These are the Baptist understanding of (1) the individual and Christian discipleship, (2) the church and its essential nature, and (3) the state and its relation to the liberty of conscience.

First, in terms of Christian discipleship, Baptists believe that God left each individual free to affirm Christ as Lord of Life. This is a voluntary act. No one imposes this on the individual, not the church, not the state, not even God. While saved completely by God's grace and not by human accomplishments, the individual must accept God's grace and submit to God's will. Baptists, therefore, believe that one does not become a Christian automatically, sacramentally, or institutionally through baptism or the Lord's Supper. For this reason, Baptists historically have baptized only "believers," those who can make a conscious, individual, and voluntary submission to the will of God. Baptist opposition to infant baptism stems from the belief that infants cannot choose and that proxy faith is not faith at all. Baptist Christians contend that the Christian faith is personal, experiential, and voluntary. Every baptismal pool in every Baptist church throughout the world is a testimony to the voluntary principle in religion.

Second, in terms of the church, Baptist voluntarism means that Christians voluntarily covenant together with others who have trusted Christ as Lord of their lives, and, under God's Spirit, create together a local believers church. Faith begins privately, in the lonely soul of the individual, but it is rooted firmly in a local congregation of believers. Thorough congregationalists in church government, Baptists vest all decision-making authority in the hands of the members of the local congregation and in no outside agency or institution, whether of church or state.

Baptist Christians who voluntarily covenant with each other to form a local church are free, under Christ's Lordship, to determine their membership, which they insist should be of believers only. Calling this a "regenerate church membership," Baptists try to safeguard the regenerate nature of that membership by practicing believer's baptism by immersion. The "believer's" part of baptism dominated among the earliest Baptists. Over the years, however, "immersion," as the mode of baptism, has also become a Baptist hallmark.

As local Baptist churches determine their membership, they also choose their own leadership, pastoral and otherwise. No outside organization of church or state can impose leaders on Baptist churches. Rather, local Baptist churches, acting only under Christ's sovereignty, ordain whom they wish to the ministry of Christ. Without priesthood or hierarchy, Baptists affirm that all church members stand on equal footing and serve as priests before God, to the church, and for the world.

Just as Baptist churches choose their own leadership, they also determine their own order of worship and work. Both the liturgy and the mission of each local church is determined by the members of that local church. Likewise, Baptists voluntarily participate in the larger Body of Christ, including denominational and ecumenical entities. Every local Baptist church in the world, with its membership, its leadership, its liturgy, its ministries, and its participation with other Christian bodies, is a testimony to the voluntary principle in religion.

Third, in terms of the state, the voluntary principle in religion shaped Baptists into ardent advocates of liberty of conscience, including freedom *of* religion, freedom *for* religion, and freedom *from* religion. Among other reasons, Baptists championed religious liberty because of their belief that God alone is Lord of the conscience. Also, Baptists confronted religious constrictionism because they believed that a freely and voluntarily chosen faith is the only valid faith.

During the first half of the seventeenth century, Baptists in England peppered both royalty and religion with some of the first and most forceful tracts ever written on religious liberty. John Smyth, Thomas Helwys, Leonard Busher, and John Murton, among others, led the Baptist parade for freedom of conscience.

In America, Baptists in the seventeenth century tangled with religious establishmentarianism at both the courthouse and the church house. Joining their British Baptist counterparts, Baptists in the colonies declared unceasing war on religious tyranny. John Clarke, Obadiah

Holmes, and especially Roger Williams articulated the Baptist position on soul liberty that would endure until the present moment.

How, therefore, could Mercer University Press better begin a new publishing series entitled *Baptists* than with the first edition in over a hundred years of *The Bloody Tenent of Persecution for Cause of Conscience* by Roger Williams? Originally published in 1644, Williams's book appeared, says eminent Baptist historian of American religion Edwin Gaustad, "not to great acclaim but to devouring flames" (xvi). Williams courageously challenged the conventional wisdom of his day on matters of church and state, arguing that compulsion in religion was contrary to mercy, peace, common sense, and the Spirit of Christ. Additionally, he rooted his arguments for voluntarism in humanitarian, biblical, and historical grounds. The thought of Roger Williams is Exhibit A of what Baptists have meant by *the voluntary principle in religion.* Anyone who knows anything at all about Baptist history understands that Roger Williams, though he established the first Baptist church in America, remained a Baptist only a matter of months. Despite that fact, Williams reflected and shaped the Baptist struggle for religious liberty in America among the Baptist people for two hundred additional years. His *Bloody Tenent* must surely find enthusiastic admission into the canon of Baptist classics. To include it as the initial publication in this series on *Baptists*, is, therefore, a delight for me as the editor of the series.

Richard Groves, who worked with Mercer University Press in 1998 to produce a significant new edition of Thomas Helwys's *A Short Declaration of The Mystery of Iniquity,* has increased our indebtedness to him with his arduous and careful editing of this classic by Roger Williams. A working pastor, Groves's editorial work challenges Baptist pastors, Baptist historians, and Baptist theologians to reengage the intellectual tradition of the Baptist people.

In securing Edwin Gaustad to write a historical introduction to this edition of *The Bloody Tenent,* Groves enormously multiplied the value of this particular volume. Gaustad is not only one of the world's finest Baptist historians, he is also one of America's ablest interpreters of American religion. Additionally, he is a devout and discerning student of Roger Williams.

In the future, you will find in this series on *Baptists* more new, critical editions of Baptist classics, such as this monumental work by Williams. You also will discover valuable secondary interpretations of Baptist life which will help clarify and focus the Baptist contributions to culture, both in America and around the world. Welcome to the *Baptists*.

Walter B. Shurden is the Callaway Professor of
Christianity in the Roberts Department of Christianity
and Executive Director of the Center for Baptist Studies,
Mercer University, Macon, GA.

HISTORICAL INTRODUCTION

EDWIN GAUSTAD

Roger Williams's *Bloudy Tenent* was not widely read in the seventeenth century for two substantial reasons: first, his ideas were so shocking that the English Parliament ordered that the book be burned; and, second, the book, hastily written and hastily printed, did not prove particularly inviting to the potential reader. And, to be perfectly honest, his book has not been widely read since the seventeenth century. It is no longer burned, just ignored, or virtually impossible to find. Richard Groves has taken a major and welcome step with respect to the accessibility of the *Bloudy Tenent*. He has given us a new edition—the first in over one hundred years—that makes the book once more widely available. But far beyond that, he has painstakingly refined the text so that the book can be actually read, not just held up for viewing as a quaint and dusty artifact. And the world, since the 1640s, has taken major and welcome steps that make the horrifying notion of religious liberty is no longer something to be suppressed, denounced, or treated with utter contempt. Thanks in no small part to Roger Williams himself. Religious liberty can even be embraced. This liberty is, in fact, what James Madison referred to as "the lustre of our country."

So one no longer has any good excuse for avoiding an exciting encounter with the book that stands at the head of the stream that flows through toleration acts in England and elsewhere, through constitutions in the United States and around the world, and through declarations of universal human rights to be proclaimed and pursued. In 1644, liberty was unleashed, to the boundless benefit of all humankind in the centuries follow.

Where does *The Bloudy Tenent* fit in the life and thought of Roger Williams? First, with respect to the life. Born in London around 1603, Williams attended Cambridge University (Pembroke College) and entered the ministry of the Church of England. He was, however, sympathetic to the Puritan wing of that national church, the faction seeking to reform Anglicanism in the direction of a more consistent Protestantism. Such Protestantism would discard the accumulated traditions of centuries, returning to the Bible, and particularly to the New Testament, in order to create a "purified" and true church of Christ. Some Puritans thought that they could reform the Church of England from within: that is, by degrees rid it of all lingering taints of Roman Catholicism and all authoritarian rule of persecuting bishops. Other Puritans despaired of ever achieving a meaningful reform in this gradual, piece-meal fashion. These Puritans advocated a clean break from the national church, a complete separation. This position may have had the force of logic behind it, but it also had the force of the state against it. For no separation from the official church was either legal or tolerable. And so Separatists had to flee, secretly to Holland, or—with some connivance—to America.

Williams would ultimately align himself with this second group: the Separatists. Initially, however, he joined with the large migration to America of Puritans who wanted to remain in England's national church, but create in a new world the model of what a New Testament church would really look like. Near the end of the year 1630, Roger, with his wife, Mary, boarded a ship in Bristol, England, and headed out across a forbidding Atlantic Ocean to the Massachusetts Bay Colony launched only a few months before. Arriving on 5 February 1631, the young married couple encountered a winter more severe than any they had known in England. They also found foodstuffs in short supply, and housing of the most primitive sort. The tiny colony teetered on the edge of survival.

Williams was prepared for hardship. He was not prepared, however, for the prevailing sentiment among these early settlers to remain with the Church of England, while trying to reform it. This "middle walking," as he called it—neither wholly in the Church nor wholly separate from it—struck Williams as an untenable position. He likened it to trying to build a square house on the keel of a ship, or in another figure, to trying to walk a straight path with one foot in the ditch and the other on the road. How much better it would be, he argued, to start afresh, not worrying about bishops or books of common prayer or kneeling or making the sign of the cross—or doing many other things that the New Testament did not require. And so, when Williams was asked to become pastor of the one and only church in Boston, he declined, saying "I durst not officiate to an unseparated people, as upon examination and conference I found them to be." Williams would not "act with a doubting Conscience," not now in 1631, nor in any of the years that followed.

So he retreated from Boston to Salem, where a church founded three years earlier showed more signs of independence and a leaning toward Separatism. He and Mary soon moved even farther southwest from Boston to the Plymouth Colony that had been founded by Separatists ten years before. For about two years the young couple lived there and welcomed their firstborn, a son, into the world in August 1633. All the while Roger Williams reflected upon what Separatism required, what allegiance to the New Testament demanded, and what a liberty of the soul or of the conscience meant in terms of both church and civil life. When he returned to Salem late in 1633, it was to engage in controversy after controversy, winning the attention and raising the alarm of the authorities in Boston.

Not every controversy that Williams engaged in dealt directly with religious liberty, but most of them did. He expressed opposition, for example, to the civil magistrates exercising any authority over the churches. Religion must be kept wholly separate from the civil order, and the civil order from religion. Failure to maintain this separation had, since the days of the Roman Emperor Constantine, resulted in countless bloody persecutions, innumerable religious wars, and the senseless slaughter of innocent men, women, and children. If the lessons of history taught us anything at all, Williams maintained, they taught us that an officially enforced religion was contrary not only to all mercy and peace, but also contrary to the spirit of Christ. Nation after nation has brought compulsion into religion, "but so did never the Lord Jesus bring any unto his most pure worship." Demanding that men or women believe in a certain doctrine or worship in a certain way was, said Williams, like requiring "an unwilling Spouse...to enter into a forced bed." That defied all humanity, all common sense, all decency.

In the struggle to get across his shocking new ideas, even symbols were important. The English flag at this time had a bright red cross in its design, the presence of this Christian icon in the nation emblem being a clear mixing of politics and religion, of nationalism and faith. Some citizens of Salem grew so agitated over this issue that they rudely cut the cross out of the flag, an act that again caught the uneasy attention of the Boston fathers. Whether Williams had personally performed this surgery on the national flag was never examined: it was simply assumed that he stood behind every radical act or thought coming out of Salem. And certainly in most cases this was true.

Another mixing of politics and religion troubled Williams: the requirement that every oath of office or of loyalty to the colony conclude with the words, "so help me God." Fine for those that believe in God, said Williams, but what sense does it make to demand of the unbeliever that he too swear, "so help me God"? Was this not taking the name of "the Lord thy God" in vain? But, his opponents sputtered in reply, the name of God is invoked as a witness to all legal contracts, to all treaties and testimonies, and who is to inquire whether all parties to such agreements are believers or not? Beside, what possible difference could it make? No difference at all, Williams would readily concede, if the liberty of conscience made no difference. But if a pure heart and a sincere faith ranked above empty form and ritual, then the difference was monumental. The magistrate should deal with all citizens as equal members of a civil society, keeping his clumsy hands out of all matters related to a religious conscience. The church, on its part, should strive to keep itself unspotted from the world—pure and undefiled, in the words of the New Testament.

If the governor and his assistants in the Massachusetts Bay Colony were keeping count of the "absurdities" pouring forth from Williams's mind and mouth (and they were), Williams obligingly gave them even more grounds for moving against him. The Massachusetts colonists claimed their lands, he declared, without a proper legal title, for the land belonged—not to King Charles I—but to the Indians! Until and unless the Boston authorities paid an appropriate price to the Indians for *their* land, the colonists were trespassers and their charter was void. What folly! Governor John Winthrop responded that land which "lies common, and hath been replenished or subdued is free to any that possess or improve it." And his ministerial ally in the growing contest with Williams, John Cotton of Boston's church, scornfully observed: "We did not conceive that it is a just title to so vast a continent, to make no other improvement of millions of acres in it, but only to burn it up for pastime." But why waste time trying to reason with a man who was clearly beyond the reach of reason? The time had come for action, not words.

The General Court of Massachusetts, the ultimate legislative, executive, and judicial authority of the Bay Colony, summoned Williams to appear before it (and not for the first time) in October, 1635. In a colony only five years old and still struggling for its survival, if not its place in history, this radical insurgent could be tolerated no longer. He had defied all civil authorities, had questioned the purity and integrity of the colony's churches, and had even challenged the validity of the charter itself. He had been warned, repeatedly. Now, he was given one last chance to recant and repent, but he would not. Again, he would not "act with a doubting Conscience." Therefore, the Court would act, with the assurance that it had no other choice. "Whereas Mr. Roger Williams, one of the elders of the church at Salem, hath broached & divulged diverse new & dangerous opinions," the Court began, and whereas he had questioned and defamed both magisterial and clerical authority without hint of retraction or repentance, "it is therefore ordered that the said Mr. Williams shall depart out of this jurisdiction within six weeks."

Exile and rejection. From those with whom he had labored and to whom he had brought his most earnest reflection and pastoral instruction, he received not bread but a stone. Massachusetts Bay Colony would have nothing more to do with him. And so in a story that has become a familiar epic in American history, the solitary Roger Williams made his way through the winter snows and a "howling wilderness" to the headwaters of Narragansett Bay where he purchased some land from the Indians and named the tiny settlement Providence, "in a sense of God's merciful Providence to me in my distress." Thus was Rhode Island born, and the first haven of religious liberty in the new world created.

Much of what followed is not directly relevant to this introduction to the *Bloudy Tenent*, but it is important to note that in his controversy with the Bay Colony authorities lay the seeds of the book that would emerge nine years later. His letters written and received in the late 1630s and early 1640s (many of them unfortunately lost) reveal that his stance on behalf of religious liberty had softened not one whit. It only intensified, partly because now it had become so personal. Williams resented his expulsion in 1635 and never stopped resenting it for the remainder of his life. He could perhaps understand if his ideas were such that the church in Salem saw fit to excommunicate him. But why did that require that he also be expelled from the "common earth and air" of his fellow citizens? Why, indeed, unless the church and the Bay Colony were one? And that, of course, was the very point Williams had labored to make: politics and religion, church and state, have come together in one great and costly confusion. "The Commonwealth and the Church is yet but one," Williams wrote, "and he that is banished from the one, must necessarily be banished from the other also."

In these years immediately after the exile, Pastor John Cotton of Boston emerges as the chief antagonist of Roger Williams—as he is in *The Bloudy Tenent* itself. Cotton saw Williams as one suffering from a "holier than thou complex." He would be more faithful to the New Testament than anyone else, more dedicated to a pure church than anyone else, and certainly more concerned about the liberty of conscience than anybody else. He charges us with "middle walking," Cotton noted, that we halt half-way between Christ and the Anti-Christ. But, replied Cotton, "we conceive the Lord hath guided us to walk with an even foot between two extremes." "This moderation," Cotton concluded, "we see no cause to repent of." Williams, on the other hand, Cotton charged, thinks that radical surgery is the only cure for any problem; never is he willing to consider patient instruction and gradual amelioration.

From the perspective of Roger Williams, the Bay Colony churches had started down the proper path of separation, but had suddenly stopped. They had abandoned bishops, had dropped the Book of Common Prayer, had drawn their church members only from those who could tell of their experience of saving grace. But, for heaven's sake and the churches' sake and consciences' sake, why stop there? Why allow the church and the world to get all muddled together? Why allow the sword and the spirit to intrude upon each other's domain? When God's people, Williams wrote, open "a gap in the hedge or wall of Separation between the Garden of the Church and the Wilderness of the World, God hath ever broken down the wall itself... and made his Garden a Wilderness, as at this day." So it is up to God's people to set things aright, to clear out all the weeds from His garden, to purify His church, and to keep the world's wilderness from invading the sanctity of the true church or violating the integrity of the human soul. And that, Mr. Cotton, is the sum of the controversy between us, Williams concluded in his letter of 1636.

So how much development or accommodation in the two contrasting positions occurred between 1636 and 1644? The answer is, "very little." Williams could as readily have published his views in 1636 as eight years later, if only he could have found a publisher in America. Only Boston had printing presses capable of issuing a real book (the *Bay Psalm Book* had been published in 1640 and John Eliot's Indian Bible a generation later), but Boston was in no mood to disseminate the views of Roger Williams. So the publication of *The Bloudy Tenent* had to await the trip of Roger Williams to London, primarily on other business: namely, the securing of a charter for the small and much-besieged colony of Rhode Island. At last, in 1644, Williams's book appeared, not to great acclaim but to devouring flames. More on the content of that book later, but first let us conclude with a swift summary of Williams' remaining years.

He returned to America in September of 1644, having been granted permission to dock in Boston, if he would give every assurance that he would move as quickly as possible to Providence, giving no speeches or sermons along the way. For his part, Williams was eager to be on his way, not having seen his wife in eighteen months and not having seen at all a son born soon after his departure. He carried with him not only the Parliamentary charter, but a few copies of *The Bloudy Tenent* rescued from the hands of his enemies. By November of that year, he was elected "chief officer" of his colony, and would maintain that position for three years. Now the questions of religious liberty and civil authority were more than theoretical; in the years of governance he must wrestle with the limits of each to see if a civil society could stand on a foundation of full liberty.

During his time in London, England had been plunged in a civil war, and by 1649 King Charles I was beheaded. Now, Parliament—under Oliver Cromwell—ruled. When the monarchy was restored in 1660, Williams's earlier charter, issued by Parliament would no longer suffice. Back in London as early as 1651, Williams, along with the Baptist pastor and physician in Newport, John Clarke, worked to settle territorial disputes among the Rhode Islanders themselves as well as to secure a more secure legal title to the colony's claims. (Connecticut and Massachusetts were always nipping at the heels of vulnerable Rhode Island, trying to claim its lands within their own borders.) Because the disputatious citizens of Rhode Island continued to quarrel among themselves, Williams found it necessary to return to the colony in 1654 where, now as "President," he struggled to restore some order. Clarke, meanwhile, remained in London for an astounding total of twelve years, until at last King Charles II granted Rhode Island its royal charter in

1663. That charter boldly asserted that "a most flourishing civil state may stand and best be maintained...with a full liberty in religious concernments." What a staggering proposition! What a pivotal development! John Cotton (who had died in 1652) would have been appalled; Roger Williams (who had retired from public office in 1657, but was still active in the colony's life) could only rejoice.

In 1672, Williams, though now aged and in failing health, engaged in several days of debate with the Quakers in both Newport and Providence. Because Rhode Island offered a full liberty in religion, Quakers who had been persecuted and put to death elsewhere flocked in the 1650s and 1660s to Williams's colony. Roger Williams disagreed strongly with many of the doctrines and practices of the Quakers, but—and this is the critical point—he would never allow the hand of the state to be raised against them: no fines, no whippings, no jail sentences, and no hangings. Religious liberty was for all, not just for those with whom one happened to agree.

In 1675, New England's bloodiest conflict erupted: King Philip's War. The native Americans, resentful of the growing power and numbers of the still immigrating English, struck back – with power and with effect. Roger Williams who had earlier learned the language of the New England tribes, who had often served as negotiator and diplomat between the Indians and the English, and who had in 1643 published a popular and sympathetic book on the natives (A Key Into the Language of America), now found himself helpless to halt the onslaught. Whole towns were attacked and burned to the ground, and even Roger Williams's own house in Providence was destroyed. Hundreds of lives on both sides were lost, with casualties in the thousands and property damage greater than New England had ever known, before or since. It was a dreary and sobering time for all. Trust between the English and Indians was forever broken, and Williams's hope for a different kind of relationship between the two cultures shattered.

Williams's hopes for Rhode Island also suffered many a disappointment, as "complaints and clamors," "heats and hatreds" continued to erupt among the citizens. They never seemed to recognize the opportunities afforded them, nor to revel in the fact that, as Williams pointed out, "Our Charter excels all in New England or the World, as to the Souls of Men." Sometime early in 1683, Roger Williams died. No monument marked his grave, no eulogy celebrated his life or mourned his death.

Having provided some biographical context for the publication of *The Bloudy Tenent*, we would now place that book in the intellectual context of the radical reformer's ideas. It is impossible to know when the fires of religious liberty first began to burn in the mind and heart of Roger Williams. Certainly he knew well, even as a boy, of the many Protestant martyrs burned at the stake in the reign of Mary Tudor (1553-58), known more despairingly to most Protestants as Bloody Mary as she strove to return England to the Roman Catholic fold. Some of those martyrdoms had occurred in Williams's own parish—St. Sepulchre. And virtually all of them has been memorialized, even celebrated, in John Foxe's famous *Book of Martyrs*, first published in 1563 and countless times thereafter. Religion in the sixteenth century, and even in the seventeenth, was not a matter of casual choice among roughly equal options. It was, far too often, a choice between life and death.

Williams, of course, grew up in the fold of the Church of England, the national and official church. State supported and state protected, only this Church enjoyed legal standing. Any other religious option had to be pursued privately, secretly, and at potentially great cost to both livelihood and life. To hold any office in the government, one had to be a member of this Anglican church. To be admitted to either university, Oxford or Cambridge, one had to be a member of this church. And to enjoy any social standing or hope of privilege or position, this church membership was the essential prerequisite.

If Protestants suffered under Queen Mary I, Roman Catholics suffered most thereafter. With Catholic France and Catholic Spain hovering menacingly in the background, any effort on behalf of Catholicism aroused immediate resistance and repression. After the exposure of the Gunpowder Plot in 1605 that attempted to blow up Parliament, anti-Catholicism grew even more virulent. Every November 5th, Guy Fawkes day, would be celebrated very publicly by burning the pope in effigy. Thus religion, in Williams's youthful days, was as much an affair of state as an affair of the heart.

By the time that Roger and Mary Williams boarded the Lyon in Bristol late in 1630, the newly married couple had obviously decided that much was wrong with the Church of England as it then existed. When Charles I succeeded James I on the English throne in 1625, those who hoped for more leniency or toleration in religious matters found only severe disappointment instead. King Charles believed in absolutism both

in politics and religion. And when he appointed William Laud bishop of
London in 1628 (and later Archbishop of Canterbury), he chose one who
had no sympathy at all with Puritanism or any other form of dissent.
Conformity, not freedom, was all that mattered in an England grown
increasingly hostile to reformers or troublemakers. So the young
Williams couple could only conclude, as so many other earnest English
Christians did in the 1630s, that religiously everything had to be better
three thousand miles away in a new world. Certainly, from the point of
view of Roger Williams, they could not be worse.

So with high hopes and perhaps unrealistic dreams, Williams made
the voyage to Massachusetts. Here, away from bishops and kings, one
would have the chance to create the New Testament church and give full
honor to the sacred conscience. But, of course, as we have seen, it did not
quite work out that way. Williams could not find in Massachusetts any
model that corresponded with his own image of the pure church. Later,
in Rhode Island he helped create the first Baptist church in America in
Providence in 1638. And while this church rejected infant baptism in
order to have a membership of voluntary believers only, and though it
carefully kept itself separate from the civil order, it did not long satisfy
Roger Williams as a perfect replica of the church in the New Testament.
For, after all, that church had apostles appointed directly by Christ, and
sacraments or ordinances established directly by him. No seventeenth-
century church could hope to duplicate that. So, Roger Williams
concluded after a few months in Providence's Baptist church, that one
must await the return of Christ and the re-institution of the apostolic age
in order to have the scripturally true and pure church. But one did not
need to await the return of Christ in order to seek one's own salvation,
nor did one need to wait in the effort to preserve and protect the liberty
of the soul.

So the protests in Massachusetts as well as the letters to Governor
John Winthrop and Pastor John Cotton, written from Rhode Island in
1636 and after, were promissory notes for the full payment found in *The
Bloudy Tenent*. Before calling attention to some salient points (and
powerful language) in that book, it should be noted that Williams did not
rest his case for religious liberty on humanitarian grounds alone. As he
read his scriptures, and he knew them very well in the original Hebrew
and Greek as well as in translation, the Bible demanded that its message
be propagated "armed only with the spiritual sword of the word of God,"

never by imprisonments, whippings, fines, banishment, or death (Ch. XV). In Appendix II Richard Groves has shown how frequently Williams had recourse to scripture, Old Testament and New, in his contest with John Cotton. Cotton, of course, quoted scripture at length as well, since both sides acknowledged the force of the Bible as the ultimate authority. And, as both Williams and Cotton noted, even the devil can quote scripture when it seems to his advantage to do so.

Williams, therefore, appealed to the Bible regularly and earnestly, but in addition he appealed to history, to reason, and to the essential nature of the Christian religion. Because his arguments were so novel (as well as shocking) in 1644, he came at them from every conceivable angle, repeated them often, and summarized them so that none could miss the point. The point was stated bluntly enough in his opening syllabus: "First, that the blood of so many hundred thousand souls of Protestants and papists, spilled in the wars of present and former ages for their respective consciences, is not required nor accepted by Jesus Christ, the Prince of Peace." Religious persecution has for centuries been a bloody business, the swords of conquerors and kings and magistrates of every stripe dripped with blood, and the slaying of men, women, and children for no other cause than their sincere (if differing) beliefs resulted in "oceans and oceans of blood." That is why one can only call this a *bloody* tenet. It cannot be dressed up or papered over or explained away: persecution "for cause of conscience" is about blood.

The first proposition on Williams's opening page is followed by eleven others that further shake the kingdom of England and the whole western world. The sixth, for example, is breathtaking: "It is the will and command of God that, since the coming of his Son and Lord Jesus, a permission of the most paganish, Jewish, Turkish, or anti-Christian consciences and worships be granted to all men in all nations and countries. . ." Williams is not talking about a meek and mild toleration here, where Presbyterians might be allowed to live side by side with Anglicans. He is talking about, no shouting about, FREEDOM. Even for pagans! Even for Moslems! Even for those who condemn and crusade against the Christian religion itself. No wonder that Rhode Island was regularly referred to as the sewer or latrine of New England; no wonder that it took Massachusetts over three hundred years to revoke the sentence of exile against Roger Williams. And no wonder that Parliament ordered so dangerous a book to be burned.

The final proposition is stated in less alarming tones until one considers its full implications. "Lastly, true civility and Christianity may both flourish in a state or kingdom, notwithstanding the permission of diverse and contrary consciences, either of Jew of Gentile." Here Williams takes on over a thousand years of Christian history, from the fourth century to the seventeenth, even as he takes on the near-universal practice of his day to seek or demand conformity—not diversity—in the civil order. Williams asserts, with only the example of Holland to support him, a state cannot merely survive if it offers religious liberty, it can actually flourish. Some would have been happy to burn not only the book, but its author as well.

Williams knew that this controversy concerned more than a difference of opinion between John Cotton and himself, more than a local quarrel in a puny colony or two across the Atlantic Ocean. Williams was trying to turn the tide of history, a herculean task. In also rejecting the divine right of kings and vesting governmental power in the people, he anticipated and almost certainly influenced John Locke one generation later. He was trying to move England, and others if they would follow, from a medieval world to a modern one. And he was trying to prevent future slaughters of the innocents, the past slaughters having stained so many pages of western history and having seriously soiled Christianity itself.

What, then, if his language becomes bombastic and bloody? Could anything less gain the attention of a somnolent and satisfied society all around him? If English authorities insisted on a religious conformity and persisted in persecuting all dissenters from that official approved path, then "the parliament of England has committed a greater rape than if they had forced or ravished the bodies of all the women in the world." In his preface to the "Courteous Reader," Williams notes the irony of Parliament's permitting "English Bibles in the poorest English houses," thus making it possible "for the simplest man or woman to search the scriptures." But then the tragedy: Parliament proceeded to stipulate what every one must believe. Each conscience is molded and forced in England every bit as much "as if they lived in Spain or Rome itself without the sight of a Bible." In a moving plea to his fellow countrymen, Roger Williams concludes that "Having bought truth dear, we must not sell it cheap, not the least grain of it for the whole world."

All of this merely sets the stage for the body of the book, a dialogue between Truth and Peace that enables Williams to get in as many blows as he can against Cotton and the received wisdom of the day. More than four hundred years ago, Williams pointed out, English nobles wrested a Magna Carta from a reluctant king. Now, it is time for a second Magna Carta that offers to every man, woman, and child a full liberty in religion and a total emancipation from the bloody tenet of persecution for cause of conscience. Persecution, Williams pointed out, never hits the real enemies of religion; it falls upon the "meek and peaceable of the earth" who are charged with being "rebels, factious, peace-breakers, although they deal not with the state or state matters, but matters of [a] divine and spiritual nature" (Ch. XVII). Similarly, religious oaths and religious tests never screen out the hypocrite who is prepared to swear to anything that advances his career. The sincere and the innocent suffer.

In trying to find sound scriptural basis for their respective positions, both Williams and Cotton appealed to the parable of Jesus concerning the wheat and the tares (Matthew 13:24-30). When an enemy sowed tares or weeds among a farmer's wheat, the workers said to the farmer that they should rip out the weeds. But the farmer replied, "Nay, lest while ye gather up the tares, ye root up also the wheat with them. Let both grow together until the harvest...." Since Jesus has introduced this parable by saying that "The kingdom of heaven is likened unto a man which sowed good seed in his field," both men felt justified in drawing lessons regarding saints and sinners from this story. But what were the lessons?

Williams, of course, saw the parable as a justification for leaving the heretics and the orthodox both undisturbed until the Day of Judgment for only God alone knew who were His. When men tried to root out the unbelievers, they ended up destroying the truly faithful. Naturally, civil crime can be punished by civil authority, but the civil sword is far too clumsy and crude a weapon to deal with spiritual error. Wait for God's harvest; emulate God's patience (Ch. XXVI). Cotton, on the other hand, saw all this as being taken out of context. Clearly, those who hold false doctrine may be censured by the church, or even excommunicated. But beyond that, if such persons corrupt others or are in danger of doing so, then the "Civil Sword" may be used against them. To act in any other way is to expose the Commonwealth to "a dangerous and damnable infection." None of this made any sense to Williams who saw in shedding the blood of the innocent a crime greater than the blowing up of Parliament, or slittings the throats of kings or emperors—"so precious is that valuable jewel of a soul above all the present lives and bodies of all the men in the world" (Ch. XXXIII). Furthermore, if a person is truly unredeemed, what civil punishment can possibly compare with the eternal condemnation that awaits?

The arguments between Williams and Cotton flow back and forth, with Williams apologizing for the length of his treatise. Only the extreme importance of the subject, however, justifies the vigor and the length of the argument. Williams ends the first half of his book by declaring again how the bloody tenet contradicts so totally the spirit of Jesus who never used the sword, who never called upon the civil state to enforce his teaching, who said to Peter, "Put up thy sword." But instead the persecutors, following some other light, are "so deeply guilty of the blood of souls, compelled and forced to hypocrisy in a spiritual and soul-rape; so deeply guilty of the blood of the souls under the altar, persecuted in all ages for the cause of conscience, and so destructive to the civil peace and welfare of all kingdoms, countries, and commonwealths" (Ch. LXXX).

What the John Cottons, Williams Lauds, and Charleses of this suffering age have succeeded in doing is turning the world upside down as they "pluck up the roots and foundations of all common society in the world." They have reversed the natural order of things as they turn "the garden and paradise of the church and saints into the field of the civil state of the world." They manage to bring chaos out of order, reversing the divine activity of creation (Ch. CXXXXVII). Fortunately, there is "some sand left in this one-hour glass of merciful opportunity." Read and reform; read and repent; read and re-write history from this time forward. "One grain of time's inestimable sand is worth a golden mountain; let us not lose it" (Ch. CXXXVIII).

The Bloudy Tenent all by itself might seem enough of a cannonade to destroy the enemy. But not when the enemy was found on every surrounding hilltop and in every place of power. So Williams kept up the firepower as much as he was able: in private correspondence, in published treatises (published only in London, of course, never in Boston), and one must assume in personal dialogue, though no record of this survives. About the same time that Williams published *The Bloudy Tenent,* he wrote a short essay entitled *Christenings Make Not Christians.* The subject again was religious liberty, but in this instance the soul liberty of the Native Americans. Williams objected to what he saw as the forced conversion of the Indian: a stronger culture imposing its will on a weaker one. Of course, it was possible to get the Indian to attend church, to repeat some phrases, to display an outward conformity, but what Williams saw in both North and South America was "ten thousands of poor Natives, sometimes by wiles and subtle devices, sometimes by force compelling them to submit to that which they understood not." A certain kind of evangelism or missionizing could be persecution of a subtler sort.

He also fought for the attention of the members of Parliament in this same visit to London. In *Queries of Highest Consideration,* Williams proved that he could be concise when he had too. And so he made his points briefly and swiftly. (1) The ancient nation of Israel is no pattern for modern nations since Jesus displaced Moses. (2) Religious persecution is a violation of the Christian faith and, beyond that, "opposite to the very tender Bowels of Humanity." (3) A requirement of religious conformity hinders the conversion of the Jews since it does not allow them even "a civil life or being." (4) Religious persecution is the chief disturber of civil peace, and the chief murderer of men, women, and children. (5) When the state enforces religion, the soul is violated, "ravished into a dissembled Worship, which their Hearts embrace not." (6) Although both politicians and clergy profess that they seek more light, they persecute and silence those very persons from whom more light might come. Neither Parliament nor the Westminster Assembly (that powerful gathering of Presbyterians and others) found the arguments of Roger Williams persuasive in the 1640s or in the decades that followed.

When Williams returned to London in 1651, his work had been cut out for him by none other than John Cotton who in 1647 responded to *The Bloudy Tenent* with his own large treatise: *The Bloudy Tenent, Washed, and Made White in the Bloud of the Lambe.* Not to be outdone in the matter of long titles, Williams came back in 1652 with *The Bloudy Tenent Yet More Bloudy: By Mr. Cotton's Endeavor to Wash it White in the Bloud of the Lambe.* Between 1644 and 1652, Parliament had taken two steps of which Williams approved: it had cut off the head of Archbishop William Laud in 1645 and that of King Charles in 1649. This made it possible, wrote Williams, for the "most High Eternal King of Kings" to rule over England with greater effect than ever before. But Parliament had still not embraced religious liberty. Nor had Massachusetts. Neither one understood that God had granted no authority to secular rulers to reform or discipline his church; that remained the prerogative of God and of His people alone.

As for John Cotton himself, his method of argumentation, said Williams, is devious and cunning. Whenever Cotton seemed to take a clear, unequivocal stand, he always provided himself with an escape route, with "strange Reserves, and Retreats." When Williams charged Cotton with being a persecutor of conscientious souls, Cotton replied that he never persecuted, but sometimes an obstinate and stubborn conscience convicted itself. When challenged over the magistrate's interference with the church, Cotton ran as fast as he could "into the Land of Israel" to call "up Moses and his Laws." Cotton does not know that Jesus ushered in a *new* testament and a *new* dispensation, that the Old Testament pattern of a national church was unique to that time and place and cannot now be duplicated "by any Civil State in all or any of the Nations of the World beside."

But all that is mere trifle when compared to the main point: namely, that the bloody tenet is as bloody as ever, despite the best efforts of John Cotton to wash it white. "I must profess," Williams concluded, "while Heaven and Earth lasts, that no one tenent that either London, England, or the World doth harbor, is so heretical, blasphemous, seditious, and dangerous to the corporal, to the spiritual, to the present, to the Eternal Good of all Men, as the bloudy Tenent (however washed and whited) I say, as is the bloudy Tenent of persecution for cause of conscience." He had not retreated an inch. He had only dug his position deeper into the earth and, he hoped, deeper into the human heart.

No doubt Cotton would have responded yet again, except that he died in 1652, the year when *The Bloudy Tenant Yet More Bloudy* was published. But Williams still had plenty of opponents. In England, he addressed Parliament once again in that same year, in a short tract called *The Examiner Defended.* And in Massachusetts he took on Governor John Endicott in 1651 for his having been a party to the public whipping (30 lashes) of the Baptist Obadiah Holmes who had committed the grievous sin of preaching in Massachusetts. Williams was enraged: "The Maker and Searcher of Hearts knows with what bitterness I wrote," he declared. The magistrate who persecutes is, among many other things, unbelievably arrogant, for how can he look into the human heart? How can he know that he is not persecuting Christ himself? Listen carefully, governor, for a voice that cries out: "Endicott, Endicott, why huntest thou me? Why imprisonest thou me? Why finest? Why so bloodily whippest?" You have persecuted many sorts of consciences, Williams noted; "Is it beyond all possibility and hazard that I have not fought against God, that I have not persecuted Jesus in some of them?"

Williams could put hard questions as well as sharp answers, and in his civil capacity in Providence, he tried again and again to make it clear that liberty did not mean licentiousness, that freedom did not lead to anarchy. The citizens of Providence were all too ready to embrace liberty, but also ready to dodge responsibility. That will never work, Williams explained. One must as citizen pay taxes, contribute to the common defense, and practice civility. Just as one must, in the religious realm, pursue truth earnestly, all the while protecting the rights of all others—Jew, Gentile, Moslem, pagan, unbeliever—to do precisely the same. Those tough lessons did not come easily in the seventeenth century, nor have they come easily in the centuries that have followed.

The Bloudy Tenent of Persecution for Cause of Conscience

Roger Williams

First, that the blood of so many hundred thousand souls of Protestants and papists, spilled in the wars of present and former ages for their respective consciences, is not required nor accepted by Jesus Christ the Prince of Peace.

Secondly, pregnant scriptures and arguments are throughout the work proposed against the doctrine of persecution for cause of conscience.

Thirdly, satisfactory answers are given to scriptures and objections produced by Mr. Calvin, Beza, Mr. Cotton, and the ministers of the New English churches, and others former and later, tending to prove the doctrine of persecution for cause of conscience.

Fourthly, the doctrine of persecution for cause of conscience is proved guilty of all the blood of the souls crying for vengeance under the altar.

Fifthly, all civil states, with their officers of justice, in their respective constitutions and administrations, are proved essentially civil, and therefore not judges, governors, or defenders of the spiritual, or Christian, state and worship.

Sixthly, it is the will and command of God that, since the coming of his Son the Lord Jesus, a permission of the most paganish, Jewish, Turkish, or anti-Christian consciences and worships be granted to all men in all nations and countries, and they are only to be fought against with that sword which is only, in soul matters, able to conquer, to wit, the sword of God's Spirit, the word of God.

Seventhly, the state of the land of Israel, the kings and people thereof, in peace and war, is proved figurative and ceremonial, and no pattern nor precedent for any kingdom or civil state in the world to follow.

Eighthly, God requires not a uniformity of religion to be enacted and enforced in any civil state; which enforced uniformity, sooner or later, is the greatest occasion of civil war, ravishing of conscience, persecution of Christ Jesus in his servants, and of the hypocrisy and destruction of millions of souls.

Ninthly, in holding an enforced uniformity of religion in a civil state, we must necessarily disclaim our desires and hopes of the Jews' conversion to Christ.

Tenthly, an enforced uniformity of religion throughout a nation or civil state confounds the civil and religious, denies the principles of Christianity and civility, and that Jesus Christ is come in the flesh.

Eleventhly, the permission of other consciences and worships than a state professes only can, according to God, procure a firm and lasting peace; good assurance being taken, according to the wisdom of the civil state, for uniformity of civil obedience from all sorts.

Twelfthly, lastly, true civility and Christianity may both flourish in a state or kingdom, notwithstanding the permission of divers and contrary consciences, either of Jew or Gentile.

To The Right Honorable Both Houses
of The High Court of Parliament.

Right honorable and renowned patriots:
next to the saving of your own souls in the lamentable shipwreck of mankind, your task as Christians is to save the souls, but as magistrates the bodies and goods, of others.

Many excellent discourses have been presented to your fathers' hands and yours, in former and present parliaments. I shall be humbly bold to say that in what concerns your duties as magistrates towards others a more necessary and seasonable debate was never yet presented.

Two things your honors here may please to view in this controversy of persecution for cause of conscience, beyond what is extant.

First, the whole body of this controversy formed and pitched in true *battalia*.

Secondly, although in respect of myself it be *impar congressus*, yet, in the power of that God who is *Maximus in Minimis*, your honors shall see the controversy is discussed with men as able as most, eminent for ability and piety—Mr. Cotton, and the New English ministers.

When the prophets in scripture have given their coats of arms and escutcheons to great men, your honors know the Babylonian monarch has the lion, the Persian the bear, the Grecian the leopard, the Roman a compound of the former three, most strange and dreadful. (Daniel 7)

Their oppressing, plundering, ravishing, murdering, not only the bodies, but the souls of men, are large explaining commentaries of such similitudes.

Your honors have been famous to the end of the world for your unparalleled wisdom, courage, justice, mercy, in the vindicating your civil laws, liberties, etc. Yet let it not be grievous to your honors' thoughts to ponder a little why all the prayers, and tears, and fastings in this nation have not pierced the heavens, and quenched these flames; which yet who knows how far they will spread, and when they will out!

Your honors have broke the jaws of the oppressor, and taken the prey out his mouth. (Job 29:17) For which act, I believe, it has pleased the Most High God to set a guard, not only of trained men, but of mighty angels, to secure your sitting, and the city.

I fear we are not pardoned, though reprieved. Oh, that there may be a lengthening of London's tranquillity, of the parliament's safety, *by [showing] mercy to the poor.* (Daniel 4 [27])

Right honorable, soul yokes, soul oppressions, plunderings, ravishings, etc., are of a crimson and deepest dye, and I believe the chief of England's sins, unstopping the vials of England's present sorrows.

This glass presents your honors with arguments from religion, reason, experience, all proving that the greatest yokes yet lying upon English necks, the people's and your own, are of a spiritual and soul nature.

All former parliaments have changed these yokes according to their consciences, popish or Protestant. It is now your honors' turn at helm, and as your task so I hope your resolution not to change. For that is but to turn the wheel which another parliament, and the very next, may turn again; but to ease the subjects and yourselves from a yoke (as was once spoke in a case not unlike, Acts 15) which neither you nor your fathers were ever able to bear.

Most noble senators, your fathers, whose seats you fill, are moldered, and moldering their brains, their tongues, etc., to ashes in the pit of rottenness. They and you must shortly, together with two worlds of men, appear at the great bar. It shall then be no grief of heart that you have now attended to the cries of souls, thousands oppressed, millions ravished by the acts and statutes concerning souls not yet repealed, of bodies impoverished, imprisoned, etc., for their souls' belief, yea, slaughtered on heaps for religious controversies, in the wars of present and former ages.

"Notwithstanding the success of later times, wherein sundry opinions have been hatched about the subject of religion, a man may clearly discern with his eye, and, as it were, touch with his finger, that according to the verity of holy scripture, etc., men's consciences ought in no sort to be violated, urged, or constrained. And whensoever men have attempted any thing by this violent course, whether openly or by secret means, the issue has been pernicious, and the cause of great and wonderful innovations in the principallest and mightiest kingdoms and countries."[1]

---

[1] "The famous saying of a late king of Bohemia." Williams's footnote. *Tracts on Liberty of Conscience and Persecution, p. 217.* Hanserd Knollys Society, 1846.

It cannot be denied to be a pious and prudential act for your honors, according to your conscience, to call for the advice of faithful counselors in the high debates concerning your own, and the souls of others.

Yet, let it not be imputed as a crime for any suppliant to the God of heaven for you, if, in the humble sense of what their souls believe, they pour forth, among others, these three requests at the throne of grace.

First, that neither your honors, nor those excellent and worthy persons whose advice you seek, limit the Holy One of Israel to their apprehensions, debates, conclusions, rejecting or neglecting the humble and faithful suggestions of any, though as base as spittle and clay, with which sometimes Christ Jesus opens the eyes of them that are born blind.

Secondly, that the present and future generations of the sons of men may never have cause to say that such a parliament, as England never enjoyed the like, should model the worship of the living, eternal, and invisible God after the bias of any earthly interest, though of the highest concernment under the sun. And yet says the learned Sir Francis Bacon (however otherwise persuaded, yet thus he confesses), "Such as hold pressure of conscience are guided therein by some private interests of their own."[2]

Thirdly, whatever way of worshipping God your own consciences are persuaded to walk in, yet, from any bloody act of violence to the consciences of others it may never be told at Rome nor Oxford that the parliament of England has committed a greater rape than if they had forced or ravished the bodies of all the women in the world.

And that England's parliament, so famous throughout all Europe and the world, should at last turn papists, prelatists, Presbyterians, Independents, Socinians, Familists, Antinomians, etc., by confirming all these sorts of consciences by civil force and violence to their consciences.[3]

---

[2] *Essay of Religion,* Essay 3, "Unity in Religion."

[3] "It is rarely seen that ever persons were persecuted for their conscience, but by such persecution they were confirmed and hardened in their conscience." Williams's footnote.

TO EVERY COURTEOUS READER

While I plead the cause of truth and innocency against the bloody doctrine of persecution for cause of conscience, I judge it not unfit to give alarm to myself and men to prepare to be persecuted or hunted for cause of conscience.

Whether you stand charged with ten or but two talents, if you hunt any for cause of conscience, how can you say you follow the Lamb of God, who so abhorred that practice?

If Paul, if Jesus Christ, were present here at London, and the question were proposed, what religion would they approve of? The papists, prelatists, Presbyterians, Independents, etc., would each say, "Of mine, of mine"?

But put the second question: If one of the several sorts should by major vote attain the sword of steel, what weapons does Christ Jesus authorize them to fight with in his cause? Do not all men hate the persecutor, and every conscience, true or false, complain of cruelty, tyranny, etc.?

Two mountains of crying guilt lie heavy upon the backs of all men that name the name of Christ, in the eyes of Jews, Turks, and pagans.

First, the blasphemies of their idolatrous inventions, superstitions, and most unchristian conversations.

Secondly, the bloody, irreligious, and inhuman oppressions and destructions under the mask or veil of the name of Christ, etc.

Oh! how like is the jealous Jehovah, the consuming fire, to end these present slaughters of the holy witnesses in a greater slaughter! (Rev. 5)

Six years preaching of so much truth of Christ as that time afforded in King Edward's days kindles the flames of Queen Mary's bloody persecutions.

Who can now but expect that after so many scores of years preaching and professing of more truth, and among so many great contentions among the very best of Protestants, a fiery furnace should be heat, and who sees not now the fires kindling?

I confess I have little hopes, till those flames are over, that this discourse against the doctrine of persecution for cause of conscience should pass current, I say not among the wolves and lions, but even among the sheep of Christ themselves. Yet, *liberavi animam meam,* I have not hid within my breast my soul's belief. And, although sleeping on the bed either of the pleasures or profits of sin, think you your conscience bound to smite at him that dares to waken you? Yet in the midst of all these civil and spiritual wars, I hope we shall agree in these particulars.

First, however the proud (upon the advantage of a higher earth or ground) overlook the poor, and cry out schismatics, heretics, etc., shall blasphemers and seducers escape unpunished? Yet there is a sorer punishment in the gospel for despising of Christ than Moses, even when the despiser of Moses was put to death without mercy. (Hebrews 10: 28, 29.) *He that believes not shall be damned.* (Mark 16:16)[4]

Secondly, whatever worship, ministry, ministration, the best and purest are practiced without faith and true persuasion that they are the true institutions of God, they are sin, sinful worships, ministries, etc. And however in civil things we may be servants unto men, yet in divine and spiritual things the poorest peasant must disdain the service of the highest prince. *Be ye not the servants of men.* (1 Cor. 7 [23]).

Thirdly, without search and trial no man attains this faith and right persuasion. *Try all things.* (I Thessalonians 5 [21])

In vain have English parliaments permitted English Bibles in the poorest English houses, and the simplest man or woman to search the scriptures, if yet against their souls' persuasion from the scripture they should be forced, as if they lived in Spain or Rome itself without the sight of a Bible, to believe as the church believes.

Fourthly, having tried, we must hold fast (I Thessalonians 5 [21]), upon the loss of a crown. (Rev. 3 [2]). We must not let go for all the fleabitings of the present afflictions, etc. Having bought truth dear, we must not sell it cheap, not the least grain of it for the whole world; no, not for the saving of souls, though our own most precious; least of all for the bitter sweetening of a little vanishing pleasure—for a little puff of credit and reputation from the changeable breath of uncertain sons of men, for the broken bags of riches on eagles' wings, for a dream of these—any or all of these, which on our death-bed vanish and leave tormenting stings behind them. Oh! how much better is it from the love of truth, from the love of the Father of lights from whence it comes, from the love of the Son of God, who is the way and the truth, to say as he, *For*

---

[4] Underhill misquotes this verse, saying, "He that believes shall not be damned."

this end was I born, and for this end came I into the world, that I might bear witness to the truth. (John 18:37)

SCRIPTURES AND REASONS,
WRITTEN LONG SINCE BY A WITNESS OF JESUS CHRIST, CLOSE PRISONER IN NEWGATE, AGAINST PERSECUTION IN CAUSE OF CONSCIENCE; AND SENT SOME WHILE SINCE TO MR. COTTON BY A FRIEND, WHO THUS WROTE:

In the multitude of counselors there is safety; it is therefore humbly desired to be instructed in this point, viz.:

Whether persecution for cause of conscience
   be not against the doctrine of Jesus Christ, the king of kings.
The scriptures and reasons are these.[5]

1. Because Christ commands that the tares and wheat, which some understand are those that walk the truth and those that walk in lies, should be let alone in the world, and not plucked up until the harvest, which is the end of the world. (Matthew 13:30, 38, etc.)
2. The same commands (Matthew 15:14) that they that are blind (as some interpret, led on in false religion and are offended with him for

---

[5] Chapters 6-9 of a work printed in 1620, titled, "A most Humble Supplication of the King's Majesty's Loyal Subjects, ready to testify all Civil Obedience, by the Oath of Allegiance, or otherwise, and that of Conscience; who are persecuted (only for differing in Religion) contrary to Divine and Human Traditions." Published in *Tracts on Liberty of Conscience, 1614-1661*, Hanserd Knollys Society, London, 1848; edited by E. B. Underhill. Underhill conjectures that the author was John Murton (Morton), who was associated with Thomas Helwys in the Netherlands and in England. One of Cotton's controversial works, "A Defense of the Doctrine Propounded by the Synod of Dort," was directed against "John Murton and his Associates."

teaching true religion) should be let alone, referring their punishment unto their falling into the ditch.

3. Again, he reproved his disciples who would have had fire come down from heaven and devour those Samaritans who would not receive him, in these words: *You know not of what Spirit you are; the Son of man is not come to destroy men's lives, but to save them.* (Luke 9:54, 55)

4. Paul, the apostle of our Lord, teaches *that the servant of the Lord must not strive, but must be gentle toward all men, suffering the evil men, instructing them with meekness that are contrary minded, proving if God at any time will give them repentance, that they may acknowledge the truth, and come to amendment out of that snare of the devil,* etc. (II Timothy 2:24-26)[6]

5. According to these blessed commandments, the holy prophets foretold that when the law of Moses concerning worship should cease and Christ's kingdom be established, *They shall break their swords into mattocks, and their spears into scythes.* (Isaiah 2:4; Micah 4:3,4) And Isaiah 9:9, *Then shall none hurt nor destroy in all the mountain of my holiness,* etc. And when he came, the same he taught and practiced as before. So did his disciples after him. *For the weapons of his warfare are not carnal,* says the apostle. (2 Corinthians 10:4)

But he charges straightly that his disciples should be so far from persecuting those that would not be of their religion that when they were persecuted they should pray (Matthew 5:44), when they were cursed, they should bless, etc.

And the reason seems to be because they who now are tares may hereafter become wheat; they who are now blind, may hereafter see; they that now resist him, may hereafter receive him; they that are now in the devil's snare, in adverseness to the truth, may hereafter come to repentance; they that are now blasphemers and persecutors, as Paul was, may in time become faithful as he; they that are now idolaters, as the Corinthians once were (1 Corinthians 6:9), may hereafter become true worshippers as they; they that are now no people of God, nor under mercy, as the saints sometimes were (1 Peter 2:10), may hereafter become the people of God, and obtain mercy, as they.

---

[6] Williams mistakenly cites 2 Timothy 24:2.

Some come not till the eleventh hour (Matthew 20:6); if those that come not till the last hour should be destroyed, because they come not at the first, then should they never come, but be prevented.

All which premises are in all humility referred to your godly wise consideration.

II. Because this persecution for cause of conscience is against the profession and practice of famous princes.[7]

First, you may please to consider the speech of King James, in his majesty's speech in parliament, 1609.[8] He says, "It is a sure rule in divinity that God never loves to plant his church by violence and bloodshed."

And in his highness' Apology, p. 4, speaking of such papists that took the oath, thus: "I gave good proof that I intended no persecution against them for conscience' cause, but only desired to be secured for civil obedience, which for conscience' cause they are bound to perform."

And, p. 60, speaking of Blackwell,[9] the archpriest, his majesty says, "It was never my intention to lay any thing to the said archpriest's charge, as I have never done to any for cause of conscience."[10]

And in his highness' exposition on Revelation 20, printed 1588, and after in 1603, his majesty writes thus: "Sixthly, the compassing of the saints, and the besieging of the beloved city, declares unto us a certain note of a false church to be persecution; for they come to seek the faithful, the faithful are them that are sought: the wicked are the besiegers, the faithful are the besieged."[11]

---

[7] The document should begin with "I," for the first section deals with scriptures which argue against persecution for cause of conscience, while this section catalogues "the opinions of famous princes" in opposition to persecution for cause of conscience. The next section is: "Thirdly, because persecution for cause of conscience is condemned by ancient and later writers...."

[8] *The Works of the Most High and Mighty Prince James.* Published by James, Bishop of Winton, etc., London, 1616, p. 544.

[9] George Blackwell was commissioned to act as archbishop over the secular clergy in England by Cardinal Cajetan, March 7, 1598, and was confirmed and approved by a bull from Pope Clement VIII, April 6, 1599. He took the oath of allegiance enacted in consequence of the Gunpowder Plot, and openly expressed his approbation of it, though Paul V had condemned it. His superiors at Rome could not endure his attempts to induce Roman Catholics to take the oath, and he was superseded in 1508.

[10] *The Works of the Most High and Mighty Prince James,* p. 268.

[11] Ibid., p. 79.

Secondly, the saying of Stephen, king of Poland: "I am a king of men, not of consciences; a commander of bodies, not of souls."[12]

Thirdly, the king of Bohemia has thus written: "And, notwithstanding the success of the later times, wherein sundry opinions have been hatched about the subject of religion, may make one clearly discern with his eye, and (as it were) to touch with his finger, that according to the verity of holy scriptures, and a maxim heretofore told and maintained by the ancient doctors of the church, that men's consciences ought in no sort to be violated, urged, or constrained, and whensoever men have attempted any thing by this violent course, whether openly or by secret means, the issue has been pernicious, and the cause of great and wonderful innovations in the principallest and mightiest kingdoms and countries of all Christendom."

And further, his majesty says: "So that once more we do profess, before God and the whole world, that from this time forward we are firmly resolved not to persecute, or molest, or suffer to be persecuted or molested, any person whosoever for matter of religion; no, not they that profess themselves to be of the Romish church, neither to trouble or disturb them in the exercise of their religion, so they live conformable to the laws of the states," etc.[13]

And for the practice of this, where is persecution for cause of conscience, except in England and where popery reigns, and there neither in all places, as appears by France, Poland, and other places?

Nay, it is not practiced among the heathen that acknowledge not the true God, as the Turk, Persian, and others.

Thirdly, because persecution for cause of conscience is condemned by ancient and later writers; yea, and the papists themselves.

Hilary against Auxentius, says thus: "The Christian church does not persecute, but is persecuted. And lamentable it is to see the great folly of these times and to sigh at the foolish opinion of this world, in that men think by human aid to help God, and with worldly pomp and power to

---

[12] Stephen Bathori, King of Poland, 1575-1586. Caldwell cites *Lardner's Cabinet Cyclopedia, Poland*, p. 167: "I reign over persons; but it is God who rules the conscience. Know that God has reserved three things to himself: the creation of something out of nothing; the knowledge of futurity; and the government of the conscience."

[13] From the manifesto issued by Frederick the Fifth, King of Bohemia, against Frederick the Second, Archduke of Austria and Emperor of Germany, at the beginning of the Thirty Years War.

undertake to defend the Christian church. I ask of you bishops, what help used the apostles in the publishing of the gospel? With the aid of what power did they preach Christ and convert the heathen from their idolatry to God? When they were in prisons, and lay in chains, did they praise and give thanks to God for any dignities, graces, and favors received from the court? Or do you think that Paul went about with regal mandates, or kingly authority, to gather and establish the church of Christ? Sought he protection from Nero, Vespasian? The apostles wrought with their hands for their own maintenance, travelling, by land and water, from town to city, to preach Christ; yea, the more they were forbidden, the more they taught and preached Christ. But now, alas! human help must assist and protect the faith, and give the same countenance. To and by vain and worldly honors do men seek to defend the church of Christ, as if he by his power were unable to perform it."[14]

The same, against the Arians: "The church now, which formerly by enduring misery and imprisonment was known to be a true church, does now terrify others by imprisonment, banishment, and misery, and boasts that she is highly esteemed of the world; when as the true church cannot but be hated of the same."

Tertullian ad Scapulam: "It agrees both with human reason, and natural equity, that every man worship God uncompelled, and believe what he will; for another man's religion and belief neither hurts nor profits anyone: neither beseems it any religion to compel another to be of their religion, which willingly and freely should be embraced, and not by constraint: forasmuch as the offerings were required of those that freely and with good will offered, and not from the contrary."[15]

Jerome in *Proem. lib, 4. in Jeremiam:* "Heresy must be cut off with the sword of the Spirit; let us strike through with the arrows of the Spirit all sons and disciples of misled heretics, that is, with testimonies of holy scriptures. The slaughter of heretics is by the word of God."[16]

Brentius upon I Corinthians 3: "No man has power to make or give laws to Christians, whereby to bind their consciences; for willingly, freely,

---

[14] S. Hilarii Opera, Lib. I, Contra Arianos vel Auxentium, Cap. 3,4, pp. 465-466; Ventiis, 1749.
[15] Tertullian. "To Scapula." *The Fathers of the Church.* Washington, D.C.: Catholic University of America, 1950, p. 152.
[16] S. Hieronymi Opera, in proemium lib. 4, in Jeremiam, pp. 615-616, Parifiis, 1704.

and uncompelled, with a ready desire and cheerful mind, must those that come, run unto Christ."[17]

Luther, in his book of the civil magistrate, says, "The laws of the civil magistrate's government extend no further than over the body or goods, and to that which is external: for over the soul God will not suffer any man to rule; only he himself will rule there. Wherefore, whosoever does undertake to give laws unto the souls and consciences of men, he usurps that government himself which appertains unto God," etc.[18]

Therefore, upon I Kings 6: "In the building of the temple there was no sound of iron heard, to signify that Christ will have in his church a free and a willing people, not compelled and constrained by laws and statutes."[19]

Again, he says upon Luke 22: "It is not the true catholic church which is defended by the secular arm or human power, but the false and feigned church, which although it carries the name of a church, yet it denies the power thereof."[20]

And upon Psalm 17 he says, "For the true church of Christ knows not *brachium seculare*, which the bishops nowadays chiefly use."

Again, in *Postil. Dom. 1. post. Epiphan*, he says, "Let not Christians be commanded, but exhorted; for he that willingly will not do that whereunto he is friendly exhorted, he is no Christian; whereof they that do compel those that are not willing show thereby that they are not Christian preachers, but worldly beadles."[21]

Again, upon I Peter 3 he says, "If the civil magistrate shall command me to believe thus and thus, I should answer him after this manner: Lord, or sir, look you to your civil or worldly government, your power extends not so far as to command any thing in God's kingdom; therefore herein I

---

[17] Johannes Brenz (1499-1570), a Swabian reformer. *Operum reverendi et clarissimi theologi D. Joannis Brentii* (Tübingen: Excudebat Georgius Gruppenbachius, 1576-1590). Caldwell notes, "The Works of Brentius, 8 vols. Folio, Tübeingen, 157501590, are not within the editor's reach, nor on the catalogues of any of the public libraries of the country, so far as examined."

[18] *The Works of Martin Luther, Vol. III* (Philadelphia: Muhlenburg Press, 1930) 251.

[19] "Secular Authority," *Martin Luther: Selections from His Writings*. Ed. John Dillenberger (Garden City: Doubleday & Co., 1962) 372.

[20] Auflegung des Evangelii am Bartholomews Tag, Luke xxii: 24-30. *D. Martin Luthers Werke: Kritische Gesamtausgabe* (WA) (Weimar, 1883), Bd. 1, 79-81.

[21] "Auflegung der Epistelam ersten Sonntag nach Epiphania." *D. Martin Luthers Werke: Kritische Gesamtausgabe* (WA) (Weimar, 1883), Bd. 17 (2), 5-15.

may not hear you. For if you cannot bear it, that any should usurp authority where you have to command, how do you think that God should suffer you to thrust him from his seat, and to seat yourself therein?"[22]

Lastly, the papists, the inventors of persecution, in a wicked book of theirs, set forth in King James his reign, thus: "Moreover, the means which Almighty God appointed his officers to use in the conversion of kingdoms, and nations, and people, was humility, patience, charity, saying, *'Behold, I send you as sheep in the midst of wolves.'* (Matthew 10:16) He did not say, 'Behold, I send you as wolves among sheep, to kill, imprison, spoil, and devour those unto whom they were sent.'

"Again, verse 17, he says, *'They to whom I send you will deliver you up into councils, and in their synagogues they will scourge you; and to presidents and to kings shall you be led for my sake.'* He does not say, 'You, whom I send, shall deliver the people, whom you ought to convert, unto councils, and put them in prisons, and lead them to presidents, and tribunal seats, and make their religion felony and treason.'

"Again he says, ver. 32, *'When you enter into an house, salute it, saying, Peace be unto this house.'* He does not say, 'You shall send pursuivants[23] to ransack or spoil the house.'

"Again he says, John 10, *'The good pastor gives his life for his sheep; the thief comes not but to steal, kill, and destroy.'* He does not say, 'The thief gives his life for his sheep, and the good pastor comes not but to steal, kill, and destroy.'"

So that we holding our peace, our adversaries themselves speak for us, or rather for the truth.

TO ANSWER SOME MAIN OBJECTIONS.

And first, that it is no prejudice to the commonwealth if liberty of conscience were suffered to such as do fear God indeed, as is or will be manifest in such men's lives and conversations.

Abraham abode among the Canaanites a long time, yet contrary to them in religion. (Gen. 13: 7; 16:13) Again, he sojourned in Gerar, and King Abimelech gave him leave to abide in his land. (Gen. 20:21, 23, 24)

---

[22] *Luther's Works, Vol. 30* (St. Louis: Concordia Publishing House, 1967) 81.
[23] An officer of arms ranking below a herald but having similar duties.

Isaac also dwelt in the same land, yet contrary in religion. (Gen. 26)

Jacob lived twenty years in one house with his uncle Laban, yet differed in religion. (Gen. 31)

The people of Israel were about four hundred and thirty years in that infamous land of Egypt, and afterwards seventy years in Babylon, all which time they differed in religion from those states. (Exod. 12; 2 Chron. 36)

Come to the time of Christ, where Israel was under the Romans, where lived divers sects of religions, as Herodians, scribes and Pharisees, Sadducees and libertines, Theudaeans and Samaritans, beside the common religion of the Jews, Christ, and his apostles, all which differed from the common religion of the state, which is like the worship of Diana, which almost the whole world then worshipped. (Acts 19:20)

All these lived under the government of Caesar, being nothing hurtful unto the commonwealth, giving unto Caesar that which was his. And for their religion and consciences towards God he left them to themselves, as having no dominion over their souls and consciences. And when the enemies of the truth raised up any tumults, the wisdom of the magistrate most wisely appeased them. (Acts 18:14; 19:35)

THE ANSWER OF MR. JOHN COTTON, OF BOSTON, IN NEW ENGLAND, TO THE AFORESAID ARGUMENTS AGAINST PERSECUTION FOR CAUSE OF CONSCIENCE, PROFESSEDLY MAINTAINING PERSECUTION FOR CAUSE OF CONSCIENCE

The question which you put is, whether persecution for cause of conscience be not against the doctrine of Jesus Christ, the King of Kings?

Now, by persecution for cause of conscience, I conceive you mean either for professing some point of doctrine which you believe in conscience to be the truth, or for practicing some work which in conscience you believe to be a religious duty.

Now in points of doctrine some are fundamental, without right belief whereof a man cannot be saved; others are circumstantial, or less principal, wherein men may differ in judgment without prejudice of salvation on either part.

In like sort, in points of practice, some concern the weightier duties of the law, as, what God we worship, and with what kind of worship, whether such as, if it be right, fellowship with God is held, if corrupt, fellowship with him is lost.

Again, in points of doctrine and worship less principal, either they are held forth in a meek and peaceable way, though the things be erroneous or unlawful, or they are held forth with such arrogance and impetuousness as tends and reaches (even of itself) to the disturbance of civil peace.

Finally, let me add this one distinction more: when we are persecuted for conscience' sake, it is either for conscience rightly informed, or for erroneous and blind conscience.

These things premised, I would lay down mine answer to the question in certain conclusions.

First, it is not lawful to persecute any for conscience' sake rightly informed; for in persecuting such, Christ himself is persecuted in them. (Acts 9:4)

Secondly, for an erroneous and blind conscience (even in fundamental and weighty points), it is not lawful to persecute any, till after admonition once or twice; and so the apostle directs (Titus 3:10), and gives the reason that in fundamental and principal points of doctrine or worship the word of God in such things is so clear that he cannot but be convinced in conscience of the dangerous error of his way after once or twice admonition, wisely and faithfully dispensed. And then, if anyone persist, it is not out of conscience, but against his conscience, as the apostle says (verse 11), he "is subverted, and sins, being condemned of himself," that is, of his own conscience. So that if such a man, after such admonition, shall still persist in the error of his way, and be therefore punished, he is not persecuted for cause of conscience, but for sinning against his own conscience.

Thirdly, in things of lesser moment, whether points of doctrine or worship, if a man hold them forth in a spirit of Christian meekness and love, though with zeal and constancy, he is not to be persecuted, but tolerated, till God may be pleased to manifest his truth to him. (Phil. 3:17; Rom. 14:1-4)

But if a man hold forth, or profess any error or false way, with a boisterous and arrogant spirit, to the disturbance of civil peace, he may justly be punished according to the quality and measure of the disturbance caused by him.

Now let us consider of your reasons or objections to the contrary. Your first head of objections is taken from the scripture.

Objection 1. Because Christ commands to let alone the tares and wheat to grow together unto the harvest. (Matt. 13:30, 38)

Answer. Tares are not briars and thorns, but partly hypocrites, like unto the godly, but indeed carnal, as the tares are like to wheat, but are not wheat; or partly such corrupt doctrines or practices as are indeed unsound, but yet such as come very near the truth (as tares do to the wheat), and so near that good men may be taken with them; and so the persons in whom they grow cannot be rooted out but good will be rooted up with them. And in such a case Christ calls for toleration, not for penal prosecution, according to the third conclusion.

Objection 2. In Matthew15:14 Christ commands his disciples to let the blind alone till they fall into the ditch; therefore he would have their punishment deferred till their final destruction.

Answer. He there speaks not to public officers, whether in church or commonweal, but to his private disciples, concerning the Pharisees, over whom they had no power. And the command he gives to let them alone is spoken in regard of troubling themselves, or regarding the offence which they took at the wholesome doctrine of the gospel. As who should say, Though they be offended at this saying of mine, yet do not you fear their fear, nor be troubled at their offence, which they take at my doctrine, not out of sound judgment, but out of their blindness. But this makes nothing to the cause in hand.

Objection 3. In Luke 9:54,55 Christ reproves his disciples, who would have had fire come down from heaven to consume the Samaritans, who refused to receive Him.

Objection 4. And Paul teaches Timothy not to strive, but to be gentle towards all men, suffering evil patiently.

Answer. Both these are directions to ministers of the gospel, how to deal, not with obstinate offenders in the church that sin against conscience, but either with men without, as the Samaritans were, and many unconverted Christians in Crete, whom Titus, as an evangelist, was to seek to convert, or at best with some Jews or Gentiles in the church, who, though carnal, yet were not convinced of the error of their way. And it is true, it became not the spirit of the gospel to convert aliens to the faith of Christ, such as the Samaritans were, by fire and brimstone; nor to deal harshly in public ministry, or private conference, with all such contrary-minded men, as either had not yet entered into church-fellowship, or if they had, yet did hitherto sin of ignorance, not against conscience.

But neither of both these texts do hinder the ministers of the gospel to proceed in a church-way against church members, when they become scandalous offenders either in life or doctrine; much less do they speak at all to civil magistrates.

Objection 5. From the prediction of the prophets, who foretold that carnal weapons should cease in the days of the gospel. (Isa. 2:4; 11:9; Mic. 4:3,4) And the apostle professes, *The weapons of our warfare are not carnal.* (2 Cor. 10:4) And Christ is so far from persecuting those that would not be of his religion that he charges them, when they are persecuted themselves, they should pray, and when they are cursed they should bless. The reason whereof seems to be that they who are now persecutors and wicked persons, may become true disciples and converts.

Answer. Those predictions in the prophets do only show, first, with what kind of weapons he will subdue the nations to the obedience of the faith of the gospel, not by fire and sword, and weapons of war, but by the power of his word and Spirit, which no man doubts of.

Secondly, those predictions of the prophets show what the meek and peaceable temper will be of all the true converts to Christianity, not lions or leopards, etc., not cruel oppressors, nor malignant opposers, nor biters of one another. But do not forbid them to drive ravenous wolves from the sheepfold, and to restrain them from devouring the sheep of Christ.

And when Paul says, *The weapons of our warfare are not carnal but spiritual,* he denies not civil weapons of justice to the civil magistrate (Rom. 13), but only to church officers. And yet the weapons of such officers he acknowledges to be such, as though they be spiritual, yet are ready to take vengeance of all disobedience (2 Cor. 10:6), which has reference, among other ordinances, to the censure of the church against scandalous offenders.

When Christ commands his disciples to bless them that curse them and persecute them, he gives not therein a rule to public officers, whether in church or commonweal, to suffer notorious sinners, either in life or doctrine, to pass away with a blessing; but to private Christians to suffer persecution patiently, yea, and to pray for their persecutors.

Again, it is true Christ would have his disciples to be far from persecuting, for that is a sinful oppression of men for righteousness' sake; but that hinders not but that he would have them execute upon all disobedience the judgment and vengeance required in the word. (2 Cor. 10:6; Rom. 13:4)

Though it be true that wicked persons now may by the grace of God become true disciples and converts, yet we may not do evil that good may come thereof. And evil it would be to tolerate notorious evil doers, whether seducing teachers, or scandalous livers. Christ had something against the angel of the church of Pergamos for tolerating them that held the doctrine of Balaam, and against the church of Thyatira for tolerating Jezebel to teach and seduce. (Rev. 2:14, 20)

Your second head of reasons is taken from the profession and practice of famous princes, King James, Stephen of Poland, king of Bohemia. Thereunto a treble answer may briefly be returned.

First, we willingly acknowledge that none is to be persecuted at all, no more than they may be oppressed for righteousness' sake.

Again, we acknowledge that none is to be punished for his conscience, though misinformed, as has been said, unless his error be fundamental, or seditiously and turbulently promoted, and that after due conviction of his conscience, that it may appear he is not punished for his conscience, but for sinning against his conscience.

Furthermore, we acknowledge none is to be constrained to believe or profess the true religion till he be convinced in judgment of the truth of it; but yet restrained he may from blaspheming the truth, and from seducing any unto pernicious errors.

2. We answer, what princes profess or practice is not a rule of conscience. They many times tolerate that in point of state policy which cannot justly be tolerated in point of true Christianity.

Again, princes many times tolerate offenders out of very necessity, when the offenders are either too many, or too mighty for them to punish; in which respect David tolerated Joab and his murders: but against his will.

3. We answer further that for those three princes named by you, who tolerated religion, we can name you more and greater who have not tolerated heretics and schismatics, notwithstanding their pretence of conscience, and arrogating the crown of martyrdom to their sufferings.

Constantine the Great, at the request of the General Council of Nicea, banished Arius, with some of his fellows. (Sozomen, *Ecclesicatical History*, Book I, chapters 19, 20)[24] The same Constantine made a severe law against the Donatists. And the like proceedings against them were used by Valentinian, Gratian, and Theodosius, as Augustine reports in Epistle 166.[25] Only Julian the Apostate granted liberty to heretics as well as to pagans, that he might, by tolerating all weeds to grow, choke the

---

[24] *Nicene and Post-Nicene Fathers, Vol. II* (Buffalo, New York: The Christian Literature Company, 1890) pp. 179ff.

[25] Perhaps a reference to Epistle 185, "A Treatise Concerning the Correction of the Donatists," *Nicene and Post-Nicene Fathers, Vol. IV* (Buffalo, New York: The Christian Literature Company, 1887).

vitals of Christianity, which was also the practice and sin of Valens the Arian.

Queen Elizabeth, as famous for her government as any of the former, it is well known what laws she made and executed against papists. Yea, and King James, one of your own witnesses, though he was slow in proceeding against papists, as you say, for conscience' sake, yet you are not ignorant how sharply and severely he punished those whom the malignant world calls Puritans, men of more conscience and better faith than he tolerated.

I come now to your third and last argument, taken from the judgment of ancient and later writers, yea, even of papists themselves, who have condemned persecution for conscience' sake.

You begin with Hilary, whose testimony we might admit without any prejudice to the truth; for it is true, the Christian church does not persecute, but is persecuted. But to excommunicate an heretic is not to persecute; that is, it is not to punish an innocent, but a culpable and damnable person, and that not for conscience, but for persisting in error against light of conscience, whereof it has been convinced.

It is true also what he says, that neither the apostles did, nor may we, propagate Christian religion by the sword; but if pagans cannot be won by the word, they are not to be compelled by the sword. Nevertheless, this hinders not but if they or any others should blaspheme the true God and his true religion, they ought to be severely punished; and no less do they deserve, if they seduce from the truth to damnable heresy or idolatry.

Your next writer, which is Tertullian, speaks to the same purpose in the place alleged by you. His intent is only to restrain Scapula, the Roman governor of Africa, from the persecution of Christians, for not offering sacrifice to their gods: and for that end fetches an argument from the law of natural equity, not to compel any to any religion, but to permit them either to believe willingly, or not to believe at all, which we acknowledge, and accordingly permit the Indians to continue in their unbelief. Nevertheless, it will not therefore be lawful openly to tolerate the worship of devils, or idols, or the seduction of any from the truth.

When Tertullian says, "Another man's religion neither hurts nor profits any," it must be understood of private worship, and religion professed in private; otherwise a false religion professed by the members of a church, or by such as have given their names to Christ, will be the ruin and desolation of the church, as appears by the threats of Christ to the churches of Asia. (Rev. 2)

Your next author, Hierom, crosses not the truth, nor advantages your cause; for we grant what he says, that heresy must be cut off with the sword of the Spirit. But this hinders not, but that being so cut down, if the heretic still persist in his heresy to the seduction of others, he may be cut off by the civil sword to prevent the perdition of others. And that to be Hierom's meaning appears by his note upon that of the apostle, "A little leaven leavens the whole lump." "Therefore," says he, "a spark, as soon as it appears, is to be extinguished, and the leaven to be removed from the rest of the dough, rotten pieces of flesh are to be cut off, and a scabbed beast is to be driven from the sheepfold, lest the whole house, mass of dough, body, and flock, be set on fire with the spark, be soured with the leaven, be putrified with the rotten flesh, perish by the scabbed beast."[26]

Brentius, whom you next quote, speaks not to your cause. We willingly grant him and you that man has no power to make laws to bind conscience. But this hinders not, but that men may see the laws of God observed which do bind conscience.

The like answer may be returned to Luther, whom you next allege. First, that the government of the civil magistrate extends no further than over the bodies and goods of their subjects, not over their souls; and therefore they may not undertake to give laws to the souls and consciences of men.

Secondly, that the church of Christ does not use the arm of secular power to compel men to the faith or profession of the truth, for this is to be done by spiritual weapons, whereby Christians are to be exhorted, not compelled.

But this hinders not that Christians, sinning against light of faith and conscience, may justly be censured by the church with excommunication, and by the civil sword also, in case they shall corrupt others to the perdition of their souls.

As for the testimony of the popish book, we weigh it not, as knowing whatsoever they speak for toleration of religion where themselves are under hatches, when they come to sit at stern, they judge and practice

---

[26] S. Hieronymi Opera, tom. iv, 291, Parisiis, 1706.

quite contrary: as both their writings and judicial proceedings have testified to the world these many years.

To shut up this argument from testimony of writers. It is well known Augustine retracted this opinion of yours, which in his younger times he had held, but in after riper age reversed and refuted, as appears in the second book of his *Retractations,* chapter 5, and in his Epistles, 48, 50. And in his first book *Against Parmenianus,* chapter 7, he shows that if the Donatists were punished with death they were justly punished. And in his eleventh Tractate upon John, "They murder," says he, "souls, and themselves are afflicted in body. They put men to everlasting death, and yet they complain when themselves are put to suffer temporal death."[27]

Optatus, in his third book,[28] justifies Macarius, who had put some heretics to death, that he had done no more herein than what Moses, Phineas, and Elias had done before him.

Bernard, in his sixty-sixth Sermon in Cantica:[29] "Out of doubt," says he, "it is better that they should be restrained by the sword of him who bears not the sword in vain than that they should be suffered to draw many others into their error. For he is the minister of God for wrath to every evil doer."

Calvin's judgment is well known, who procured the death of Michael Servetus for pertinacity in heresy, and defended his fact by a book written of that argument.[30]

Beza also wrote a book, *De Haereticis Morte Plectendis,* that heretics are to be punished with death.[31] Aretius likewise took the like course about the death of Valentinis Gentilis, and justified the magistrate's proceeding against him, in a history written of that argument.[32]

---

[27] "St.. Augustine, Retractation," *The Fathers of the Church, Vol.* , (Washington, D.C.: Catholic University of America, 1968) pp. 129ff; "St. Augustine, Letters, Vol. I, *The Fathers of the Church, Vol.* , (Washington, D.C.: Catholic University of America, 1951) pp. 231ff, 237ff; Contra Epistolam Parmeniani, lib. i, cap. 8, tom. ix, 19; "St. Augustine, Tractates on the Gospel of John, 11-27," (Washington, D.C.: Catholic University of America, (date?) (page?)

[28] S. Optati Opera. p. 75. Parisiis, 1679. Microfilm EC reel 6722 no. 06.

[29] Bernardi Opera, i, tom. 4. p. 1499, Parisiis, 1680.

[30] Calvini Opera, tom.viii, p. 510, Amsterdam, 1667.

[31] *De Haerteticis Morte Plectendis.* Beza Tract. Theol. tom. i. p. 85. edit. 1582.

[32] Benedictus Aretius. "A Short History of Valentinus the Tritheist, Tried, condemned and put to Death by the Protestant Reformed City and Church of Bern in

Finally, you come to answer some main objections, as you call them, which yet are but one, and that one objects nothing against what we hold. It is, say you, no prejudice to the commonwealth, if liberty of conscience were suffered to such as fear God indeed, which you prove by the examples of the patriarchs and others.

But we readily grant you liberty of conscience is to be granted to men that fear God indeed, as knowing they will not persist in heresy, or turbulent schism, when they are convinced in conscience of the sinfulness thereof.

But the question is, whether an heretic, after once or twice admonition, and so after conviction, or any other scandalous and heinous offender, may be tolerated, either in the church without excommunication, or in the commonwealth without such punishment as may preserve others from dangerous and damnable infection.

Thus much I thought needful to be spoken, for avoiding the grounds of your error.

I forbear adding reasons to justify the truth, because you may find that done to your hand, in a treatise sent to some of the brethren late of Salem, who doubted as you do.[33]

The Lord Jesus lead you by a Spirit of truth into all truth, through Jesus Christ.

Switzerland, for asserting the Three Divine Persons of the Trinity to be Three Distinct, Eternal Spirits," etc. (Geneva, 1567).

[33] "A Model of Church and Civil Power," which is "examined and answered" in this work, beginning with chapter lxxxii.

A REPLY TO THE
AFORESAID ANSWER OF MR. COTTON,
IN A CONFERENCE BETWEEN TRUTH AND PEACE

CHAPTER I

Truth. In what dark corner of the world, sweet Peace, are we two met? How has this present evil world banished me from all the coasts and quarters of it? And how has the righteous God in judgment taken you from the earth? (Rev. 6:4)

Peace. It is lamentably true, blessed Truth, the foundations of the world have long been out of course; the gates of earth and hell have conspired together to intercept our joyful meeting and our holy kisses. With what a wearied, tired wing have I flown over nations, kingdoms, cities, towns, to find out precious Truth!

Truth. The like inquiries in my flights and travels have I made for Peace, and still am told she has left the earth, and fled to heaven.

Peace. Dear Truth, what is the earth but a dungeon of darkness, where Truth is not?

Truth. And what is the peace thereof but a fleeting dream, your ape and counterfeit?

Peace. Oh! Where is the promise of the God of heaven, that righteousness and peace shall kiss each other?

Truth. Patience, sweet Peace, these heavens and earth are growing old, and shall be changed like a garment. (Psalm 102 [26]) They shall melt away, and be burnt up with all the works that are therein; and the Most High Eternal Creator shall gloriously create new heavens and new earth, wherein dwells righteousness. (2 Pet. 3 [13]) Our kisses then shall have their endless date of pure and sweetest joys. Till then both you and I must hope, and wait, and bear the fury of the dragon's wrath, whose monstrous lies and furies shall with himself be cast into the lake of fire, the second death. (Rev. 20 [10, 14])

Peace. Most precious Truth, you know we are both pursued and laid for. Mine heart is full of sighs, mine eyes with tears. Where can I better vent my full, oppressed bosom than into yours, whose faithful lips may for these few hours revive my drooping, wandering spirits, and here begin to wipe tears from mine eyes, and the eyes of my dearest children?

Truth. Sweet daughter of the God of peace, begin. Pour out your sorrows, vent your complaints. How joyful am I to improve these precious minutes to revive our hearts, both yours and mine, and the hearts of all that love the truth and peace. (Zach. 8 [19])

Peace. Dear Truth, I know your birth, your nature, your delight. They that know you will prize you far above themselves and lives, and sell themselves to buy you. Well spoke that famous Elizabeth to her famous attorney, Sir Edward Coke:[34] "Mr. Attorney, go on as you have begun, and still plead, not *pro Domina Regina*, but *pro Domina Veritate.*"

Truth. It is true, my crown is high; my scepter is strong to break down strongest holds, to throw down highest crowns of all that plead, though but in thought, against me. Some few there are, but oh! how few are valiant for the truth, and dare to plead my cause, as my witnesses in sackcloth (Rev. 11); while all men's tongues are bent like bows to shoot out lying words against me!

Peace. Oh! how could I spend eternal days and endless dates at your holy feet, in listening to the precious oracles of your mouth! All the words of your mouth are truth, and there is no iniquity in them. Your lips drop as the honey-comb. But oh! since we must part anon, let us, as you said, improve our minutes, and, according as you promised, revive me with your words, which are sweeter than the honey and the honey-comb.

---

[34] Jurist and politician whose defense of the supremacy of the common law against claims of royal prerogatives had a profound influence on the development of English law. A patron of Williams in his youth. According to a tradition reported by Underhill, Coke noticed the young Williams in church, and, impressed by the accuracy of the notes the boy took on the sermon, sent him to Oxford. (vii) Underhill conjectures that Williams' early decision to study law was influenced by his patron, and that he became early attached to "those rights of liberty which found so able a defender in the aged Coke." (viii)

CHAPTER II

Peace. Dear Truth, I have two sad complaints.

First, the most sober of your witnesses that dare to plead your cause, how are they charged to be mine enemies—contentions, turbulent, seditious!

Secondly, your enemies, though they speak and rail against you, though they outrageously pursue, imprison, banish, kill your faithful witnesses, yet how is all vermillioned over for justice against the heretics! Yea, if they kindle coals, and blow the flames of devouring wars that leave neither spiritual nor civil state, but burn up branch and root, yet how do all pretend an holy war! He that kills, and he that is killed, they both cry out, "It is for God, and for their conscience."

It is true, nor one nor other seldom dare to plead the mighty prince Christ Jesus for their author, yet both (both Protestant and papist) pretend they have spoke with Moses and the prophets, who all, say they, before Christ came, allowed such holy persecutions, holy wars against the enemies of holy church.

Truth. Dear Peace, to ease your first complaint, it is true, your dearest sons, most like their mother, peacekeeping, peace-making sons of God, have borne and still must bear the blurs of troublers of Israel, and turners of the world upside down. And it is true again, what Solomon once spoke: *The beginning of strife is as when one lets out water; therefore,* says he, *leave off contention before it be meddled with.*[35] This caveat should keep the banks and sluices firm and strong, that strife, like a breach of waters, break not in upon the sons of men.

Yet strife must be distinguished: it is necessary, or unnecessary, godly or ungodly, Christian or unchristian, etc.

It is unnecessary, unlawful, dishonorable, ungodly, unchristian, in most cases in the world: for there is a possibility of keeping sweet peace in most cases, and, if it be possible, it is the express command of God that peace be kept. (Romans 12:18)[36]

Again, it is necessary, honorable, godly, etc., with civil and earthly weapons to defend the innocent, and to rescue the oppressed from the

---

[35] Proverbs 17:14.
[36] Williams mistakenly cites Romans 13.

violent paws and jaws of oppressing, persecuting Nimrods. (Psalm 73; Job 29)

It is as necessary, yea, more honorable, godly, and Christian to fight the fight of' faith with religious and spiritual artillery, and to contend earnestly for the faith of Jesus, once delivered to the saints, against all opposers, and the gates of earth and hell, men or devils, yea, against Paul himself, or an angel from heaven, if he bring any other faith or doctrine. (Jude 4; Galatians 1:8)

Peace. With a clashing of such arms am I never wakened. Speak once again, dear Truth, to my second complaint of bloody persecution, and devouring wars, marching under the colors of upright justice and holy zeal, etc.

Truth. Mine ears have long been filled with a threefold doleful outcry.

First, of one hundred forty-four thousand virgins (Rev. 14), forced and ravished by emperors, kings, governors, to their beds of worship and religion, set up like Absalom's on high, in their several states and countries.

Secondly, the cry of those precious souls under the altar (Rev. 6[9]), the souls of such as have been persecuted and slain for the testimony and witness of Jesus, whose blood has been spilled like water upon the earth; and that because they have held fast the truth and witness of Jesus, against the worship of the states and times, compelling to an uniformity of state religion.

These cries of murdered virgins, who can sit still and hear? Who can but run, with zeal inflamed, to prevent the deflowering of chaste souls, and spilling of the blood of the innocent? Humanity stirs up and prompts the sons of men to draw material swords for a virgin's chastity and life against a ravishing murderer; and piety and Christianity must needs awaken the sons of God to draw the spiritual sword, the word of God, to preserve the chastity and life of' spiritual virgins, who abhor the spiritual defilements of false worship. (Rev. 14)

Thirdly, the cry of the whole earth, made drunk with the blood of its inhabitants, slaughtering each other in their blinded zeal for conscience, for religion, against the Catholics, against the Lutherans, etc.

What fearful cries, within these twenty years, of hundred thousands, men, women, children, fathers, mothers, husbands, wives, brothers, sisters, old and young, high and low, plundered, ravished, slaughtered, murdered, famished! And hence these cries, that men fling away the spiritual sword and spiritual artillery in spiritual and religious causes, and rather trust for the suppressing of each other's gods, conscience, and religion, as they suppose, to an arm of flesh and sword of steel.

Truth. Sweet Peace, what have you there?

Peace. Arguments against persecution for cause of conscience.

Truth. And what there?

Peace. An answer to such arguments, contrarily maintaining such persecution for cause of conscience.

Truth. These arguments against such persecution, and the answer pleading for it, written, as love hopes, from godly intentions, hearts, and hands, yet in a marvelously different style and manner—the arguments against persecution in milk, the answer for it, as I may say, in blood.

The author of these arguments against persecution, as I have been informed, being committed by some then in power close prisoner to Newgate for the witness of some truths of Jesus, and having not the use of pen and ink, wrote these arguments in milk, in sheets of paper brought to him by the woman, his keeper, from a friend in London as the stopples of his milk bottle.

In such paper, written with milk, nothing will appear; but the way of reading it by fire being known to this friend who received the papers, he transcribed and kept together the papers, although the author himself could not correct nor view what himself had written.

It was in milk, tending to soul nourishment, even for babes and sucklings in Christ; it was in milk, spiritually white, pure and innocent, like those white horses of the word of truth and meekness, and the white linen or armor of righteousness, in the army of Jesus (Rev. 6,19); it was in milk, soft, meek, peaceable, and gentle, tending both to the peace of souls, and the peace of states and kingdoms.

Peace. The answer, though I hope out of milky pure intentions, is returned in blood --bloody and slaughterous conclusions—bloody to the souls of' all men, forced to the religion and worship which every civil state or commonweal agrees on, and compels all subjects to, in a dissembled uniformity; bloody to the bodies, first, of the holy witnesses of Christ Jesus, who testify against such invented worships, secondly, of the nations and peoples slaughtering each other for their several respective religions and consciences.

CHAPTER III

Truth. In the answer, Mr. Cotton first lays down several distinctions and conclusions of his own, tending to prove persecution.

Secondly, answers to the scriptures and arguments proposed against persecution.

Peace. The first distinction is this: by persecution for cause of conscience, "I conceive you mean either for professing some point of doctrine which you believe in conscience to be the truth, or for practicing some work which you believe in conscience to be a religious duty."

Truth. I acknowledge that to molest any person, Jew or Gentile, for either professing doctrine, or practicing worship merely religious or spiritual, it is to persecute him; and such a person, whatever his doctrine or practice be, true or false, suffers persecution for conscience.

But withal I desire it may be well observed that this distinction is not full and complete.[37] For beside this, that a man may be persecuted because he holds or practices what he believes in conscience to be a truth, as Daniel did, for which he was cast into the lions' den (Daniel 6:16), and many thousands of Christians, because they dare not cease to preach and practice what they believed, was by God commanded, as the apostles answered (Acts 4,5), I say, besides this, a man may also be persecuted because he dares not be constrained to yield obedience to such doctrines and worships as are by men invented and appointed. So the three famous Jews, who were cast into the fiery furnace for refusing to fall down in a nonconformity to the whole conforming world, before the golden image. (Daniel 3:21) So thousands of Christ's witnesses, and of late in those bloody Marian days, have rather chosen to yield their bodies to all sorts of torments than to subscribe to doctrines, or practice worships unto which the states and times (as Nebuchadnezzar to his golden image) have compelled and urged them.

A chaste wife will not only abhor to be restrained from her husband's bed as adulterous and polluted, but also abhor (if not much more) to be constrained to the bed of a stranger. And what is abominable in corporal is much more loathsome in spiritual whoredom and defilement.

---

[37] "Conscience will not be restrained from its own worship, nor constrained to another." (Williams's footnote)

'The spouse of Christ Jesus, who could not find her soul's beloved in the ways of his worship and ministry (Canticles 1,3,5), abhorred to turn aside to other flocks, worships, etc., and to embrace the bosom of a false Christ. (Canticles 1:8)

CHAPTER IV

Peace. The second distinction is this: "In points of doctrine some are fundamental, without right belief whereof a man cannot be saved; others are circumstantial and less principal, wherein a man may differ in judgment without prejudice of salvation on either part."

Truth. To this distinction I dare not subscribe, for then I should everlastingly condemn thousands, and ten thousands, yea, the whole generation of the righteous, who since the falling away from the first primitive Christian state or worship, have and do err fundamentally concerning the true matter, constitution, gathering, and governing of the church. And yet, far be it from any pious breast to imagine that they are not saved and that their souls are not bound up in the bundle of eternal life.

We read of four sorts of spiritual, or Christian, foundations in the New Testament.

First, the foundation of all foundations, the cornerstone itself, the Lord Jesus, on whom all depend—persons, doctrines, practices. (1 Cor. 3 [11])

2. Ministerial foundations. The church is built upon the foundation of the apostles and prophets. (Eph. 2: 20)

3. The foundation of future rejoicing in the fruits of obedience. (1 Tim. 6 [19])

4. The foundation of doctrines, without the knowledge of which there can be no true profession of Christ, according to the first institution—the foundation, or principles *of repentance from dead works, faith towards God, the doctrine of baptism, laying on of hands, the resurrection, and eternal judgment.* (Heb. 6 [1,2]) In some of these, to wit, those concerning baptisms and laying on of hands, God's people will be found to be ignorant for many hundred years; and I yet cannot see it

proved that light is risen, I mean the light of the first institution, in practice.[38]

God's people, in their persons, heart-waking (Canticles 5: 2), in the life of personal grace, will yet be found fast asleep in respect of public Christian worship.

God's people, in their persons, are his, most dear and precious. Yet in respect of the Christian worship they are mingled among the Babylonians, from whence they are called to come out, not locally, as some have said, for that belonged to a material and local Babel, and literal Babel and Jerusalem have now no difference, but spiritually and mystically to come out from her sins and abominations.

If Mr. Cotton maintain the true church of Christ to consist of the true matter of holy persons called out from the world (and the true form of union in a church government), and that also neither national, provincial, nor diocesan churches are of Christ's institution, how many thousands of God's people of all sorts, clergy and laity, as they call them, will they find, both in former and later times, captivated in such national, provincial, and diocesan churches? Yea, and so far from living in, yea, or knowing of any such churches, for matter and form, as they conceive now only to be true, that until of late years how few of God's people knew any other church than the parish church of dead stones or timber, it being a late marvelous light revealed by Christ Jesus, the Sun of Righteousness, that his people are a company or church of living stones? (I Peter 2:9)

And, however his own soul, and the souls of many others, precious to God, are persuaded to separate from national, provincial, and diocesan churches, and to assemble into particular churches, yet, since there are parish churches in England, but what are made up of the parish bounds within such and such a compass of houses, and that such churches have been and are in constant dependence on, and subordination to the national church, how can the New English particular churches join with the old English parish churches in so many ordinances of word, prayer, singing, contribution, etc., but they must needs confess, that as yet their souls are far from the knowledge of the foundation of a true Christian

---

[38] The laying on of hands was practiced by some churches in Rhode Island. In the 1650's there was a division within the Baptist church in Providence over the practice. About 1670 eighteen-twenty churches which practiced the laying on of hands formed a separate association. (Caldwell, p. 65)

church, whose matter must not only be living stones, but also separated from the rubbish of anti-Christian confusions and desolations?[39]

CHAPTER V

Peace. With lamentation, I may add, how can their souls be clear in this foundation of the true Christian matter, who persecute and oppress their own acknowledged brethren, presenting light unto them about this point? But I shall now present you with Mr. Cotton's third distinction. "In points of practice," says he, "some concern the weightier duties of the law, as what God we worship, and with what kind of worship; whether such, as if it be right, fellowship with God is held; if false, fellowship with God is lost."

Truth. It is worth the inquiry what kind of worship he intends. For worship is of various signification. Whether in general acceptation he mean the rightness or corruptness of the church, or the ministry of the church, or the ministrations of the word, prayer, seals, etc.

And because it pleases the Spirit of God to make the ministry one of the foundations of the Christian religion (Hebrews 6:1, 2), and also to make the ministry of the word and prayer in the church to be two special works, even of the apostles themselves (Acts 6: 2), I shall desire it may be well considered in the fear of God.

First, concerning the ministry of the word. The New English ministers, when they were new elected and ordained ministers in New England, must undeniably grant that at that time they were no ministers, notwithstanding their profession of standing so long in a true ministry in old England, whether received from the bishops, which some have maintained true, or from the people, which Mr. Cotton and others better liked, and which ministry was always accounted perpetual and indelible. I apply, and ask, will it not follow, that if their new ministry and ordination be true, the former was false? And if false, that in the exercise of it, notwithstanding abilities, graces, intentions, labors, and, by God's gracious, unpromised, and extraordinary blessing, some success, I say,

---

[39] "Mr. Cotton and all the half-Separatists, halting between true and false churches, and consequently not yet clear in the fundamental matter of a Christian church." (Williams's footnote)

will it not according to this distinction follow that, according to visible rule, fellowship with God was lost?

Secondly, concerning prayer. The New English ministers have disclaimed and written against that worshipping of God by the common or set forms of prayer, which yet themselves practiced in England, notwithstanding they knew that many servants of God, in great sufferings, witnessed against such a ministry of the word, and such a ministry of prayer.

Peace. I could name the persons, time, and place, when some of them were faithfully admonished for using of the Common Prayer, and the arguments presented to them, then seeming weak, but now acknowledged sound; yet, at that time, they satisfied their hearts with the practice of the author of the Council of Trent, who used to read only some of the choicest selected prayers in the mass-book, which I confess was also their own practice in their using of the Common Prayer. But now, according to this distinction, I ask whether or no fellowship with God in such prayers was lost?

Truth. I could particularize other exercises of worship, which cannot be denied, according to this distinction, to be of the weightier points of the law—to wit, what God we worship, and with what kind of worship?—wherein fellowship with God, in many of our unclean and abominable worships, has been lost. Only upon these premises I shall observe: first, that God's people, even the standard bearers and leaders of them, according to this distinction, have worshipped God in their sleepy ignorance, by such a kind of worship as wherein fellowship with God is lost; yea also, that it is possible for them to do, after much light is risen against such worship, and in particular, brought to the eyes of such holy and worthy persons.

Secondly, there may be inward and secret fellowship with God in false ministries of word and prayer (for that to the eternal praise of infinite mercy, beyond a word or promise of God, I acknowledge), when yet, as the distinction says, in such worship, not being right, fellowship with God is lost, and such a service or ministration must be lamented and forsaken.[40]

Thirdly, I observe that God's people may live and die in such kinds of worship, notwithstanding that light from God, publicly and privately,

---

[40] "It pleases God sometimes, beyond his promise, to convey blessings and comfort to his, in false worships." (Williams's footnote)

has been presented to them, able to convince; yet, not reaching to their conviction, and forsaking of such ways, contrary to a conclusion afterward expressed; to wit, "that fundamentals are so clear, that a man cannot but be convinced in conscience, and therefore that such a person not being convinced, he is condemned of himself, and may be persecuted for sinning against his conscience."

Fourthly, I observe, that in such a maintaining a clearness of fundamentals or weightier points, and upon that ground a persecuting of men because they sin against their consciences, Mr. Cotton measures that to others which himself, when he lived in such practices, would not have had measured to himself. As first, that it might have been affirmed of him that in such practices he did sin against his conscience, having sufficient light shining about him.

Secondly, that he should or might lawfully have been cut off by death or banishment, as an heretic, sinning against his own conscience.

And in this respect the speech by King James was notable to a great nonconformitant converted to conformity, and counseling the king to persecute the nonconformists even unto death. "You beast," quotes the king, "if I had dealt so with you in your nonconformity, where had you been?"

CHAPTER VI

Peace. The next distinction concerns the manner of persons holding forth the aforesaid practices, not only the weightier duties of the law, but points of doctrine and worship less principal.

"Some," says he, "hold them forth in a meek and peaceable way; some with such arrogance and impetuousness, as of itself tends to the disturbance of civil peace."

Truth. In the examination of this distinction we shall discuss, first, what is civil peace (wherein we shall vindicate your name the better); secondly, what it is to hold forth a doctrine, or practice, in this impetuousness or arrogancy.

First, for civil peace, what is it but *pax civitatis*, the peace of the city, whether an English city, Scotch, or Irish city, or further abroad, French, Spanish, Turkish city, etc.

Thus it pleased the Father of lights to define it (Jeremiah 29:7), *Pray for the peace of the city,* which peace of the city, or citizens, so compacted in a civil way of union, may be entire, unbroken, safe, etc., notwithstanding so many thousands of God's people, the Jews, were there in bondage, and would neither be constrained to the worship of the city Babel, nor restrained from so much of the worship of the true God as they then could practice, as is plain in the practice of the three worthies, Shadrach, Meshach, and Abednego, as also of Daniel (Daniel 3, 6)—the peace of the city or kingdom being a far different peace from the peace of the religion, or spiritual worship, maintained and professed of the citizens. This peace of their worship, which worship also in some cities being various, being a false peace, God's people were and ought to be nonconformitants, not daring either to be restrained from the true, or constrained to false worship; and yet without breach of the civil or city peace, properly so called.

Peace. Hence it is that so many glorious and flourishing cities of the world maintain their civil peace; yea, the very Americans and wildest pagans keep the peace of their towns or cities, though neither in one nor the other can any man prove a true church of God in those places, and consequently no spiritual and heavenly peace, the peace spiritual, whether true or false, being of a higher and far different nature from the peace of the place or people, being merely and essentially civil and human.

Truth. Oh! how lost are the sons of men in this point! To illustrate this: the church, or company of worshippers, whether true or false, is like unto a body or college of physicians in a city, like unto a corporation, society, or company of East India or Turkey merchants, or any other society or company in London, which companies may hold their courts, keep their records, hold disputations, and in matters concerning their society may dissent, divide, break into schisms and factions, sue and implead each other at the law, yea, wholly break up and dissolve into pieces and nothing, and yet the peace of the city not be in the least measure impaired or disturbed, because the essence or being of the city, and so the well being and peace thereof, is essentially distinct from those particular societies; the city courts, city laws, city punishments distinct from theirs. The city was before them, and stands absolute and entire when such a corporation or society is taken down. Again, the church of Christ in Ephesus, which were God's people, converted and called out from the worship of that city unto Christianity, or worship of God in Christ, was distinct from both.

Now suppose that God remove the candlestick from Ephesus, yea, though the whole worship of the city of Ephesus should be altered; yet, if men be true and honestly ingenuous to city covenants, combinations, and principles, all this might be without the least impeachment or infringement of the peace of the city of Ephesus.

Thus in the city of Smyrna was the city itself or civil estate one thing, the spiritual or religious state of Smyrna another; the church of Christ in Smyrna distinct from them both. And the synagogue of the Jews, whether literally Jews as some think, or mystically false Christians as others called the synagogue of Satan (Rev. 2), distinct from all these. And notwithstanding these spiritual oppositions in point of worship and religion, yet hear we not the least noise, nor need we, if men keep but the bond of civility, of any civil breach, or breach of civil peace among them; and to persecute God's people there for religion, that only was a breach of civility itself.

CHAPTER VII

Peace. Now to the second query, what it is to hold forth doctrine or practice in an arrogant or impetuous way?

Truth. Although it has not pleased Mr. Cotton to declare what is this arrogant or impetuous holding forth of doctrine or practice trending to disturbance of civil peace, I cannot express my sad and sorrowful observation, how it pleases God to leave him as to take up the common reproachful accusation of God's children, to wit, that they are arrogant and impetuous. Which charge, together with that of obstinacy, pertinacity, pride, troublers of the city, etc., Satan commonly loads the meekest of the saints and witnesses of Jesus with.

To wipe off, therefore, these foul blurs and aspersions from the fair and beautiful face of the spouse of Jesus, I shall select and propose five or six cases, for which God's witnesses in all ages and generations of men have been charged with arrogance, impetuousness, etc., and yet the God of heaven and judge of all men has graciously discharged them from such crimes, and maintained and avowed them for his faithful and peaceable servants.

First, God's people have proclaimed, taught, disputed, for divers months together, a new religion and worship, contrary to the worship projected in the town, city, or state where they have lived, or where they have traveled, as did the Lord Jesus himself over all Galilee, and the apostles after him in all places, both in the synagogues and market-places, as appears Acts 17:2,17 and Acts 18:4,8. Yet there is no arrogance or impetuousness.

Secondly, God's servants have been zealous for their Lord and Master, even to the very faces of the highest, and concerning the persons of the highest, so far as they have opposed the truth of God. So Elijah to the face of Ahab: *It is not I, but you and your father's house, that troubles Israel.* (1 Kings 18:18) So the Lord Jesus concerning Herod: *Go, tell that fox.* (Luke 13:3) So Paul: *God delivered me from the mouth of the lion;* [2 Tim. 4:17] and to Ananias, *You whited wall.* (Acts 23:3) And yet in all this no arrogance, nor impetuousness.

Thirdly, God's people have been immovable, constant, and resolved to the death in refusing to submit to false worships, and in preaching and professing the true worship, contrary to the express command of public authority. So the three famous worthies against the command of Nebuchanezzar, and the uniform conformity of all nations agreeing upon a false worship (Dan. 3). So the apostles (Acts 4, 5), and so the witnesses of Jesus in all ages, who loved not their lives to the death (Rev. 12), not regarding sweet life nor bitter death, and yet not arrogant, nor impetuous.

Fourthly, God's people, since the coming of the King of Israel, the Lord Jesus, have openly and constantly professed that no civil magistrate, no king, nor Caesar, have any power over the souls or consciences of their subjects in the matters of God and the crown of Jesus, but the civil magistrates themselves, yea, kings and Caesars, are bound to subject their own souls to the ministry and church, the power and government of this Lord Jesus, the King of Kings. Hence was the charge against the apostles (false in civil but true in spirituals) that they affirmed that there was another King, one Jesus. (Acts 17:7) And indeed, this was the great charge against the Lord Jesus himself which the Jews laid against him, and for which he suffered death, as appears by the accusation written over his head upon the gallows (John 19:19), *Jesus of Nazareth, King of the Jews.*

This was and is the sum of all true preaching of the gospel, or glad news, viz., that God anointed Jesus to be the sole King and Governor of

all the Israel of God in spiritual and soul causes (Psalm 2:6; Acts 2:36).
Yet this kingly power of his he resolved not to manage in his own person,
but ministerially in the hands of such messengers which he sent forth to
preach and baptize, and to such as believed that word they preached.
(John 17) And yet here no arrogance, nor impetuousness.

5. God's people, in delivering the mind and will of God concerning
the kingdoms and civil states where they have lived, have seemed in all
show of common sense and rational policy, if men look not higher with
the eye of faith, to endanger and overthrow the very civil state, as appears
by all Jeremiah's preaching and counsel to King Zedekiah, his princes and
people, insomuch that the charge of the princes against Jeremiah was that
he discouraged the army from fighting against the Babylonians, and
weakened the land from its own defense; and this charge in the eye of
reason seemed not to be unreasonable, or unrighteous. (Jer. 37, 38) And
yet in Jeremiah no arrogance, nor impetuousness.

6. Lastly, God's people, by their preaching, disputing, etc., have
been, though not the cause, yet accidentally the occasion of great
contentions and divisions, yea, tumults and uproars, in towns and cities
where they have lived and come; and yet neither their doctrine nor
themselves arrogant nor impetuous, however so charged. For thus the
Lord Jesus discovers men's false and secure suppositions, *Suppose you
that I am come to give peace on the earth? I tell you, nay; but rather division;
for from henceforth shall there be five in one house divided, three against
two, and two against three, the father shall be divided against the son and
the son against the father*, etc. (Luke 12:61) And thus upon the occasion of
the apostles' preaching the kingdom and worship of God in Christ were
most commonly uproars and tumults wherever they came. For instance,
those strange and monstrous uproars at Iconium, at Ephesus, at
Jerusalem. (Acts 14: 4; 19:29, 40; 21:30, 31)

CHAPTER VIII

Peace. It will be said, dear Truth, what the Lord Jesus and his
messengers taught was truth; but the question is about error.

Truth. I answer, this distinction now in discussion concerns not
truth or error, but the manner of holding forth or divulging.

I acknowledge that such may be the way and manner of holding forth, either with railing or reviling, daring or challenging speeches, or with force of arms, swords, guns, prisons, etc., that it may not only tend to break, but may actually break the civil peace, or peace of the city.

Yet these instances propounded are cases of great opposition and spiritual hostility, and occasions of breach of civil peace; and yet as the borders, or matter, were of gold, so the specks, or manner, (Cant. 1) were of silver: both matter and manner pure, holy, peaceable, and inoffensive.

Moreover, I answer, that it is possible and common for persons of soft and gentle nature and spirits to hold out falsehood with more seeming meekness and peaceableness than the Lord Jesus or his servants did or do hold forth the true and everlasting gospel. So that the answerer would be requested to explain what he means by this arrogant and impetuous holding forth of any doctrine which very manner of holding forth tends to break civil peace, and comes under the cognizance and correction of the civil magistrate, lest he build the sepulchre of the prophets, and say, If we had been in the Pharisees' days, the Roman emperor's days, or the bloody Marian days, we would not have been partakers with them in the blood of the prophets (Matt. 23:30), who were charged with arrogance and impetuousness.

CHAPTER IX

Peace. It will here be said, whence then arise civil dissentions and uproars about matters of religion?

Truth. I answer: When a kingdom or state, town or family, lies and lives in the guilt of a false god, false Christ, false worship, no wonder if sore eyes be troubled at the appearance of the light, be it never so sweet. No wonder if a body full of corrupt humors be troubled at strong, though wholesome, physic—if persons sleepy and loving to sleep be troubled at the noise of shrill, though silver, alarms. No wonder if Adonijah and all his company be amazed and troubled at the sound of the right heir, King Solomon (1 Kings 1)—if the husbandmen were troubled when the Lord of the vineyard sent servant after servant, and at last his only son, and they beat, and wounded, and killed even the son himself, because they meant themselves to seize upon the inheritance, unto which they had no right. (Matt. 21:38) Hence all those tumults about the apostles in the

Acts, etc. Whereas, good eyes are not so troubled at light; vigilant and watchful persons, loyal and faithful, are not so troubled at the true, no, nor at a false religion of Jew or Gentile.

Secondly, breach of civil peace may arise when false and idolatrous practices are held forth, and yet no breach of civil peace from the doctrine or practice, or the manner of holding forth, but from that wrong and preposterous way of suppressing, preventing, and extinguishing such doctrines or practices by weapons of wrath and blood, whips, stocks, imprisonment, banishment, death, etc., by which men commonly are persuaded to convert heretics, and to cast out unclean spirits, which only the finger of God can do, that is, the mighty power of the Spirit in the word.

Hence, the town is in an uproar, and the country takes the alarm to expel that fog or mist of error, heresy, blasphemy, as is supposed, with swords and guns. Whereas it is light alone, even light from the bright shining Sun of Righteousness, which is able, in the souls and consciences of men, to dispel and scatter such fogs and darkness.

Hence the sons of men, as David speaks in another case (Psalm 39 [6]), disquiet themselves in vain, and unmercifully disquiet others, as, by the help of the Lord, in the sequel of this discourse shall more appear.

CHAPTER X

Peace. Now the last distinction is this: "Persecution for conscience is either for a rightly informed conscience, or a blind and erroneous conscience."

Truth. Indeed, both these consciences are persecuted; but lamentably blind and erroneous will those consciences shortly appear to be which out of zeal for God, as is pretended, have persecuted either. And heavy is the doom of those blind guides and idol shepherds, whose right eye God's finger of jealousy has put out, who flattering the ten horns, or worldly powers, persuade them what excellent and faithful service they perform to God in persecuting both these consciences; either hanging up a rightly informed conscience, and therein the Lord Jesus himself, between two malefactors, or else killing the erroneous and the blind, like Saul, out of zeal to the Israel of God, the poor Gibeonites, whom it pleased God to permit to live; and yet that hostility and cruelty used against them, as the repeated judgment year after year upon the whole land after told them, could not be pardoned until the death of the persecutor, Saul [and] his sons, had appeased the Lord's displeasure. (2 Sam. 21)

CHAPTER XI

Peace. After explication in these distinctions, it pleases the answerer to give his resolution to the question in four particulars.

First, that he holds it "not lawful to persecute any for conscience' sake rightly informed, for in persecuting such," says he, "Christ himself is persecuted." For which reason, truly rendered, he quotes Acts 9:4, *Saul, Saul, why persecutest thou me?*

Truth. He that shall read this conclusion over a thousand times, shall as soon find darkness in the bright beams of the sun, as in this so clear and shining a beam of truth; viz., that Christ Jesus, in his truth, must not be persecuted.

Yet, this I must ask, for it will be admired by all sober men, what should be the cause or inducement to the answerer's mind to lay down such a position or thesis as this is, It is not lawful to persecute the Lord Jesus?

Search all scriptures, histories, records, monuments; consult with all experiences; did ever Pharaoh, Saul, Ahab, Jezebel, scribes and Pharisees, the Jews, Herod, the bloody Neros, Gardiners,[41] Bonners,[42] pope, or devil himself, profess to persecute the Son of God, Jesus as Jesus, Christ as Christ without a mask or covering?

No, says Pharaoh, the Israelites are idle, and therefore speak they of sacrificing. David is risen up in a conspiracy against Saul, therefore

---

[41] Stephen Gardiner (11483?-1555), Bishop of Windsor. His patron was Thomas, Cardinal Wolsey, Lord Chancellor of England under Henry VIII. After being excluded from the Privy Council under Edward VI, he was made Lord Chancellor under Mary. Along with Bonner, he was largely responsible for the cruelties imposed on Protestants during Mary's reign.

[42] Edmund Bonner (1500?-1569), Bishop of London. Subscribed to the principle of the supremacy of the monarch, was deprived of the bishopric under Edward VI, and imprisoned until the reign of Mary in 1553. Foxe's *Book of Martyrs* says that he "burned heretics cheerfully." He refused to take the oath of supremacy under Elizabeth, and was deprived of the bishopric and imprisoned again. He died in prison.

persecute him. Naboth has blasphemed God and the king, therefore stone him. Christ is a seducer of the people, a blasphemer against God, and traitor against Caesar, therefore hang him. Christians are schismatical, factious, heretical, therefore persecute them. The devil has deluded John Huss, therefore crown him with a paper of devils, and burn him, etc.

Peace. One thing I see apparently in the Lord's overruling the pen of this worthy answerer, viz., a secret whispering from heaven to him, that although his soul aim at Christ, and has wrought much for Christ in many sincere intentions, and God's merciful and patient acceptance, yet he has never left the tents of such who think they do God good service in killing the Lord Jesus in his servants. And yet they say, if we had been in the days of' our fathers, in Queen Mary's days, etc., we would never have consented to such persecution. And therefore, when they persecute Christ Jesus in his truths or servants, they say, "Do not say you are persecuted for the word, for Christ's sake: for we hold it not lawful to persecute Jesus Christ."

Let me also add it second: So far as he has been a guide, by preaching for persecution, I say, wherein he has been a guide and leader, by misinterpreting and, applying the writings of' truth, so far, I say, his own mouth and hands shall judge (I hope not his person, but) his actions; for the Lord Jesus has suffered by him. (Acts 9:5) And if the Lord Jesus himself were present, himself should suffer that in his own person, which his servants witnessing his truth do suffer for his sake.

CHAPTER XII

Peace. Their second conclusion is this: "It is not lawful to persecute an erroneous and blind conscience, even in fundamental and weighty points, till after admonition once or twice (Titus 3: 11), and then such consciences may be persecuted; because the word of God is so clear in fundamental and weighty points, that such a person cannot but sin against his conscience, and so being condemned of himself, that is, of his conscience, he may be persecuted for sinning against his own conscience."

Truth. I answer, in that great battle between the Lord Jesus and the devil, it is observable that Satan takes up the weapons of scripture, and such scripture which in show and color was excellent for his purpose; but in this third of Titus, as Solomon speaks of the birds of heaven (Prov. 1 [17]), a man may evidently see the snare: and I know the time is coming wherein it shall be said, *Surely in vain the net is laid in the sight of the saints (heavenly birds).*

So palpably gross and thick is the mist and fog which Satan has raised about this scripture, that he that can but see men as trees in matters of God's worship may easily discern what a wonderful deep sleep God's people are fallen into concerning the visible kingdom of Christ; insomuch that this third of Titus, which through fearful profanations has so many hundred years been the pretended bulwark and defense of all the bloody wolves, dens of lions, and mountains of leopards, hunting and devouring the witnesses of Jesus, should now be the refuge and defense of (as I hope) the lambs and little ones of Jesus; yet, in this point, so preaching and practicing so unlike to themselves, to the Lord Jesus, and lamentably too like to his and their persecutors.

CHAPTER XIII

Peace. Bright Truth, since this place of Titus is such a pretended bulwark for persecuting of heretics, and under that pretence of persecuting all your followers, I beseech you by the bright beams of the Sun of Righteousness, scatter these mists, and unfold these particulars out of the text:

First, what this man is that is an heretic.

Secondly, how this heretic is condemned of himself.

Thirdly, what is this first and second admonition, and by whom it is supposed to be given.

Fourthly, what is this rejecting of him, and by whom it is supposed this rejection was to be made.

Truth. First, what is this heretic? I find him commonly defined to be such an one as is obstinate in fundamentals, and so also I conceive the answerer seems to resent him, saying, that the apostle renders this reason why after once and twice admonition he ought to be persecuted; because in fundamental and principal points of doctrine and worship, the word of God is so clear that the heretic cannot but be convinced in his own conscience.

But of this reason, I find not one tittle mentioned in this scripture. For although he says such an one is condemned of himself, yet he says not, nor will it follow, that fundamentals are so clear that after first and second admonition a person that submits not to them is condemned of himself, any more than in lesser points. This eleventh verse has reference to the former verses. Titus, an evangelist, a preacher of glad news, abiding here with the church of Christ at Crete, is required by Paul to avoid, to reject, and to teach the church to reject, genealogies, disputes, and unprofitable questions about the law. Such a like charge it is as he gave to Timothy, left also an evangelist at Ephesus. (I Timothy 1: 4)

If it should be objected, what is to be done to such contentious, vain strivers about genealogies and questions unprofitable? The apostle seems plainly to answer, Let him be once and twice admonished.

Objection. Yea, but what if once and twice admonition prevail not?

The apostle seems to answer, (αιρετικον ανθρωπον); and that is, the man that is willfully obstinate after such once and twice admonition, reject him.

With this scripture agrees that of 1 Timothy 6: 4, 6, where Timothy is commanded to withdraw himself from such who dote about questions and strifes of words.

All which are points of a lower and inferior nature, not properly falling within the terms or notions of those (στοιχεια) first principles, and (θεμελιους) foundations of the Christian profession, to wit, repentance from dead works, faith towards God, the doctrine of baptism, and of laying on of hands, the resurrection, and eternal judgment. (Heb. 6: 2, etc.)

Concerning these fundamentals (although nothing is so little in the Christian worship, but may be referred to one of these six, yet) does not Paul to Timothy or Titus speak in those places by me alleged, or of any of these, as may evidently appear by the context and scope.

The beloved spouse of Christ is no receptacle for any filthy person, obstinate in any filthiness against the purity of the Lord Jesus, who has commanded his people to purge out the old leaven, not only greater portions, but a little leaven which will leaven the whole lump; and therefore this heretic, or obstinate person in these vain and unprofitable questions, was to be rejected, as well as if his obstinacy had been in greater matters.

Again, if there were a door or window left open to vain and unprofitable questions, and sins of smaller nature, how apt are persons to cover with a silken covering, and to say, Why, I am no heretic in fundamentals, spare me in this or that little one, this or that opinion or practice; these are of an inferior circumstantial nature, etc.

So that the coherence with the former verses, and the scope of the Spirit of God in this and other like scriptures being carefully observed, this Greek word *heretic* is no more in true English, and in truth, than an obstinate and willful person in the church of Crete, striving and contending about those unprofitable questions and genealogies, etc.; and is not such a monster intended in this place, as most interpreters run upon, to wit, one obstinate in fundamentals, and, as the answerer makes the apostle to write, in such fundamentals and principal points wherein the word of God is so clear that a man cannot but be convinced in conscience, and therefore is not persecuted for matter of conscience, but for sinning against his conscience.

CHAPTER XIV

Peace. Now, in the second place, what is this self-condemnation?

Truth. The apostle seems to make this a ground of the rejecting of such a person—because he is subverted and sins, being condemned of himself. It will appear upon due search that this self-condemning is not here intended to be in heretics (as men say) in fundamentals only; but, as it is meant here, in men obstinate in the lesser questions, etc.

First, he is subverted, or turned crooked, αμαρτανει, a word opposite to straightness, or rightness. So that the scope is, as I conceive, upon true and faithful admonition once or twice, the pride of heart, or heat of wrath, draws a veil over the eyes and heart, so that the soul is turned and loosed from the checks of truth.

Secondly, he sins, εξεστραπται; that is, being subverted, or turned aside, he sins, or wanders from the path of truth, and is condemned by himself, αυτοκατακριτος; that is, by the secret checks and whisperings of his own conscience, which will take God's part against a man's self in smiting, accusing, etc.

Which checks of conscience we find even in God's own dear people, as is most admirably opened in the fifth of Canticles, in those sad, drowsy, and unkind passages of the spouse, in her answer to the knocks and calls of the Lord Jesus; which God's people, in all their awakenings, acknowledge how slightly they have listened to the checks of their own consciences. This the answerer pleases to call sinning against his conscience, for which he may lawfully be persecuted: to wit, for sinning against his conscience.

Which conclusion—though painted over with the vermilion of mistaken scripture, and that old dream of Jew and Gentile that the crown of Jesus will consist of outward material gold, and his sword be made of iron or steel, executing judgment in his church and kingdom by corporal punishment—I hope, by the assistance of the Lord Jesus, to manifest it to be the overturning and rooting up the very foundations and roots of all true Christianity, and absolutely denying the Lord Jesus, the great anointed, to be yet come in the flesh.

CHAPTER XV

This will appear, if we examine the two last queries of this place of Titus; to wit,

First, what this admonition is?

Secondly, what is the rejection here intended? Reject him.

First, then, Titus, unto whom this epistle and these directions were written, and in him to all that succeed men in the like work of the gospel to the world's end, was no minister of the civil state, armed with the majesty and terror of a material sword, who might for offences against the civil state inflict punishments upon the bodies of men by imprisonments, whippings, fines, banishment, death. Titus was a minister of the gospel, or glad tidings, armed only with the spiritual sword of the word of God, and with such spiritual weapons as (yet) through God were mighty to the casting down of strongholds, yea, every high thought of the highest head and heart in the world (II Corinthians 10:4)

Therefore, these first and second admonitions were not civil or corporal punishments on men's persons or purses, which courts of men may lawfully inflict upon malefactors; but they were the reprehensions, convictions, exhortations, and persuasions of the word of the eternal God, charged home to the conscience in the name and presence of the

Lord Jesus, in the midst of the church. Which being despised and not hearkened to, in the last place follows rejection; which is not a cutting off by heading, hanging, burning, etc., or an expelling of the country and coasts; neither which (no, nor any lesser civil punishment) Titus, nor the church at Crete, had any power to exercise. But it was that dreadful cutting off from that visible head and body, Christ Jesus and his church; that purging out of the old leaven from the lump of the saints; the putting away of the evil and wicked person from the holy land and commonwealth of God's Israel, (1 Cor. 5 [6, 7] where it is observable, that the same word used by Moses for putting a malefactor to death, in typical Israel, by sword, stoning, etc. (Deut. 13:6), here used by Paul for the spiritual killing, or cutting off by excommunication, *Put away that evil person, etc.* (1 Cor. 5:13)

Now, I desire the answerer, and any in the holy awe and fear of God, to consider that from whom the first and second admonition was to proceed, from them also was the rejecting or casting out to proceed as before. But not from the civil magistrate to whom Paul writes not this epistle, and who also is not bound once and twice to admonish, but may speedily punish, as he sees cause, the persons or purses of delinquents against his civil state; but from Titus, the minister or angel of the church, and from the church with him, were these first and second admonitions to proceed.

And, therefore, at last also, this rejecting, which can be no other but a casting out, or excommunicating of him from their church society.

Indeed, this rejecting is no other than that avoiding which Paul writes of to the church of Christ at Rome (Rom. 16:17); which avoiding, however woefully perverted by some to prove persecution, belonged to the governors of Christ's church and kingdom in Rome and not to the Roman emperor, for him to rid and avoid the world of them by bloody and cruel persecution.

CHAPTER XVI

Peace. The third conclusion is in points of lesser moment there ought to be a toleration.

Which though I acknowledge to be the truth of God, yet three things are very observable in the manner of laying it down: for Satan uses excellent arrows to bad marks, and sometimes beyond the intent, and hidden from eye of the archer.

First, says he, such a person is to be tolerated till God may be pleased to reveal his truth to him.

Truth. This is well observed by you: for indeed this is the very ground why the apostle calls for meekness and gentleness toward all men, and toward such as oppose themselves (2 Tim. 2 [25]); because there is a peradventure, or it may be; *It may be God may give them repentance.* That God that has shown mercy to one, may show mercy to another. It may be that eye salve that anointed one man's eye who was blind and opposite, may anoint another as blind and opposite. He that has given repentance to the husband, may give it to his wife, etc.

Hence the soul that is lively and sensible of mercy received to itself in former blindness, opposition, and in their enmity against God, cannot but be patient and gentle toward the Jews, who yet deny the Lord Jesus to be come, and justify their forefathers in murdering of him: toward the Turks, who acknowledge Christ a great prophet, yet less than Mahomet: yea, to all the several sorts of anti-Christians, who set up many a false Christ instead of him: and, lastly, to the pagans, and wildest sorts of the sons of men, who have not yet heard of the Father, nor the Son: and to all these sorts, Jews, Turks, anti-Christians, pagans, when they oppose the light presented to them, in sense of its own former opposition, and that God peradventure may at last give repentance. I add, such a soul will not only be patient, but earnestly and constantly pray for all sorts of men, that out of them God's elect may be called to the fellowship of Christ Jesus; and, lastly, not only pray, but endeavour, to its utmost ability, their participation of the same grace and mercy.

That great rock upon which so many gallant ships miscarry, viz., that such persons, false prophets, heretics, etc., were to be put to death in Israel, I shall, with God's assistance, remove. As also that fine silken covering of the image, viz., that such persons ought to be put to death, or banished, to prevent the infecting and seducing of others, I shall, with God's assistance, in the following discourse pluck off.

Secondly, I observe from the scriptures he quotes for this toleration (Phil. 3[17] and Rom. 14[1-4]), how closely, yet I hope unadvisedly, he makes the churches of Christ at Philippi and Rome all one with the cities Philippi and Rome, in which the churches were, and to whom only Paul wrote. As if what these churches in Philippi and Rome must tolerate

among themselves, that the cities Philippi and Rome must tolerate in
their citizens: and what these churches must not tolerate, that these cities,
Philippi and Rome, must not tolerate within the compass of the city,
state, and jurisdiction.

Truth. Upon that ground, by undeniable consequence, these cities,
Philippi and Rome, were bound not to tolerate themselves, that is, the
cities and citizens of Philippi and Rome, in their own civil life and being;
but must kill or expel themselves from their own cities, as being
idolatrous worshippers of other gods than the true God in Jesus Christ.

But as the lily is among the thorns, so is Christ's among the
daughters; and as the apple tree among the trees of the forest, so is her
beloved among the sons; so great a difference is there between the church
in a city or country, and the civil state, city, or country in which it is.

No less then (as David in another case, Psalm 103 [11], *as far as the
heavens are from the earth*) are they that are truly Christ's (that is,
anointed truly with the Spirit of Christ) from many thousands who love
not the Lord Jesus Christ, and yet are and must be permitted in the
world, or civil state, although they have no right to enter into the gates of
Jerusalem, the church of God.

And this is the more carefully to be minded, because whenever a
toleration of others' religion and conscience is pleaded for, such as are (I
hope in truth) zealous for God, readily produce plenty of scriptures
written to the church, both before and since Christ's coming, all
commanding and pressing the putting forth of the unclean, the cutting
off the obstinate, the purging out the leaven, rejecting of heretics. As if
because briars, thorns, and thistles may not be in the garden of the
church, therefore they must not be plucked up out of the wilderness.
Whereas he that is a briar, that is, a Jew, a Turk, a pagan, an anti-
Christian, today, may be, when the word of the Lord run freely, a
member of Jesus Christ tomorrow, cut out of the wild olive and planted
into the true.

Peace. Thirdly, from this toleration of persons but holding lesser
errors, I observe the unmercifulness of such doctrines and hearts, as if
they had forgotten the blessedness; *Blessed are the merciful for they shall
obtain mercy.* (Matt. 5[7]) He that is slightly and but a little hurt, shall be
suffered, and means vouchsafed for his cure. But the deep wounded
sinners, and leprous, ulcerous, and those of bloody issues twelve years
together, and those which have been bowed down thirty-eight years of

their life, they must not be suffered, until peradventure God may give them repentance. But either it is not lawful for a godly magistrate to rule and govern such a people, as some have said, or else if they be under government, and reform not to the state religion after the first and second admonition, the civil magistrate is bound to persecute, etc.

Truth. Such persons have need, as Paul to the Romans (12:1), to be besought by the mercy of God to put on bowels of mercy toward such as have neither wronged them in body nor goods, and therefore justly should not be punished in their goods or persons.

CHAPTER XVII

Peace. I shall now trouble you, dear Truth, but with one conclusion more, which is this, viz., that if a man hold forth error with a boisterous and arrogant spirit, to the disturbance of the civil peace, he ought to be punished, etc.

Truth. To this I have spoken to, confessing that if any man commit aught of those things which Paul was accused of (Acts 25:11), he ought not to be spared, yea, he ought not, as Paul says, in such cases to refuse to die.

But if the matter be of another nature, a spiritual and divine nature, I have written before in many cases, and might in many more, that the worship which a state professes may be contradicted and preached against, and yet no breach of civil peace. And if a breach follow, it is not made by such doctrines, but by the boisterous and violent opposers of them.

Such persons only break the city's or kingdom's peace, who cry out for prison and swords against such who cross their judgment or practice in religion. For as Joseph's mistress accused Joseph of uncleanness, and calls out for civil violence against him, when Joseph was chaste and herself guilty, so, commonly, the meek and peaceable of the earth are traduced as rebels, factious, peace-breakers, although they deal not with the state or state matters, but matters of divine and spiritual nature, when their traducers are the only unpeaceable, and guilty of breach of civil peace.

Peace. We are now come to the second part of the answer, which is a particular examination of such grounds as are brought against such persecution.

The first sort of grounds are from the scriptures.

CHAPTER XVIII

First, Because Christ commands to let alone the tares to grow up together with the wheat, until the harvest. (Matthew 13:30, 38)

Unto which he answers: "That the tares are not briars and thorns, but partly hypocrites, like unto the godly, but indeed carnal, as the tares are like to wheat, but are not wheat ; or partly such corrupt doctrines or practices as are indeed unsound, but yet such as come very near the truth (as tares do to the wheat), and so near that good men may be taken with them; and so the persons in whom they grow cannot be rooted out but good wheat will be rooted out with them. In such a case," says he, "Christ calls for peaceable toleration, and not for penal prosecution, according to the third conclusion."

Truth. The substance of this answer I conceive to be, first negative; that by tares are not meant persons of another religion and worship, that is, says he, "they are not briars and thorns."

Secondly, affirmative; by tares are meant either persons, or doctrines, or practices; persons, as hypocrites, like the godly; doctrines or practices corrupt, yet like the truth.

For answer hereunto, I confess that not only those worthy witnesses, whose memories are sweet with all that fear God, Calvin, Beza, etc., but of later times many conjoin with this worthy answerer to satisfy themselves and others with such an interpretation.

But, alas! how dark is the soul left that desires to walk with God in holy fear and trembling, when in such a weighty and mighty point as this is, that in matters of conscience concerns the spilling of the blood of thousands, and the civil peace of the world in the taking up arms to suppress all false religions!—when, I say, no evidence, or demonstration of the Spirit is brought to prove such an interpretation, nor arguments from the place itself or the scriptures of truth to confirm it; but a bare affirmation that these tares must signify persons, or doctrines and practices.

I will not imagine any deceitful purpose in the answerer's thoughts in the proposal of these three—persons, doctrines, or practices; yet dare I confidently avouch that the old serpent has deceived their perilous souls, and by tongue and pen would deceive the souls of others by such a method of dividing the word of truth. A threefold cord, and so a threefold snare, is strong; and too like it is that one of the three, either persons, doctrines, or practices, may catch some feet.

CHAPTER XIX

Peace. The place then being of such importance as concerning the truth of God, the blood of thousands, yea, the blood of saints, and of the Lord Jesus in them, I shall request your more diligent search, by the Lord's holy assistance, into this scripture.

Truth. I shall make it evident that by these tares in this parable are meant persons in respect of their religion and way of worship, open and visible professors, as bad as briars and thorns; not only suspected foxes, but as bad as those greedy wolves which Paul speaks of (Acts 20 [29]), who with perverse and evil doctrines labor spiritually to devour the flock, and to draw away disciples after them, whose mouths must be stopped, and yet no carnal force and weapon to be used against them; but their mischief to be resisted with those mighty weapons of the holy armory of the Lord Jesus, wherein there hangs a thousand shields. (Cant. 4 [4])

That the Lord Jesus intends not doctrines, or practices, by the tares in this parable, is clear; for, first, the Lord Jesus expressly interprets the good seed to be persons, and those the children of the kingdom; and the tares also to signify men, and those the children of the wicked one. ([Matt. 13] 38)

Secondly, such corrupt doctrines or practices are not to be tolerated now, as those Jewish observations, the Lord's own ordinances, were for a while to be permitted. (Romans 14) Nor so long as till the angels, the reapers, come to reap the harvest in the end of the world. For can we think that because the tender consciences of the Jews were to be tendered in their differences of meats that therefore persons must now be tolerated in the church (for I speak not of the civil state), and that to the world's end, in superstitious forbearing and forbidding of flesh in popish Lents, and superstitious Fridays, etc.; and that because they were to be tendered in their observation of Jewish holidays, that therefore until the harvest, or world's end, persons must now be tolerated (I mean in the church) in the observation of popish Christmas, Easter, Whitsuntide, and other superstitious popish festivals?

I willingly acknowledge that if the members of a church of Christ shall upon some delusion of Satan kneel at the Lord's Supper, keep Christmas, or any other popish observation, great tenderness ought to be used in winning his soul from the error of his way; and yet I see not that persons so practicing were fit to be received into the churches of Christ now, as the Jews, weak in the faith, that is, in the liberties of Christ, were to be received. (Rom. 14:1) And least of all (as before) that the toleration or permission of such ought to continue till doomsday, or the end of the world, as this parable urges the toleration: *Let them alone until the harvest.*

CHAPTER XX

Again, hypocrites were not intended by the Lord Jesus in this famous parable.[43]

First, the original word ζιζανια, signifying all those weeds which spring up with the corn, as cockle, darnel, tares, etc., seems to imply such a kind of people as commonly and generally are known to be manifestly different from, and opposite to, the true worshippers of God, here called the children of the kingdom: as these weeds, tares, cockle, darnel, etc., are commonly and presently known by every husbandman to differ from the wheat, and to be opposite, and contrary, and hurtful unto it.

Now whereas it is pleaded that these tares are like the wheat, and so like that this consimilitude, or likeness, is made the ground of this

---

[43] "Tares proved not to signify hypocrites. Hence were the witnesses of Christ, Wyclif and others, in H. 4 his reign [the reign of Henry IV] called Lollards, (as some say) from Lolia, weeds known well enough, hence taken for the sign of barrenness: *infelix lolium & steriles,inantur avenae.* [Virgil, *Georgics*] Others conceive they were so called from one Lollard, etc., but all papists accounted them as tares because of their profession." (Williams's footnote)

interpretation, viz., that tares must needs signify hypocrites, or doctrines, or practices, who are like God's children, truth, etc., I answer, first, the parable holds forth no such thing, that the likeness of the tares should deceive the servants to cause them to suppose for a time that they were good wheat; but that as soon as ever the tares appeared (verse 26), the servants came to the householder about them (verse 27). The scripture holds forth no such time wherein they doubted or suspected what they were.

Peace. It may be said they did not appear to be tares until the corn was in the blade, and put forth its fruit.

Truth. I answer, the one appeared as soon as the other; for so the word clearly carries it, that seed of both having been sown, when the wheat appeared and put forth its blade and fruit, the tares also were as early, and put forth themselves, or appeared also.

Secondly, there is such a dissimilitude, or unlikeness, I say such a dissimilitude, that as soon as the tares and wheat are sprung up to blade and fruit, every husbandman can tell which is wheat, and which are tares and cockle, etc.

Peace. It may be said, True: so when the hypocrite is manifested, then all may know him, etc.; but before hypocrites be manifested by fruits they are unknown.

[Truth]. I answer: search into the parable, and ask when was it that the servants first complained of the tares to the householder, but when they appeared or came in sight, there being no interim wherein the servants could not tell what to make of them, but doubted whether they were wheat or tares, as the answerer implies.

Secondly, when was it that the householder gave charge to let them alone, but after that they appeared, and were known to be tares; which should imply by this interpretation of the answerer, that when men are discovered and known to be hypocrites, yet, still such a generation of hypocrites in the church must be let alone and tolerated until the harvest, or end of the world; which is contrary to all order, piety, and safety, in the church of the Lord Jesus, as doubtless the answerer will grant. So that these tares being notoriously known to be different from the corn, I conclude that they cannot here be intended by the Lord Jesus to signify secret hypocrites, but more open and apparent sinners.

CHAPTER XXI

The second reason why these tares cannot signify hypocrites in the church, I take from the Lord Jesus' own interpretation of the field in which both wheat and tares are sown, which, says he, is the world, out of which God chooses and calls his church.[44]

The world lies in wickedness, is like a wilderness, or a sea of wild beasts innumerable, fornicators, covetous, idolaters, etc., with whom God's people may lawfully converse and cohabit in cities, towns, etc., else must they not live in the world, but go out of it. In which world as soon as ever the Lord Jesus had sown the good seed, the children of the kingdom, true Christianity, or the true church, the enemy, Satan, presently, in the night of security, ignorance, and error, while men slept, sowed also these tares which are anti-Christians, or false Christians. These strange professors of the name of Jesus the ministers and prophets of God beholding, they are ready to run to heaven to fetch fiery judgments from thence to consume these strange Christians, and to pluck them by the roots out of the world. But the Son of man, the meek Lamb of God—for the elect's sake which must be gathered out of Jew and Gentile, pagan, anti-Christian – commands a permission of them in the world until the time of the end of the world, when the goats and sheep, the tares and wheat, shall be eternally separated each from other.

Peace. You know some excellent worthies, dead and living, have labored to turn this field of the world into the garden of the church.

Truth. But who can imagine that the wisdom of the Father, the Lord Jesus Christ, would so open this parable, as he professedly does, as that it should be closer shut up, and that one difficulty or lock should be opened by a greater and harder, in calling the world the church? Contrary also to the way of the light and love that is in Jesus, when he would purposely teach and instruct his scholars; contrary to the nature of parables and similitudes; and lastly, to the nature of the church or garden of Christ.

---

[44] "Two sorts of hypocrites: 1. In the church, as Judas, Simon Magnus, and these must be tolerated until discovered, and no longer. 2. Hypocrites in the world, which are false Christians, false churches, and these the Lord Jesus will have let alone unto harvest." (Williams's footnote)

CHAPTER XXII

In the former parable, the Lord Jesus compared the kingdom of heaven to the sowing of seed. The true messengers of Christ are the sowers, who cast the seed of the word of the kingdom upon four sorts of ground. Which four sorts of ground, or hearts of men, cannot be supposed to be of the church, nor will it ever be proved that the church consists of any more sorts or natures of ground properly but one, to wit, the honest and good ground. And the proper work of the church concerns the flourishing and prosperity of this sort of ground, and not the other unconverted three sorts; who, it may be, seldom or never come near the church, unless they be forced by the civil sword, which the pattern or first sower never used; and being forced, they are put into a way of religion by such a course—if not so, they are forced to live without a religion: for one of the two must necessarily follow, as I shall prove afterward.

In the field of the world, then, are all those sorts of ground: highway hearers, stony and thorny ground hearers, as well as the honest and good ground; and I suppose it will not now be said by the answerer, that those three sorts of bad grounds were hypocrites, or tares, in the church.

Now after the Lord Jesus had propounded that great leading parable of the sower and the seed, he is pleased to propound this parable of the tares with admirable coherence and sweet consolation to the honest and good ground; who, with glad and honest hearts, having received the word of the kingdom, may yet seem to be discouraged and troubled with so many anti-Christians and false professors of the name of Christ.

The Lord Jesus, therefore, gives direction concerning these tares, that unto the end of the world, successively in all the sorts and generations of them, they must be (not approved or countenanced, but) let alone, or permitted in the world.

Secondly, he gives to his own good seed this consolation: that those heavenly reapers, the angels, in the harvest, or end of the world, will take an order and course with them, to wit, they shall bind them into bundles, and cast them into the everlasting burnings; and to make the cup of their consolation run over, he adds (verse 43), *Then*, then at that time, *shall the righteous shine forth as the sun in the kingdom of their Father.*

These tares, then, neither being erroneous doctrines, nor corrupt practices, nor hypocrites, in the true church, intended by the Lord Jesus in this parable, I shall, in the third place, by the help of the same Lord Jesus, evidently prove that these tares can be no other sort of sinners but, false worshippers, idolaters, and in particular properly, anti-Christians.

CHAPTER XXIII

First, then, these tares are such sinners as are opposite and contrary to the children of the kingdom, visibly so declared and manifest (verse 38). Now the kingdom of God below is the visible church of Christ Jesus, according to Matthew 8:12. The children of the kingdom, which are threatened to be cast out, seem to be the Jews, which were then the only visible church in covenant with the Lord, when all other nations followed other gods and worships. And more plain is that fearful threatening (Matt. 21:43), *The kingdom of God shall be taken from you, and given to a nation that will bring forth the fruits thereof.*

Such, then, are the good seed, good wheat, children of the kingdom, as are the disciples, members, and subjects of the Lord Jesus Christ, his church and kingdom: and therefore, consequently, such are the tares, as are opposite to these, idolaters, will-worshippers, not truly but falsely submitting to Jesus: and in especial, the children of the wicked one, visibly so appearing. Which wicked one I take not to be the devil; for the Lord Jesus seems to make them distinct: *He that sows the good seed,* says he, *is the Son of man; the field is the world; the good seed are the children of the kingdom ; but the tares are the children of the wicked,* or wickedness; *the enemy that sows them is the devil.* [Matt. 13:37-39]

The original here του πονηρου, agrees with that (Luke 11:4), *Deliver us απο του πονηρου from evil,* or wickedness; opposite to the children of the kingdom and the righteousness thereof.

CHAPTER XXIV

Peace. It is true that all drunkards, thieves, unclean persons, etc., are opposite to God's children.

Truth. Answer. Their opposition here against the children of the kingdom is such an opposition as properly fights against the religious state, or worship, of the Lord Jesus Christ.

Secondly, it is manifest that the Lord Jesus in this parable intends no other sort of sinners: unto whom he says, Let them alone, in church or state; for then he should contradict other holy and blessed ordinances for the punishment of offenders, both in Christian and civil state.

First, in civil state. From the beginning of the world, God has armed fathers, masters, magistrates, to punish evil doers; that is such of whose actions fathers, masters, magistrates are to judge, and accordingly to punish such sinners as transgress against the good and peace of their civil state, families, towns, cities, kingdoms—their states, governments, governors, laws, punishments, and weapons being all of a civil nature; and therefore neither disobedience to parents or magistrates, nor murder, nor quarrelling, uncleanness, nor lasciviousness, stealing nor extortion, neither aught of that kind ought to be let alone, either in lesser or greater families, towns, cities, kingdoms (Romans 13), but seasonably to be suppressed, as may best conduce to the public safety.

Again, secondly, in the kingdom of Christ Jesus, whose kingdom, officers, laws, punishments, weapons, are spiritual and of a soul nature, he will not have anti-Christian idolaters, extortioners, covetous, etc., to be let alone; but the unclean and lepers to be thrust forth, the old leaven purged out, the obstinate in sin spiritually stoned to death, and put away from Israel; and this by many degrees of gentle admonition in private and public, as the case requires.

Therefore, if neither offenders against the civil laws, state, and peace ought to be let alone; nor the spiritual estate, the church of Jesus Christ ought to bear with them that are evil. (Rev. 2:2) I conclude that these are sinners of another nature—idolaters, false worshippers, anti-Christians—who without discouragement to true Christians must be let alone, and permitted in the world to grow and fill up the measure of their sins, after the image of him that has sown them, until the great harvest shall make the difference.

CHAPTER XXV

Thirdly, in that the officers unto whom these tares are referred are the angels, the heavenly reapers at the last day, it is clear as the light that, as before, these tares cannot signify hypocrites in the church, who, when they are discovered and seen to be tares, opposite to the good fruit of the good seed, are not to be let alone to the angels at harvest, or end of the world, but purged out by the governors of the church, and the whole church of Christ. Again, they cannot be offenders against the civil state and common welfare, whose dealing with is not suspended unto the coming of the angels, but unto men, who, although they know not the Lord Jesus Christ, yet are lawful governors and rulers in civil things.

Accordingly, in the fourth and last place, in that the plucking up of these tares out of this field must be let alone unto the very harvest or end, of the world, it is apparent from thence, that, as before, they could not signify hypocrites in the church, who, when they are discovered to be so, as these tares were discovered to be tares, are not to be suffered, after the first and second admonition, but to be rejected, and every brother that walks disorderly to be withdrawn or separated from. So likewise no offender against the civil state, by robbery, murder, adultery, oppression, sedition, mutiny, is forever to be connived at, and to enjoy a perpetual toleration unto the world's end, as these tares must.

Moses for a while held his peace against the sedition of Korah, Dathan, and Abiram. David for a season tolerated Shimei, Joab, Adonijah. But till the harvest, or the end of the world, the Lord never intended that any but these spiritual and mystical tares should be so permitted.

CHAPTER XXVI

Truth. Now if any imagine that the time or date is long, that in the mean season they may do a world of mischief before the world's end, as by infection, etc.[45]

First, I answer that as the civil state keeps itself with a civil guard, in case these tares shall attempt aught against the peace and welfare of it, let such civil offenses be punished; and yet, as tares opposite to Christ's kingdom, let their worship and consciences be tolerated.

Secondly, the church, or spiritual state, city, or kingdom, has laws, and orders, armories, *whereon there hang a thousand bucklers* (Cant. 4:4),

---

[45] "The danger of infection by these tares assoiled. Lamentable experience has proved this true of late in Europe, and lamentably true in the slaughter of some hundred thousands of the English." (Williams's footnote)

weapons and ammunition, able to break down the strongest holds (2 Cor. 10:4), and so to defend itself against the very gates of earth or hell.

Thirdly, the Lord himself knows who are his, and his foundation remains sure; his elect or chosen cannot perish nor be finally deceived.

Lastly, the Lord Jesus here, in this parable, lays down two reasons, able to content and satisfy our hearts to bear patiently this their contradiction and anti-Christianity, and to permit or let them alone.

First, lest the good wheat be plucked up and rooted up also out of this field of the world. If such combustions and fightings were as to pluck up all the false professors of the name of Christ, the good wheat also would enjoy little peace, but be in danger to be plucked up and torn out of this world by such bloody storms and tempests.

And, therefore, as God's people are commanded (Jer. 29:7) to pray for the peace of material Babel, wherein they were captivated, and (1 Tim. 2:1,2) to pray for all men, and specially kings and governors, that in the peace of the civil state they may have peace: so, contrary to the opinion and practice of most, drunk with the cup of the whore's fornication, yea, and of God's own people, fast asleep in anti-Christian Delilah's hip, obedience to the command of Christ to let the tares alone will prove the only means to preserve their civil peace, and that without obedience to this command of Christ, it is impossible (without great transgressions against the Lord in carnal policy, which will not long hold out) to preserve the civil peace.

Beside, God's people, the good wheat, are generally plucked up and persecuted, as well as the vilest idolaters, whether Jews or anti-Christians: which the Lord Jesus seems in this parable to foretell.

The second reason noted in the parable, which may satisfy any man from wondering at the patience of God, is this: when the world is ripe in sin, in the sins of anti-Christianism (as the Lord spoke of the sins of the Amorites, Gen. 15:6),[46] then those holy and mighty officers and executioners, the angels, with their sharp and cutting sickles of eternal vengeance, shall down with them, and bundle them up for the everlasting burnings.

Then shall that man of sin (2 Thess. 2 [8]) be consumed by the breath of the mouth of the Lord Jesus; and all that worship the beast and his picture, and receive his mark into their forehead or their hands, *shall*

---

[46] Williams mistakenly cites Genesis 12.

drink of the wine of the wrath of God, which is poured out without mixture into the cup of his indignation, and he shall be tormented with fire and brimstone in the presence of the holy angels, and in the presence of the Lamb, and the smoke of their torment shall ascend up for ever and ever. (Rev. 14:10, 11)

CHAPTER XXVII

Peace. You have been larger in vindicating this scripture from the violence offered unto it, because, as I said before, it is of such great consequence; as also, because so many excellent hands have not rightly divided it, to the great misguiding of many precious feet which otherwise might have been turned into the paths of more peaceableness in themselves and towards others.

Truth. I shall be briefer in the scriptures following.

Peace. Yet before you depart from this, I must crave your patience to satisfy one objection, and that is: These servants to whom the householder answers seem to be the ministers or messengers of the gospel, not the magistrates of the civil state, and therefore this charge of the Lord Jesus is not given to magistrates, to let alone false worshippers and idolaters.

Again, being spoken by the Lord Jesus to his messengers, it seems to concern hypocrites in the church, as before was spoken, and not false worshippers in the state, or world.

Truth. I answer, first, I believe I have sufficiently and abundantly proved that these tares are not offenders in the civil state. Nor, secondly, hypocrites in the church, when once discovered so to be; and that therefore the Lord Jesus intends a grosser kind of hypocrites, professing the name of churches and Christians in the field of the world, or commonwealth.

Secondly, I acknowledge this command, *Let them alone,* was expressly spoken to the messengers or ministers of the gospel, who have no civil power or authority in their hand, and therefore not to the civil magistrate, king, governor, to whom it pleased not the Lord Jesus, by himself or by his apostles, to give particular rules or directions concerning their behavior and carriage in civil magistracy, as they have done expressly concerning the duty of fathers, mothers, children, masters, servants, yea, and of subjects towards magistrates (Eph. 5,6; Col. 3, 4 etc.)

I conceive not the reason of this to be, as some weakly have done, because the Lord Jesus would not have any followers of his to hold the place of civil magistracy, but rather that he foresaw, and the Holy Spirit in the apostles foresaw, how few magistrates, either in the first persecuted or apostated state of Christianity, would embrace his yoke. In the persecuted state, magistrates hated the very name of Christ, or Christianity. In the state apostate, some few magistrates, in their persons holy and precious, yet as concerning their places, as they have professed to have been governors or heads of the church, have been so many false heads, and have constituted so many false visible Christs.

Thirdly, I conceive this charge of the Lord Jesus to his messengers, the preachers and proclaimers of' his mind, is a sufficient declaration of the mind of the Lord Jesus, if any civil magistrate should make question what were his duty concerning spiritual things.

The apostles, and in them all that succeed them, being commanded not to pluck up the tares, but let them alone, received from the Lord Jesus a threefold charge.

First, to let them alone, and not to pluck them up by prayer to God for their present temporal destruction.

Jeremy had a commission to plant and build, to pluck up and destroy kingdoms (Jer. 1:10); therefore he is commanded not to pray for that people whom God had a purpose to pluck up (Jer. 14:11), and he plucks up the whole nation by prayer. (Lam. 3:66) Thus Elijah brought fire from heaven to consume the captains and the fifties. (2 Kgs 1) And the apostles desired also so to practice against the Samaritans (Luke 9:54), but were reproved by the Lord Jesus. For, contrarily, the saints, and servants, and churches of Christ, are to pray for all men, especially for all magistrates, of what sort or religions soever, and to seek the peace of the city, whatever city it be, because in the peace of the place God's people have peace also. (Jer. 29:7; 2 Tim. 2, etc.)

Secondly, God's messengers are herein commanded not to prophesy, or denounce, a present destruction or extirpation of all false professors of the name of Christ, which are whole towns, cities, and kingdoms full.

Jeremy did thus pluck up kingdoms, in those fearful prophecies he poured forth against all the nations of' the world, throughout his chapters 24-26, etc., as did also the other prophets in a measure, though none comparably to Jeremy and Ezekiel.

Such denunciations of present temporal judgments are not the messengers of the Lord Jesus to pour forth. It is true, many sore and fearful plagues are poured forth upon the Roman emperors and Roman popes in the Revelation, yet not to their utter extirpation or plucking up until the harvest.

Thirdly, I conceive God's messengers are charged to let them alone, and not pluck them up, by exciting and stirring up civil magistrates, kings, emperors, governors, parliaments, or general courts, or assemblies to punish and persecute all such persons out of their dominions and territories as worship not the true God, according to the revealed will of God in Christ Jesus. It is true, Elijah thus stirred Ahab to kill all the priests and prophets of Baal; but that was in that figurative state of the land of Canaan, as I have already and shall further manifest, not to be matched or paralleled by any other state, but the spiritual state or church of Christ in all the world, putting the false prophets and idolaters spiritually to death by the two-edged sword and power of the Lord Jesus, as that church of Israel did corporally.

And therefore says Paul expressly (1 Cor. 5:10), we must go out of the world, in case we may not company in civil converse with idolaters, etc.

Peace. It may be said, some sorts of sinners are there mentioned, as drunkards, railers, extortioners, who are to be punished by the civil sword—why not idolaters also? For although the subject may lawfully converse, buy and sell, and live with such, yet the civil magistrates shall nevertheless be justly blamed in suffering of them.

Truth. I answer, the apostle, in this scripture, speaks not of permission of either, but expressly shows the difference between the church and the world, and the lawfulness of conversation with such persons in civil things, with whom it is not lawful to have converse in spirituals: secretly withal foretelling that magistrates and people, whole states and kingdoms, should be idolatrous and anti-Christian, yet with whom, notwithstanding, the saints and churches of God might lawfully cohabit, and hold civil converse and conversation.

Concerning their permission of what they judge idolatrous, I have and shall speak at large.

Peace. Oh! how contrary unto this command of the Lord Jesus have
such as have conceived themselves the true messengers of the Lord Jesus,
in all ages, not let such professors and prophets alone, whom they have
judged tares; but have provoked kings and kingdoms (and some out of
good intentions and zeal to God) to prosecute and persecute such even
unto death! Among whom God's people, the good wheat, have also been
plucked up, as all ages and histories testify, and too, too oft the world laid
upon bloody heaps in civil and intestine[47] desolations on this occasion.
All which would be prevented, and the greatest breaches made up in the
peace of our own or other countries were this command of the Lord Jesus
obeyed, to wit, to let them alone until the harvest.

CHAPTER XXVIII

I shall conclude this controversy about this parable in this brief sum
and recapitulation of what has been said. I hope, by the evident
demonstration of God's Spirit to the conscience, I have proved,
negatively, first, that the tares in this parable cannot signify doctrines or
practices, as was affirmed, but persons.

Secondly, the tares cannot signify hypocrites in the church, either
undiscovered or discovered.

Thirdly, the tares here cannot signify scandalous offenders in the
church.

Fourthly, nor scandalous offenders, in life and conversation, against
the civil state.

Fifthly, the field in which these tares are sown is not the church.

Again, affirmatively, first, the field is properly the world, the civil
state, or commonwealth.

Secondly, the tares here intended by the Lord Jesus are anti-
Christian idolaters, opposite to the good seed of the kingdom, true
Christians.

Thirdly, the ministers or messengers of the Lord Jesus ought to let
them alone to live in the world, and neither seek by prayer, or prophecy,
to pluck them up before the harvest.

---

[47] Relating to the internal affairs of a state or country.

Fourthly, this permission or suffering of them in the field of the world is not for hurt, but for common good, even for the good of the good wheat, the people of God.

Lastly, the patience of God is that the patience of man ought to be exercised toward them; and yet notwithstanding, their doom is fearful at the harvest, even gathering, bundling, and everlasting burnings, by the mighty hand of the angels in the end of the world.

CHAPTER XXIX

Peace. The second scripture brought against such persecution for cause of conscience is Matthew 15:14, where the disciples being troubled at the Pharisees' carriage toward the Lord Jesus and his doctrines, and relating how they were offended at him, the Lord Jesus commanded his disciples to let them alone, and gives this reason—that the blind lead the blind, and both should fall into the ditch.

Unto which, answer is made, "That it makes nothing to the cause, because it was spoken to his private disciples, and not to public officers in church or state: and also, because it was spoken in regard of troubling themselves, or regarding the offence which the Pharisees took."

Truth. I answer—to pass by his assertion of the privacy of the apostles, in that the Lord Jesus commanding to let them alone, that is, not only not to be offended themselves, but not to meddle with them—it appears it was no ordinance of God, nor Christ, for the disciples to have gone further, and have complained to, and excited, the civil magistrate to his duty: which if it had been an ordinance of God and Christ, either for the vindicating of Christ's doctrine, or the recovering of the Pharisees, or the preserving of others from infection, the Lord Jesus would never have commanded them to have tended to these holy ends.

CHAPTER XXX

Peace. It may be said that neither the Roman Caesar, nor Herod, nor Pilate knew aught of the true God, or of Christ; and it had been in vain to have made complaint to them who were not fit and competent, but ignorant and opposite judges.[48]

Truth. I answer, first, this removes, by the way, that stumbling-block which many fall at, to wit, Paul's appealing to Caesar; which since he could not in common sense do unto Caesar as a competent judge in such cases, and wherein he should have also denied his own apostleship or office, in which regard, to wit, in matters of Christ, he was higher than Caesar himself—it must needs follow that his appeal was merely in respect of' his civil wrongs, and false accusations of sedition, etc.

Secondly, if it had been an ordinance of God, that all civil magistrates were bound to judge in causes spiritual or Christian, as to suppress heresies, defend the faith of Jesus, although that Caesar, Herod, Pilate were wicked, ignorant, and opposite, yet the disciples, and the Lord Christ himself, had been bound to have performed the duty of faithful subjects, for the preventing of further evil, and the clearing of themselves, and so to have left the matter upon the magistrates' care and conscience, by complaining unto the magistrate against such evils. For every person is bound to go as far as lies in his power for the preventing and the redressing of evil; and where it stops in any, and runs not clear, there the guilt, like filth or mud, will lie.

Thirdly, had it been the holy purpose of God to have established the doctrine and kingdom of his Son this way, since his coming he would have furnished commonweals, kingdoms, cities, etc., then and since, with such temporal powers and magistrates as should have been excellently fit and competent: for he that could have had legions of angels, if he so pleased, could as easily have been, and still be furnished with legions of good and gracious magistrates to this end and purpose.

CHAPTER XXXI

[Peace]. It is generally said that God has in former times, and does still, and will hereafter stir up kings and queens, etc.

[Truth]. I answer, that place of Isaiah 49:23 will appear to be far from proving such kings and queens judges of ecclesiastical causes: and if not judges, they may not punish.

---

[48] "Christ never directed his disciples to the civil magistrate for help in his cause." (Williams's footnote)

In spiritual things, themselves are subject to the church and censures of it, although in civil respects superior. How shall those kings and queens be supreme governors of the church, and yet lick the dust of the church's feet, as it is there expressed?

Thirdly, God's Israel of old were earnest with God for a king, for an arm of flesh, for a king to protect them, as other nations had: God's Israel still have ever been restless with God for an arm of flesh.

God gave them Saul in his anger, and took him away in his wrath: and God has given many a Saul in his anger, that is, an arm of flesh in the way of his providence: though I judge not all persons whom Saul in his calling typed out to be of Saul's spirit, for I speak of a state and outward visible power only.

I add, God will take away such stays, on whom God's people rest, in his wrath: that king David, that is, Christ Jesus the antitype, in his own spiritual power in the hands of the saints, may spiritually and for ever be advanced.

And therefore I conclude, it was in one respect that the Lord Jesus said, *Let them alone*; because it was no ordinance for any disciple of Jesus to prosecute the Pharisees at Caesar's bar.

Beside, let it be seriously considered by such as plead for present corporal punishments, as conceiving that such sinners, though they break not civil peace, should not escape unpunished—I say, let it be considered, though for the present their punishment is deferred, yet the punishment inflicted on them will be found to amount to a higher pitch than any corporal punishment in the world beside, and that in these four respects:

CHAPTER XXXII

First, by just judgment from God, false teachers are stark blind. God's sword has struck out the right eye of their mind and spiritual understanding, ten thousand times a greater punishment than if the magistrate should command both the right and left eye of their bodies to be bored or plucked out; and that in so many fearful respects if the blindness of the soul and of the body were a little compared together—whether we look at that want of guidance, or the want of joy and pleasure, which the light of the eye affords; or whether we look at the damage, shame, deformity, and danger, which blindness brings to the outward man; and much more true in the want of the former, and misery of the latter, in spiritual and soul blindness to all eternity.

Secondly, how fearful is that wound that no balm in Gilead can cure! How dreadful is that blindness which for ever to all eye-salve is incurable! For if persons be willfully and desperately obstinate, after light shining forth, *Let them alone,* says the Lord. So spoke the Lord once of Ephraim: *Ephraim is joined to idols, let him alone.* (Hos. 4:17) What more lamentable condition, than when the Lord has given a poor sinner over as a hopeless patient, incurable, which we are wont to account it sorer affliction than if a man were torn and racked, etc.

And this I speak, not that I conceive that all whom the Lord Jesus commands his servants to pass from and let alone, to permit and tolerate, when it is in their power corporally to molest them, I say, that all are thus incurable; yet that sometimes that word is spoken by Christ Jesus to his servants to be patient, for neither can corporal or spiritual balm or physic ever heal or cure them.

Thirdly, their end is the ditch, that bottomless pit of everlasting separation from the holy and sweet presence of the Father of lights, goodness, and mercy itself—endless, easeless, in extremity, universality, and eternity of torments; which most direful and lamentable downfall, should strike a holy fear and trembling into all that see the pit whither these blind Pharisees are tumbling, and cause us to strive, so far as hope may be, by the spiritual eye-salve of the word of God, to heal and cure them of this their soul-destroying blindness.

Fourthly, of those that fall into this dreadful ditch both leader and follower, how deplorable in more especial manner is the leader's case, upon whose neck the followers tumble—the ruin, not only of his own soul, being horrible, but also the ruin of the followers' souls eternally galling and tormenting.

Peace. Some will say these things are indeed full of horror; yet such is the state of all sinners, and of many malefactors, whom yet the state is bound to punish, and sometimes by death itself.

Truth. I answer, the civil magistrate bears not the sword in vain, but to out off civil offences, yea, and the offenders too in case. But what is this to a blind Pharisee, resisting the doctrine of Christ, who happily may be as good a subject, and as peaceable and profitable to the civil state as any. And for his spiritual offence against the Lord Jesus, in denying him to be the true Christ, he suffers the vengeance of a dreadful judgment, both present and eternal, as before.

CHAPTER XXXIII

Peace. Yea, but it is said that the blind Pharisees, misguiding the subjects of a civil state, greatly sin against a civil state, and therefore justly suffer civil punishments; for shall the civil magistrate take care of outsides only, to wit, of the bodies of men, and not of souls, in laboring to procure their everlasting welfare?

Truth. I answer, it is a truth: the mischief of a blind Pharisee's blind guidance is greater than if he acted treasons, murders, etc.; and the loss of one soul by his seduction is a greater mischief than if he blew up parliaments, and cut the throats of kings or emperors, so precious is that invaluable jewel of a soul above all the present lives and bodies of all the men in the world! And therefore I affirm that justice, calling for eye for eye, tooth for tooth, life for life, calls also soul for soul; which the blind-guiding, seducing Pharisee, shall truly pay in that dreadful ditch, which the Lord Jesus speaks of. But this sentence against him, the Lord Jesus only pronounces in his church, his spiritual judicature, and executes this sentence in part at present, and hereafter to all eternity. Such a sentence no civil judge can pass, such a death no civil sword can inflict.

I answer, secondly, dead men cannot be infected. The civil state, the world, being in a natural state, dead in sin, whatever be the state-religion unto which persons are forced, it is impossible it should be infected. Indeed, the living, the believing, the church and spiritual state, that and that only is capable of infection; for whose help we shall presently see what preservatives and remedies the Lord Jesus has appointed.

Moreover, as we see in a common plague or infection the names are taken how many are to die, and not one more shall be struck than the destroying angel has the names of; so here, whatever be the soul-infection breathed out from the lying lips of a plague-sick Pharisee, yet the names are taken, not one elect or chosen of God shall perish. God's sheep are safe in his eternal hand and counsel, and he that knows his material, knows also his mystical stars, their numbers, and calls them every one by name. None fall into the ditch on the blind Pharisee's back but such as were ordained to that condemnation, both guide and followers. (1 Peter

2:8; Jude 4) The vessels of wrath shall break and split, and only they, to the praise of God's eternal justice. (Rom. 9:22)

CHAPTER XXXIV

Peace. But it is said, be it granted that in a common plague or infection none are smitten and die but such as are appointed, yet it is not only every man's duty, but the common duty of the magistrate to prevent infection, and to preserve the common health of the place; likewise, though the number of the elect be sure, and God knows who are his, yet has he appointed means for their preservation from perdition, and from infection, and therefore the angel is blamed for suffering Balaam's doctrine, and Jezebel, to seduce Christ Jesus' servants (Rev. 2[14,20]; Titus 3:10; Rom. 16:17)

Truth. I answer, Let the scripture, that of Titus, *Reject an heretic,* and Romans 16:17, *Avoid them that are contentious,* &c., let them, and all of like nature, be examined, and it will appear that the great and good physician, Christ Jesus, the head of the body, and king of the church, has not been unfaithful in providing spiritual antidotes and preservatives against the spiritual sickness, sores, weaknesses, dangers, of his church and people. But he never appointed the civil sword for either antidote or remedy, as an addition to those spirituals which he has left with his wife, his church or people.

Hence how great is the bondage, the captivity of God's own people to Babylonish or confused mixtures in worship, and unto worldly and earthly policies to uphold state religions or worships: since that which is written to the angel and church at Pergamos shall be interpreted as sent to the governor and city of Pergamos, and that which is sent to Titus and the church of Christ at Crete must be delivered to the civil officers and city thereof.

But as the civil magistrate has his charge of the bodies and goods of the subject, so have the spiritual officers, governors, and overseers of Christ's city or kingdom, the charge of their souls, and soul-safety. Hence, that charge of Paul to Timothy (1 Tim. 5:20), *Them that sin rebuke before all, that others may learn to fear.* This is, in the church of Christ, a spiritual means for the healing of a soul that has sinned, or taken infection, and for the preventing of the infecting of others, that others may learn to fear, etc.

CHAPTER XXXV

Peace. It is said true that Titus and Timothy, and so the officers of the church of Christ, are bound to prevent soul-infection: but what hinders that the magistrate should not be charged also with this duty?

Truth. I answer, many things I have answered, and more shall. At present I shall only say this: if it be the magistrate's duty or office, then is he both a temporal and ecclesiastical officer: contrary to which most men will affirm. And yet we know the policy of our own land and country has established to the kings and queens thereof the supreme heads or governors of the church of England.

That doctrine and distinction, that a magistrate may punish a heretic civilly, will not here avail; for what is Babel if this be not, confusedly to punish corporal or civil offences with spiritual or church censures (the offender not being a member of it), or to punish soul or spiritual offences with corporal or temporal weapons, proper to delinquents against the temporal or civil state.

Lastly, woe were it with the civil magistrate—and most intolerable burdens do they lay upon their backs that teach this doctrine—if together with the common care and charge of the commonwealth, the peace and safety of the town, city, state, or kingdom, the blood of every soul that perishes should cry against him; unless he could say with Paul (Acts 20 [26]) in spiritual regards, *I am clear from the blood of all men*, that is, the blood of souls, which was his charge to look after, so far as his preaching went, not the blood of bodies which belongs to the civil magistrate.

I acknowledge he ought to cherish, as a foster-father, the Lord Jesus (in his truth) in his saints, to cleave unto them himself, and to countenance them even to the death, yea, also, to break the teeth of the lions who offer civil violence and injury unto them.

But, to see all his subjects Christians, to keep such church or Christians in the purity of worship, and see them do their duty, this belongs to the head of the body, Christ Jesus, and such spiritual officers as he has to this purpose deputed, whose right it is, according to the true pattern. Abimelech, Saul, Adonijah, Athalia, were but usurpers: David,

Solomon, Joash, etc., they were the true heirs and types of Christ Jesus, in his true power and authority in his kingdom.

CHAPTER XXXVI

Peace. The next scripture brought against such persecution is Luke 9:54, 55, where the Lord Jesus reproved his disciples, who would have had fire come down from heaven, and devour those Samaritans that would not receive him, in these words: *You know not of what spirit you are. The Son of man is not come to destroy men's lives, but to save them.*

With this scripture Mr. Cotton joins the fourth, and answers both in one, which is this (2 Tim. 2:24 [25-26]), *The servant of the Lord must not strive, but must be gentle toward all men, suffering the evil men, instructing them with meekness that are contrary-minded and oppose themselves; proving if God peradventure will give them repentance that they may acknowledge the truth, and that they may recover themselves out of the snare of the devil, who are taken captive by him at his will.*

Unto both these scriptures it pleased him thus to answer: "Both these are directions to ministers of' the gospel how to deal, not with obstinate offenders in the church who sin against conscience, but either with men without, as the Samaritans were, and many unconverted Christians in Crete, whom Titus, as an evangelist, was to seek to convert: or at best with some Jews or Gentiles in the church, who, though carnal, yet were not convinced of the error of their way. And it is true, it became not the spirit of' the gospel to convert aliens to the faith, as the Samaritans were, by fire and brimstone, nor to deal harshly in public ministry, or private conference, with all such several minded men, as either had not yet entered into church fellowship, or if they had, did hitherto sin of ignorance, not against conscience. But neither of both these texts do hinder the minister of the gospel to proceed in a church way against church members, when they become scandalous offenders, either in life or doctrine, much less do they speak at all to the civil magistrate."[49]

---

[49] "An excellent saying of persecutors themselves." (Williams's footnote)

CHAPTER XXXVII

Truth. This perplexed and ravelled answer, wherein so many things and so doubtful are wrapped up and entangled together, I shall take in pieces.

First, concerning that of the Lord Jesus rebuking his disciples for their rash and ignorant bloody zeal (Luke 9), desiring corporal destruction upon the Samaritans for refusing the Lord Jesus, etc., the answerer affirms, that hinders not the ministers of the gospel to proceed in a church way against scandalous offenders; which is not here questioned, but maintained to be the holy will of the Lord, and a sufficient censure and punishment, if no civil offence against the civil state be committed.

Secondly, says he, "Much less does this speak at all to the civil magistrate."

Where I observe that he implies that beside the censure of the Lord Jesus, in the hands of his spiritual governors, for any spiritual evil in life or doctrine, the civil magistrate is also to inflict corporal punishment upon the contrary minded: whereas, first, if the civil magistrate be a Christian, a disciple or follower of the meek Lamb of God, he is bound to be far from destroying the bodies of men for refusing to receive the Lord Jesus Christ: for otherwise he should not know, according to this speech of the Lord Jesus, what spirit he was of, yea, and to be ignorant of the sweet end of the coming of the Son of Man, which was not to destroy the bodies of men, but to save both bodies and souls. (verses 55-56)

Secondly, if the civil magistrate being a Christian, gifted, prophesy in the church (1 Cor. 14:1) – although the Lord Jesus Christ, whom they in their own persons hold forth, shall be refused—yet they are here forbidden to call for fire from heaven, that is, to procure or inflict any corporal judgment upon such offenders, remembering the end of the Lord Jesus' coming not to destroy men's lives, but to save them.

Lastly, this also concerns the conscience of the civil magistrate. As he is bound to preserve the civil peace and quiet of the place and people under him, he is bound to suffer no man to break the civil peace, by laying hands of violence upon any, though as vile as the Samaritans, for not receiving of the Lord Jesus Christ.

It is indeed the ignorance and blind zeal of the second beast, the false prophet (Rev. 13:13), to persuade the civil powers of the earth to persecute the saints, that is, to bring fiery judgments upon men in a judicial way, and to pronounce that such judgments of imprisonment, banishment, death, proceed from God's righteous vengeance upon such heretics. So dealt divers bishops in France, and England, too, in Queen Mary's days, with the saints of God at their putting to death, declaiming against them in their sermons to the people, and proclaiming that these persecutions, even unto death, were God's just judgments from heaven upon these heretics.

CHAPTER XXXVIII

Peace. Doubtless such fiery spirits, as the Lord Jesus said, are not of God. I pray, speak to the second place out of Timothy, second epistle 2:25, 26.

Truth. I acknowledge this instruction to be meek and patient, etc., is properly an instruction to the ministers of the gospel. Yet divers arguments from hence will truly and fairly be collected to manifest and evince how far the civil magistrate ought to be from dealing with the civil sword in spiritual cases.

And first, by the way I desire to ask, what were these unconverted Christians in Crete, which the answerer compares with the Samaritans, whom Titus, says he, as an evangelist, was to seek to convert; and whether the Lord Jesus have any such disciples and followers who yet are visibly in an unconverted state? Oh! that it may please the Father of mercies, the Father of lights, to awaken and open the eyes of all that fear before him, that they may see whether this be the language of Canaan, or the language of Ashdod.

What is an unconverted Christian, but in truth an unconverted convert? That is, in English, one unturned turned; unholy holy; disciples, or followers of Jesus, not following of him: in a word, that is, Christians, or anointed by Christ, anti-Christians not anointed with the Spirit of Jesus Christ.

Certain it is, such they were not unto whom the Spirit of God gives that name (Acts 11 [26]. And indeed, whither can this tend but to uphold the blasphemy of so many as say they are Jews, that is Christians, but are not? (Rev. 2:2) But as they are not Christians from Christ, but from the beast and his picture, so their proper name from Antichrist is anti-Christians.

How sad yet and how true an evidence is this, that the soul of the answerer (I speak not of his outward soul and person, but of his worship) has never yet heard the call of the Lord Jesus to come out from those unconverted churches, from that unconverted, anti-Christian Christian world, and so from Antichrist, Belial, to seek fellowship with Christ Jesus and his converted Christians, disciples after the first pattern.

Again, I observe the haste and light attention of the answerer to these scriptures, as commonly the spirits of God's children in matters of Christ's kingdom are very sleepy: for these persons here spoken of were not, as he speaks, unconverted Christians in Crete, whom Titus as an evangelist was to convert, but they were such opposites as Timothy, to whom Paul writes this letter at Ephesus, should not meet withal.

CHAPTER XXXIX

Peace. But what is there in this scripture of Timothy alleged concerning the civil magistracy?

Truth. I argue from this place of Timothy in particular, thus: first, if the civil magistrates be Christians, or members of the church, able to prophesy in the church of Christ, I say as before, they are bound by this command of Christ to suffer opposition to their doctrine, with meekness and gentleness, and to be so far from striving to subdue their opposites with the civil sword that they are bound with patience and meekness to wait, if God peradventure will please to grant repentance unto their opposites.[50]

So also it pleases the answerer to acknowledge in these words: "It becomes not the spirit of the gospel to convert aliens to the faith (such as the Samaritans, and the unconverted Christians in Crete) with fire and brimstone."

Secondly, be they oppositions within, and church members, as the answerer speaks, become scandalous in doctrine, (I speak not of scandals against the civil state, which the civil magistrate ought to punish), it is the Lord only, as this scripture to Timothy implies, who is able to give them

---

[50] "1 Corinthians 14. Patience and meekness required in all that open Christ's mysteries." (Williams's footnote)

repentance, and recover them out of Satan's snare. To which end also, he has appointed those holy and dreadful censures in his church or kingdom. True it is, the sword may make, as once the Lord complained (Isa. 10), a whole nation of hypocrites; but to recover a soul from Satan by repentance, and to bring them from anti-Christian doctrine or worship to the doctrine or worship Christian in the least true internal or external submission, that only works the all-powerful God, by the sword of his Spirit in the hand of his spiritual officers.

What a most woeful proof hereof have the nations of the earth given in all ages? And to seek no further than our native soil, within a few scores of years, how many wonderful changes in religion has the whole kingdom made, according to the change of the governors thereof; in the several religions which they themselves embraced! Henry VII finds and leaves the kingdom absolutely popish. Henry VIII casts it into a mould half-popish, half-Protestant. Edward VI brings forth an edition all Protestant. Queen Mary within few years defaces Edward's work, and renders the kingdom after her grandfather Henry VII's pattern, all popish. Mary's short life and religion end together; and Elizabeth revives her brother Edward's model, all Protestant. And some eminent witnesses of God's truth against Antichrist have inclined to believe that before the downfall of that beast, England must once again bow down her fair neck to his proud usurping yoke and foot.

Peace. It has been England's sinful shame to fashion and change their garments and religions with wondrous ease and lightness, as a higher power, a stronger sword has prevailed; after the ancient pattern of Nebuchadnezzar's bowing the whole world in one most solemn uniformity of worship to his golden image. (Dan. 3)

CHAPTER XL

[Peace]. But it has been thought, or said, shall oppositions against the truth escape unpunished? Will they not prove mischievous?

Truth. I answer, as before, concerning the blind guides, in case there be no civil offence committed, the magistrates, and all men that by the mercy of God to themselves discern the misery of such opposites, have cause to lament and bewail that fearful condition wherein such are entangled: to wit, in the snares and chains of Satan, with which they are so invincibly caught and held, that no power in heaven or earth but the right hand of the Lord, in the meek and gentle dispensing of the word of truth, can release and quit them.

Those many false Christs, of whom the Lord Jesus forewarns (Matt. 24 [5,11]), have suitably their false bodies, faith, spirit, baptism, as the Lord Jesus has his true body, faith, spirit, etc., (Eph. 4[5]). Correspondent also are their weapons, and the success, issue, or operation of them. A carnal weapon or sword of steel may produce a carnal repentance, a show, an outside, a uniformity, through a state or kingdom; but it has pleased the Father to exalt the Lord Jesus only *to be a prince,* armed with power and means sufficient *to give repentance to Israel.* (Acts 5:31)

Accordingly, an unbelieving soul being dead in sin, although he be changed from one worship to another, like a dead man shifted into several changes of' apparel, cannot please God. (Heb. 11[6]) And consequently, whatever such an unbelieving and unregenerate person acts in worship or religion, it is but sin. (Rom. 14 [23] Preaching sin; praying, though without beads or book, sin; breaking of bread, or Lord's Supper, sin; yea, as odious as the oblation of swine's blood, a dog's neck, or killing of a man. (Isa. 66 [3])

But faith it is that gift which proceeds alone from the Father of' lights (Phil. 1:29), and till he please to make his light arise and open the eyes of blind sinners, their souls shall lie fast asleep—and the faster, in that a sword of steel compels them to a worship in hypocrisy—in the dungeons of spiritual darkness and Satan's slavery.

Peace. I add, that a civil sword, as woeful experience in all ages has proved, is so far from bringing, or helping forward an opposite in religion to repentance, that magistrates sin grievously against the work of God, and blood of souls, by such proceedings. Because as commonly the sufferings of false and anti-Christian teachers harden their followers, who being blind are by this means occasioned to tumble into the ditch of hell after their blind leaders, with more inflamed zeal of lying confidence. So, secondly, violence and a sword of steel beget such an impression in the sufferers that certainly they conclude (as indeed that religion cannot be true which needs such instruments of violence to uphold it so) that persecutors are far from soft and gentle commiseration of the blindness of others.[51] To this purpose it pleased the Father of spirits, of old, to constrain the emperor of Rome, Antoninus Pius, to write to all the governors of his provinces to forbear to persecute the Christians; because such dealing must needs be so far from converting the Christians from their way, that it rather begat in their minds an opinion of their cruelties, etc.[52]

CHAPTER XLI

Peace. The next scripture against such persecution, is that of the prophet Isaiah 2:4, together with Micah 4:3, *They shall beat their swords into plowshares, and their spears into pruning-hooks.* Isaiah 11:9, *There shall none hurt or destroy in all the mountain of my holiness.*

Unto which it pleased Mr. Cotton to say, "That these predictions do only show, first, with what kind of weapons he should subdue the nations to the obedience of the faith of the gospel, not by fire and sword, and weapons of war, but by the power of the word and Spirit of God, which," says he, "no man doubts of."

"Secondly, those predictions of the prophets show what the meek and peaceable temper will be of all true converts to Christianity; not lions nor leopards, not cruel oppressors nor malignant opposers, nor biters one of another: but do not forbid them to drive ravenous wolves from the sheepfold, and to restrain them from devouring the sheep of Christ."

Truth. In this first excellent and truly Christian answer, methinks the answerer may hear a voice from heaven, *Out of thine own mouth, will I judge thee.* [Luke 19:22] For what can be said more heavenly, by the tongues of men and angels, to show the heavenly, meek temper of all the soldiers of the Lamb of God, as also to set forth what are the spiritual weapons and ammunition of the holy war and battle of the gospel and

---

[51] "That cannot be a true religion which needs carnal weapons to uphold it. Persecutors beget a persuasion of their cruelties in the heads of the persecuted." (Williams's footnote)

[52] Eusebius, *The History of the Church* (New York: Dorset Press, 1965) 166. Caldwell, cites George Long, *Thoughts of M. Aurelius Antoninus,* "Any man moderately acquainted with Roman history will see at once from the style and tenor that it is a clumsy forgery."

kingdom of Jesus Christ, for the subduing of the nations of the world unto him?

Peace. And yet out of the same mouth, which should not be, says James, proceeds good and evil, sweet and sour; for he adds, "But this does not forbid them to drive ravenous wolves from the sheepfold, and to restrain them from devouring the sheep of Christ."

Truth. In these words, according to the judgment here maintained by him, he fights against the former truth, to wit, that by spiritual weapons Christ Jesus will subdue the nations of' the earth to the obedience of the gospel: for by driving away these wolves, he intends not only the resistance and violence which the shepherds of Christ ought spiritually to make, but the civil resistance of the material swords, staves, guns, etc. Whence I argue, that same power that forces the evil (or wolves) out, forces the good (the sheep) in; for of the same or like things is the same or like reason: as the same arm of' flesh that with a staff beats off a wolf, with a rod and hook brings in the sheep: the same dog that assaults and tears the wolf, frights and forces in the straggling sheep.

CHAPTER XLII

Peace. But for the clearer opening of this mystery, I pray explicate that scripture where the Spirit of God is pleased to use this similitude of wolves (Acts 20:29), out of which, keeping to the allegory, I shall propose these queries.

First, what wolves were these Paul warns of?

Truth. Answer. Wolves literally he will not say. Nor, secondly, persecutors of the flock, such as the Roman emperors were, [or] magistrates under him.

Therefore, thirdly, such as brought in other religions and worships, as the Spirit of God opens it (verse 30). Such as among themselves should speak perverse things, as many Antichrists did, and especially the Antichrist. And I ask, whether or no such as may hold forth other worships or religions, Jews, Turks, or anti-Christians, may not be peaceable and quiet subjects, loving and helpful neighbors, fair and just dealers, true and loyal to the civil government? It is clear they may, from all reason and experience in many flourishing cities and kingdoms of the world, and so offend not against the civil state and peace, nor incur the punishment of the civil sword, notwithstanding that in spiritual and mystical account they are ravenous and greedy wolves.

Peace. 2. I query, to whom Paul gave this charge to watch against them (verse 31)?

Truth. They were not the magistrates of the city of Ephesus, but the elders or ministers of the church of Christ, his mystical flock of sheep at Ephesus. Unto them was this charge of watching given, and so consequently of driving away these wolves.

And however that many of these charges and exhortations, given by that one Shepherd, Christ Jesus, to the shepherds or ministers of churches, be commonly attributed and directed, by the answerer in this discourse, to the civil magistrate; yet I desire, in the fear and holy presence of God, it may be inquired into, whether in all the will or testament of Christ there be any such word of Christ, by way of command, promise, or example, countenancing the governors of the civil state to meddle with these wolves, if in civil things peaceable and obedient.

Peace. Truly, if this charge were given to the magistrates at Ephesus, or any magistrates in the world, doubtless they must be able to discern and determine out of their own official abilities in these spiritual law questions, who are spiritual sheep, what is their food, what their poison, what their properties, who their keepers, etc. So, on the contrary, who are wolves, what their properties, their haunts, their assaults, the manner of taking, etc., spiritually:—and this beside the care and study of the civil laws, and the discerning of his own proper civil sheep, obedient sheep, etc.: as also wolfish oppressors, etc., whom he is bound to punish and suppress.

Truth. I know that civil magistrates, in some places, have declined the name of head of the church, and ecclesiastical judge; yet can they not with good conscience decline the name if they do the work, and perform the office of determining and punishing a merely spiritual wolf.

They must be sufficiently also able to judge in all spiritual causes and that with their own, and not with other men's eyes, no more than they do in civil causes, contrary to the common practice of the governors and rulers of civil states, who often set up that for a religion or worship to God, which the clergy, or churchmen, as men speak, shall in their consciences agree upon.

And if this be not so, to wit, that magistrates must not be spiritual judges, as some decline it in the title supreme head and governor, why is Gallio wont to be exclaimed against for refusing to be a judge in such matters as concerned the Jewish worship and religion? How is he censured for a profane person, without conscience, etc., in that he would be no judge or head? For that is all one in point of government.

Peace. In the third place, I query, whether the Father who gave, and the Son who keeps the sheep, be not greater than all? Who can pluck these sheep, the elect, out of his hand? Which answers that common objection of that danger of devouring, although there were no other weapons in the world appointed by the Lord Jesus. But,

CHAPTER XLIII

Fourthly, I ask, were not these elders or ministers of the church of Ephesus sufficiently furnished from the Lord Jesus to drive away these mystical and spiritual wolves?

Truth. True it is, against the inhuman and uncivil violence of persecutors, they were not, nor are God's children, able and provided; but to resist, drive away, expel, and kill spiritual and mystical wolves by the word of the Lord, none are fit to be Christ's shepherds who are not able. (Titus 1:9-11) The bishop, or overseer, must *be able by sound doctrine both to exhort and to convince the gainsayers*: which gainsayers to be by him convinced, that is, overcome or subdued, though it may be in themselves ever obstinate, they were, I say, as greedy wolves in Crete, as any could be at Ephesus. For so says Paul (verse 10): they were *unruly and vain talkers, deceivers, whose mouths must be stopped, who subverted whole houses;* and yet Titus, and every ordinary shepherd of a flock of Christ, had ability sufficient to defend the flock from spiritual and mystical wolves, without the help of the civil magistrate.

Peace. In this respect, therefore, methinks we may fitly allude to that excellent answer of Job to Bildad, the Shuhite (Job 26:1-2), *How hast thou helped him that is without power? How savest thou the arm that has no strength? How hast thou counseled him that has no wisdom? How hast thou plentifully declared the thing as it is?*

5. Lastly, I ask, whether, as men deal with wolves, these wolves at Ephesus were intended by Paul to be killed, their brains dashed out with

stones, staves, halberts,[53] guns, etc., in the hands of the elders of Ephesus, etc.?

Truth. Doubtless, comparing spiritual things with spiritual, all such mystical wolves must spiritually and mystically so be slain. And the witnesses of truth (Rev. 11 [5]) speak fire, and kill all that hurt them, by that fiery word of God, and that two-edged sword in their hand. (Psalm 149 [6])

But, oh! what streams of the blood of saints have been and must be shed, until the Lamb have obtained the victory (Rev. 17 [14]) by this unmerciful—and in the state of the New Testament, when the church is spread all the world over—most bloody doctrine, viz., the wolves (heretics) are to be driven away, their brains knocked out, and killed—the poor sheep to be preserved, for whom Christ died, etc.

Is not this to take Christ Jesus, and make him a temporal king by force? (John 6:15) Is not this to make his kingdom of this world, to set up a civil and temporal Israel, to bound out new earthly, holy lands of Canaan, yea, and to set up a Spanish Inquisition in all parts of the world, to the speedy destruction of thousands, yea, of millions of souls, and the frustrating of the sweet end of the coming of the Lord Jesus, to wit, to save men's souls (and to that end not to destroy their bodies) by his own blood?

CHAPTER XLIV

Peace. The next scripture produced against such persecution is II Corinthians 10:4, *The weapons of our warfare are not carnal, but mighty through God to the pulling down of strongholds; casting down imaginations, and every high thing that exalts itself against the knowledge of God, and bringing into captivity every thought to the obedience of Christ; and having in a readiness to avenge all disobedience, &c.*

Unto which it is answered, "When Paul says, *The weapons of our warfare are not carnal, but spiritual,* he denies not civil weapons of justice to the civil magistrate (Rom. 13), but only to church officers. And yet the weapons of church officers he acknowledges to be such, as though they be spiritual, yet are ready to take vengeance on all disobedience (2 Cor.

---

[53] A weapon of the fifteenth and sixteenth century having an ax-like blade and a steel spike mounted on the end of a long shaft.

10:6), which has reference, among other ordinances, to the censures of the church against scandalous offenders."

Truth. I acknowledge that herein the Spirit of God denies not civil weapons of justice to the civil magistrate, which the scripture he quotes (Rom. 13) abundantly testifies.

Yet withal, I must ask, why he here affirms the apostle denies not civil weapons of justice to the civil magistrate? Of which there is no question, unless that, according to his scope of proving persecution for conscience he intends withal that the apostle denies not civil weapons of justice to the civil magistrate in spiritual and religious causes: the contrary whereunto, the Lord assisting, I shall evince, both from this very scripture and his own observation, and lastly by that thirteenth of the Romans, by himself quoted.

First, then, from this scripture and his own observation. The weapons of church officers, says he, are such, which though they be spiritual, are ready to take vengeance on all disobedience; which has reference, says he, among other ordinances, to the censures of the church against scandalous offenders.

I hence observe that there being in this scripture held forth a twofold state, a civil state and a spiritual, civil officers and spiritual, civil weapons and spiritual weapons, civil vengeance and punishment and a spiritual vengeance and punishment: although the Spirit speaks not here expressly of civil magistrates and their civil weapons, yet, these states being of different natures and considerations, as far differing as spirit from flesh, I first observe, that civil weapons are most improper and unfitting in matters of the spiritual state and kingdom, though in the civil state most proper and suitable.

CHAPTER XLV

For, to keep to the similitude which the Spirit uses, for instance, to batter down a stronghold, high wall, fort tower, or castle, men bring not a first and second admonition, and, after obstinacy, excommunication, which are spiritual weapons, concerning them that be in the church: nor exhortations to repent and be baptized, to believe in the Lord Jesus, etc., which are proper weapons to them that be without, etc.; but to take a stronghold, men bring cannons, culverins,[54] saker,[55] bullets, powder, muskets, swords, pikes, etc., and these to this end are weapons effectual and proportionable.

On the other side, to batter down idolatry, false worship, heresy, schism, blindness, hardness, out of the soul and spirit, it is vain, improper, and unsuitable to bring those weapons which are used by persecutors, stocks, whips, prisons, swords, gibbets, stakes, etc., (where these seem to prevail with some cities or kingdoms, a stronger force sets up again what a weaker pulled down); but against these spiritual strongholds in the souls of men, spiritual artillery and weapons are proper, which are mighty through God to subdue and bring under the very thought to obedience, or else to bind fast the soul with chains of darkness, and lock it up in the prison of unbelief and hardness to eternity.

2. I observe that as civil weapons are improper in this business, and never able to effect aught in the soul: so although they were proper, yet they are unnecessary; for if, as the Spirit here says, and the answerer grants, spiritual weapons in the hand of church officers are able and ready to take vengeance on all disobedience, that is, able and mighty, sufficient and ready for the Lord's work, either to save the soul, or to kill the soul of whomsoever be the party or parties opposite; in which respect I may again remember that speech of Job, *How have you helped him that has no power?* (Job 26:2)

Peace. Offer this, as Malachi once spoke, to the governors, the kings of the earth, when they besiege, beleaguer, and assault great cities, castles, forts, etc., should any subject pretending his service bring store of pins, sticks, straws, bulrushes, to beat and batter down stone walls, mighty bulwarks, what might his expectation and reward be, but at least the censure of a man distract, beside himself?

Truth. What shall we then conceive of his displeasure who is the Chief or Prince of the kings of the earth, and rides upon the word of truth and meekness, which is the white horse (Rev. 6, 19) with his holy witnesses, the white troopers upon white horses, when to his help and aid men bring and add such unnecessary, improper, and weak munition?

---

[54] A long cannon (as an eighteen-pounder) of the sixteenth and seventeenth centuries.

[55] "A piece of ordinance of three and a half bore, carrying a ball of five pounds and a half weight." (Underhill)

Will the Lord Jesus (did he ever in his own person, or did he appoint to) join to his breastplate of righteousness, the breastplate of iron and steel? To the helmet of righteousness and salvation in Christ, a helmet and crest of iron, brass, or steel? A target of wood to his shield of faith? His two-edged sword, coming forth of the mouth of Jesus, the material sword, the work of smiths and cutlers? Or a girdle of shoe-leather to the girdle of truth? Excellently fit and proper is that alarm and item (Psalm 2 [10]), *Be wise, therefore, Oh, you kings*—especially those ten horns (Rev. 17), who, under pretence of fighting for Christ Jesus, give their power to the beast against him—and *be warned, you judges of the earth:* kiss the Son, that is, with subjection and affection, acknowledge him only the King and Judge of souls, in that power bequeathed to his ministers and churches, lest his wrath be kindled, yea, but a little; then, blessed are they that trust in him.

CHAPTER XLVI

Peace. Now, in the second place, concerning that scripture (Rom. 13) which it pleased the answerer to quote, and himself, and so many excellent servants of God have insisted upon to prove such persecution for conscience:—how have both he and they wrested this scripture, not as Peter writes of the wicked, to their eternal, yet to their own and others' temporal destruction, by civil wars and combustions in the world?

My humble request, therefore, is to the Father of lights, to send out the bright beams of the Sun of righteousness, and to scatter the mist which that old serpent, the great juggler, Satan, has raised about this holy scripture, and my request to you, divine Truth, is for your care and pains to enlighten and clear this scripture.

Truth. First, then, upon the serious examination of this whole scripture, it will appear, that from the ninth verse of the twelfth chapter to the end of this whole thirteenth chapter, the Spirit handles the duties of the saints in the careful observation of the second table in their civil conversation, or walking towards men, and speaks not at all of any point or matter of the first table concerning the kingdom of the Lord Jesus.

For, having in the whole epistle handled that great point of free justification by the free grace of God in Christ, in the beginning of the twelfth chapter he exhorts the believers to give and dedicate themselves unto the Lord, both in soul and body; and unto the ninth verse of* the twelfth chapter he expressly mentions their conversation in the kingdom, or body, of Christ Jesus, together with the several officers thereof.

And from the ninth verse to the end of the thirteenth he plainly discourses of their civil conversation, and walking one toward another, and with all men, from whence he has fair occasion to speak largely concerning their subjection to magistrates in the thirteenth chapter.

Hence it is that verse seven of this thirteenth chapter, Paul exhorts to performance of love to all men, magistrates and subjects (verses 7,8), *Render, therefore, to all their due; tribute to whom tribute is due; custom to whom custom; fear to whom fear; honor to whom honor. Owe nothing to any man, but to love one another: for he that loves another has fulfilled the law.*

If any man doubt, as the papists speak, whether a man may perfectly fulfil the law, every man of sound judgment is ready to answer him, that these words, *He that loves has fulfilled the law,* concerns not the whole law in the first table, that is, the worship and kingdom of God in Christ.

Secondly, that the apostle speaks not here of perfect observation of the second table, without failing in word or act toward men, but lays open the sum and substance of the law, which is love; and that he that walks by the rule of love toward all men, magistrates and subjects, he has rightly attained unto what the law aims at, and so in evangelical obedience fulfils and keeps the law.

Hence, therefore, again in the ninth verse, having discoursed of the fifth command in this point of superiors, he makes all the rest of the commandments of the second table, which concern our walking with man, viz., *Thou shalt not kill; thou shalt not commit adultery; thou shalt not steal; thou shalt not bear false witness; thou shalt not covet: and if there be any other commandment to be briefly comprehended in this saying, namely, thou shalt love thy neighbor as thyself.*

And verse ten, *Love works no ill to his neighbor, therefore, love is the fulfilling of the law,* that is, as before, the law concerning our civil conversation toward all men, magistrates or governors, and fellow subjects of all conditions.

CHAPTER XLVII

Peace. Although the scripture is sufficient to make the man of God perfect, and the fool wise to salvation, and our faith in God must be only founded upon the rock Christ, and not upon the sand of men's judgments and opinions: yet, as Paul alleges the judgment and sayings of unbelievers for their conviction, out of their own tenents and grants, so I pray you to set down the words of one or two, not unbelievers in their persons, but excellent and precious servants and witnesses of God in their times, whose names are sweet and precious to all that fear God, who, although their judgment ran in the common stream, viz., that magistrates were keepers of the two tables, defenders of' the faith against heretics, and, notwithstanding whatever they have written for defense of their judgments, yet the light of truth so evidently shined upon their souls in this scripture that they absolutely denied the thirteenth of the Romans to concern any matter of the first table.

Truth. First, I shall produce that excellent servant of God, Calvin, who, upon this thirteenth to the Romans, writes, *Tota autem haec disputatio est de civilibus praefecturis; itaque frustra inde sacrilegam suam tyrannidem stabilire moliuntur, qui dominatum in conscientias exerceant:*[56] —"But," says he, "this whole discourse concerns civil magistrates, and, therefore, in vain do they who exercise power over consciences go about from this place to establish their sacrilegious tyranny."

Peace. I know how far most men, and especially the sheep of Jesus, will fly from the thought of exercising tyranny over conscience, that happily they will disclaim the dealing of all with men's consciences: yet, if the acts and statutes which are made by them concerning the worship of God be attended to, their profession—and that out of' zeal according to the pattern of that ceremonial and figurative state of Israel—to suffer no other religion nor worship in their territories, but one—their profession and practice to defend their faith from reproach and blasphemy of heretics by civil weapons, and all that from this very thirteenth of the Romans—I say, if these particulars and others, be with fear and trembling, in the presence of the Most High, examined, the wonderful deceit of' their own hearts shall appear unto them, and how guilty they

---

[56] John Calvin, *Commentary on the Epistle to the Romans* (Philadelphia: Whetham) 322-323.

will appear to be of wresting this scripture before the tribunal of the Most High.

Truth. Again, Calvin, speaking concerning fulfilling of the law by love, writes thus on the same place: *Sed Paulus in totam legem non respicit; tantum de officiis loquitur, quae nobis erga proximum demandantur a lege;*[57] that is, "Paul has not respect unto the whole law, he speaks only of those duties which the law commands towards our neighbors." And it is manifest that in this place by our neighbors he means high and low, magistrates and subjects, unto whom we ought to walk by the rule of love, paying unto every one their due.

Again, *Caeterum Paulus hic tantum meminet secundae tabulae, quia de ea tantum erat quaestio:* "But Paul here only mentions the second table, because the question was only concerning that."[58]

And again, *Quod autem repetit, complementum legis esse dilectionem, intellige (ut prius) de ea legis parte, quod hominum societatem spectat? Prior enim legis tabula quae est de cultu Dei minime hie attingitur.*[59]—"But in that he repeats that love is the fulfilling of the law, understand as before, that he speaks of that part of the law which respects human society; for the first table of the law, which concerns the worship of God, is not in the least manner here touched."

After Calvin, his successor in Geneva, that holy and learned Beza, upon the word ανακεφαλαιουται, *if there be any other commandment it is summed up in this, thou shalt love thy neighbor as thyself,* writes thus: *Tota lex nihil aliud quam amorem Dei et proximi praecipet; sed tamen cum apostolus hoc loco de mutuis hominum officiis disserat, legis vocabulum ad secundum tabulam restringendam puto.* "The whole law," says he, "commands nothing else but the love of God, and yet, nevertheless, since the apostle in this place discourses of the duties of men one toward another, I think this term law ought to be restrained to the second table."[60]

---

[57] Ibid., 325.
[58] Ibid.
[59] Ibid.
[60] Bezae Nov. Test. in loc. edit. Londini, 1585.

CHAPTER XLVIII

Peace. I pray now proceed to the second argument from this scripture against the use of civil weapons in matters of religions and spiritual worship.

Truth. The Spirit of God here commands subjection and obedience to higher powers, even to the Roman emperors and all subordinate magistrates; and yet the emperors and governors under them were strangers from the life of God in Christ, yea, most averse and opposite, yea, cruel and bloody persecutors of the name and followers of Jesus: and yet unto these, is this subjection and obedience commanded. Now true it is, that as the civil magistrate is apt not to content himself with the majesty of an earthly throne, crown, sword, scepter, but to seat himself in the throne of David in the church: so God's people, and it may be in Paul's time, considering their high and glorious preferment and privileges by Jesus Christ, were apt to be much tempted to despise civil governors, especially such as were ignorant of the Son of God, and persecuted him in his servants.

Now then I argue, if the apostle should have commanded this subjection unto the Roman emperors and Roman magistrates in spiritual causes, as to defend the truth which they were no way able to discern, but persecuted—and upon trust from others no magistrate, not persuaded in his own conscience, is to take it—or else to punish heretics, whom then also they must discern and judge, or else condemn them, as the Jews would have Pilate condemn the Lord Jesus, upon the sentence of others—I say, if Paul should have, in this scripture, put this work upon these Roman governors, and commanded the churches of Christ to have yielded subjection in any such matters, he must, in the judgment of all men, have put out the eye of faith, and reason, and sense, at once.

CHAPTER XLIX

Peace. It is said by some, why then did Paul himself (Acts 25:11) appeal to Caesar, unless that Caesar, (though he was not, yet) he ought to have been a fit judge in such matters?

Truth. I answer, if Paul, in this appeal to Caesar, had referred and submitted simply and properly the cause of Christ, his ministry and ministration, to the Roman emperor's tribunal, knowing him to be an idolatrous stranger from the true God, and a lion-like, bloody persecutor of the Lord Jesus, the Lamb of God,—I say, let it be considered, whether or no he had committed these five evils:

The first, against the dimmest light of reason, in appealing to darkness to judge light, to unrighteousness to judge righteousness, the spiritually blind to judge and end the controversy concerning heavenly colors.

Secondly, against the cause of religion, which, if condemned by every inferior idolater, must needs be condemned by the Caesars themselves, who, Nebuchadnezzar-like, set up their state images or religions, commanding the world's uniformity of worship to them.

Thirdly, against the holy state and calling of the Christians themselves, who, by virtue of their subjection to Christ, even the least of them are in spiritual things above the highest potentates or emperors in the world who continue in enmity against, or in an ignorant, natural state without Christ Jesus. This honor, or high exaltation have all his holy ones, to bind, not literally but spiritually, their kings in chains, and their nobles in links of iron. (Ps. 149:8)[61]

Fourthly, against his own calling, apostleship, or office of ministry, unto which Caesar himself and all potentates, inspiritual and soul-matters, ought to have submitted; and unto which, in controversies of Christ's church and kingdom, Caesar himself ought to have appealed, the church of God being built upon the foundation of the apostles and prophets. (Eph. 2:20)

And, therefore, in case that any of the Roman governors, or the emperor himself, had been humbled and converted to Christianity by the preaching of Christ, were not they themselves bound to subject themselves unto the power of the Lord Jesus in the hands of the apostles and churches, and might not the apostles and churches have refused to have baptized, or washed them into the profession of Christ Jesus, upon the apprehension of their unworthiness?

Or, if received into Christian fellowship, were they not to stand at the bar of the Lord Jesus in the church, concerning either their opinions or practices? Were they not to be cast out and delivered unto Satan by the power of the Lord Jesus, if, after once and twice admonition, they persist

---

[61] Williams mistakenly cites Psalm 49:8.

obstinate, as faithfully and impartially as if they were the meanest in the empire? Yea, although the apostles, the churches, the elders, or governors thereof were poor and mean, despised persons in civil respects, and were themselves bound to yield all faithful and loyal obedience to such emperors and governors in civil things.

Were they not, if' Christians, bound themselves to have submitted to those spiritual decrees of the apostles and elders, as well as the lowest and meanest members of' Christ? (Acts 16) And if so, how should Paul appeal in spiritual things to Caesar, or write to the churches of Jesus to submit to them Christian or spiritual matters?

Fifthly, if Paul had appealed to Caesar in spiritual aspects, he had greatly profaned the holy name of God in holy things, in so improper and vain a prostitution of spiritual things to carnal and natural judgments, which are not able to comprehend spiritual matters, which are alone spiritually discerned. (1 Cor. 2 [14])

And yet Caesar, as a civil, supreme magistrate, ought to defend Paul from civil violence, and slanderous accusations about sedition, mutiny, civil disobedience, etc. And in that sense, who doubts but God's people may appeal to the Roman Caesar, an Egyptian Pharaoh, a Philistine Abimelech, an Assyrian Nebuchadnezzar, the great Mogul, Prester John,[62] the great Turk, or an Indian sachem?

CHAPTER L

Peace. Which is the third argument against the civil magistrates' power in spiritual and soul-matters out of this scripture (Rom. 13)?

Truth. I dispute from the nature of the magistrates' weapons (verse 4). He has a sword, which he bears not in vain, delivered to him, as I acknowledge' from God's appointment in the free consent and choice of the subjects for common good.

We must distinguish of swords.

We find four sorts of swords mentioned in the New Testament.

First, the sword of persecution, which Herod stretched forth against James. (Acts 12 [1, 2])

---

[62] Also called Presbyterian John or John the Elder. A legendary ruler, popularized in medieval chronicles and traditions as a hoped-for ally against the Muslims.

Secondly, the sword of God's Spirit, expressly said to be the word of God (Eph. 6 [1,7]), a sword of two edges, carried in the mouth of Christ (Rev. 1 [16]), which is of strong and mighty operation, piercing between the bones and the marrow, between the soul and the spirit. (Heb. 4 [12])

Thirdly, the great sword of war and destruction, given to him that rides that terrible red horse of war, so that he takes peace from the earth, and men kill one another, as is most lamentably true in the slaughter of so many hundred thousand souls within these few years in several parts of Europe, our own and others.

None of these three swords are intended in this scripture.

Therefore, fourthly, there is a civil sword, called the sword of civil justice, which being of a material nature, for the defense of persons, estates, families, liberties of a city or civil state, and the suppressing of uncivil or injurious persons or actions, by such civil punishment it cannot, according to its utmost reach and capacity, now under Christ, when all nations are merely civil, without any such typical, holy respect upon them, as was upon Israel, a national church—I say, cannot extend to spiritual and soul-causes, spiritual and soul-punishment, which belongs to that spiritual sword with two edges, the soul-piercing (in soul-saving, or soul-killing), the word of God.

CHAPTER LIIA[63]

Truth. A fourth argument from this scripture, I take in the sixth verse, from tribute, custom, etc., which is a merely civil reward, or recompense, for the magistrates' work. Now as the wages are, such is the work; but the wages are merely civil—custom, tribute, etc., not the contributions of the saints or churches of Christ, proper to the spiritual and Christian state. And such work only must the magistrate attend upon, as may properly deserve such civil wages, reward, or recompense.

Lastly, that the Spirit of God never intended to direct, or warrant, the magistrate to use his power in spiritual affairs and religious worship, I argue from the term or title it pleases the wisdom of God to give such civil officers, to wit, verse 6, God's ministers.

---

[63] There are two chapters numbered LII in the first edition. Underhill corrected the error; Caldwell repeated it, with an explanatory footnote. The error is repeated here, with the chapters designated a and b, in order to maintain a correlation with the first edition.

Now at the very first blush, no man denies a double ministry. The one appointed by Christ Jesus in his church, to gather, to govern, receive in, cast out, and order all the affairs of the church, the house, city, or kingdom of God. (Eph. 4; 1 Cor. 12)

Secondly, a civil ministry, or office, merely human and civil, which men agree to constitute, called therefore a human creation (1 Pet. 2 [13]), and is as true and lawful in those nations, cities, kingdoms, etc., which never heard of the true God, nor his holy Son Jesus, as in any part of the world beside, where the name of Jesus is most taken up.

From all which premises, viz., that the scope of the Spirit of God in this chapter is to handle the matters of the second table (having handled the matters of the first, in the twelfth), since the magistrates of whom Paul wrote, were natural, ungodly, persecuting, and yet lawful magistrates, and to be obeyed in all lawful civil things, since all magistrates are God's ministers, essentially civil, bounded to a civil work, with civil weapons, or instruments, and paid or rewarded with civil rewards—from all which, I say, I undeniably collect that this scripture is generally mistaken, and wrested from the scope of God's Spirit, and the nature of the place, and cannot truly be alleged by any for the power of the civil magistrate to be exercised in spiritual and soul-matters.

CHAPTER LIIB

Peace. Against this I know many object, out of the fourth verse of this chapter, that the magistrate is to avenge, or punish evil, from whence is gathered that heresy, false Christs, false churches, false ministries, false seals, being evil, ought to be punished civilly, etc.

Truth. I answer, that the word κακον is generally opposed to civil goodness, or virtue, in a commonwealth, and not to spiritual good, or religion, in the church.

Secondly, I have proved from the scope of the place that here is not intended evil against the spiritual, or Christian estate handled in the twelfth chapter, but evil against the civil state in this thirteenth, properly falling under the cognizance of the civil minister of God, the magistrate, and punishable by that civil sword of his as an incivility, disorder, or breach of that civil order, peace, and civility, unto which all the inhabitants of a city, town, or kingdom, oblige themselves.

Peace. I have heard that the elders of the New England churches, who yet out of this thirteenth of Romans maintain persecution, grant that the magistrate is to preserve the peace and welfare of the state, and therefore that he ought not to punish such sins as hurt not his peace.[64] In particular, they say, the magistrate may not punish secret sins in the soul, nor such sins as are yet handling in the church, in a private way, nor such sins which are private in families, and therefore, they say, the magistrate transgresses to prosecute complaints of children against their parents, servants against masters, wives against husbands (and yet this proper to the civil state). Nor such sins as are between the members and churches themselves.

And they confess, that if the magistrate punish, and the church punish, there will be a greater rent in their peace.

Truth. From thence, sweet Peace, may we well observe, first, the magistrate is not to punish all evil, according this their confession.

The distinction of private and public evil will not here avail; because such as urge that term evil, viz., that the magistrate is to punish evil, urge it strictly, *eo nomine*; because heresy, blasphemy, false church, false ministry, is evil, as well as disorder in a civil state.

Secondly, I observe, how they take away from the magistrate that which is proper to his cognizance, as the complaints of servants, children, wives, against their parents, masters, husbands, etc. families as families, being as stones which make up the common building, and are properly the object of the magistrates' care, in respect of civil government, civil order, and obedience.

CHAPTER LIVA[65]

Peace. I pray now, lastly, proceed to the author's reason why Christ's disciples should be so far from persecuting, that they ought to bless them that curse them, and pray for them that persecute them, because of the freeness of God's grace, and the deepness of his counsels, calling them

---

[64] "A Model of Church and Civil Power—Sent to the Church at Salem," examined by Williams at length in subsequent chapters.

[65] In the first edition there were two chapters numbered LIV. Underhill renumbered the chapters. The error is repeated here, with the chapters designated A and B, in order to maintain correlation with the first edition.

that are enemies, persecutors, no people, to become meek lambs, the sheep and people of God, according to 1 Peter 2:10,[66] *You which were not a people, are now a people,* etc., and Matthew 20:6, some come at the last hour, which if they were cut off because they came not sooner, would be prevented, and so should never come.

Unto this reasons the answerer is pleased thus to reply. First, in general, we must not do evil that good may come thereof.

Secondly, in particular, he affirms "that it is evil to tolerate seditious evil doers, seducing teachers, scandalous livers"; and for proof of this, he quotes Christ's reproof to the angel of the church at Pergamos for tolerating them that hold the doctrine of Balaam, and against the church of Thyatira, for tolerating Jezebel to teach and seduce. (Rev. 2:14, 20)[67]

Truth. I answer, first, by assenting to the general proposition, that it is most true, like unto Christ Jesus himself, a sure foundation. (1 Cor. 3 [11]) Yet what is built upon it, I hope by God's assistance to make it appear, is but hay and stubble, dead and withered, not suiting that golden foundation, nor pleasing to the Father of mercies, nor comfortable to the souls of men.

It is evil, says he, to tolerate notorious evil doers, seducing teachers, scandalous livers.

In which speech I observe two evils. First, that this proposition is too large and general, because the rule admits of exception, and that according to the will of God.

It is true that evil cannot alter its nature, but it is always evil, as darkness is always darkness, yet,

2. It must be remembered that it is one thing to command, to conceal, to counsel, to approve evil, and another thing to permit and suffer evil with protestation against it, or dislike of it, at least without approbation of it.

---

[66] Williams mistakenly cites 1 Peter 2:20.

[67] "Upon this point has Mr. Goodwin excellently of late discoursed." (Williams's footnote) "M.S. to A.S., with a Plea for Liberty of Conscience in a Church Way," (1644) by John Goodwin (c. 1593-1665), prominent English Puritan theologian and leader of the "new Arminians." In *Theomachia* (1644), he defended the Independents' views. In *A Bone for a Bishop* (1643) he opposed the divine right of kings. Neal says that Goodwin lost his position as vicar of Coleman Street "because he refused to baptize the children of his parishioners promiscuously and to administer the sacraments to his whole parish." (*History of the Puritans*) Cited by Caldwell, 185.

Lastly, this sufferance, or permission, of evil, is not for its own sake, but for the sake of good, which puts a respect of goodness upon such permission.

Hence, it is that for God's own glory's sake, which is the highest good, he endures, that is, permits, or suffers, the vessels of wrath. (Romans 9 [22]) And therefore, although he be of pure eyes and can behold no iniquity, yet his pure eye patiently and quietly beholds and permits all the idolatries and profanations, all the thefts and rapines, all the whoredoms and abominations, all the murders and poisonings; and yet, I say, for his glory's sake, he is patient, and long permits.

Hence, for his peoples' sake (which is the next good, in his Son), he is oftentimes pleased to permit and suffer the wicked to enjoy a longer reprieve. Therefore, he gave Paul all the lives that were in the ship. (Acts 27 [24])

Therefore, he would not so soon have destroyed Sodom, but granted a longer permission, had there been but ten righteous. (Genesis [18:32])[68] Therefore, (Jeremiah 5:1) had he found some to have stood in the gap, he would have spared others. Therefore gave he Jezebel a time, or space. (Rev. 2:21)

Therefore, for his glory's sake, has he permitted longer great sinners, who afterward have perished in their season, as we see in the case of Ahab, the Ninevites, and Amorites, etc.

Hence it pleased the Lord, not only to permit the many evils against his own honorable ordinance of marriage in the world, but was pleased, after a wonderful manner, to suffer that sin of many wives in Abraham, Jacob, David, Solomon, yea, with some expressions which seem to give approbation, as II Samuel 12 [8, 24].

Peace. It may be said, this is no pattern for us, because God is above law, and an absolute sovereign.

Truth. I answer, although we find him sometime dispensing with his law, yet we never find him deny himself, or utter a falsehood: and therefore when it crosses not an absolute rule to permit and tolerate—as in the case of the permission of the souls and consciences of all men in the world—I have shown, and shall show further, it does not, it will not, hinder our being holy as he is holy, in all manner of conversation.

---

[68] Williams mistakenly cites Genesis 19.

CHAPTER LIVB

Peace. It will yet be said, it pleases God to permit adulteries, murders, poisons. God suffers men, like fishes, to devour each other (Hab. 1 [14]); the wicked to flourish (Jer. 12 [1]); yea, sends the tyrants of the world to destroy the nations, and plunder them of their riches (Isa. 10 [5, 6.]). Should men do so, the world would be a wilderness; and beside we have command for zealous execution of justice, impartially, speedily.

Truth. I answer, we find two sorts of commands, both from Moses and from Christ, the two great prophets and messengers from the living God, the one the type or figure of the later. Moses gave positive rules, both spiritual and civil; yet also, he gave some not positive but permissive, for the common good. So the Lord Jesus expounded it.

For whereas the Pharisees urged it, that Moses commanded to give a bill of divorcement and to put away, the Lord Jesus expounded it, *Moses for the hardness of your hearts suffered,* or permitted. (Matt. 19:7, 8)[69]

This was a permissive command, universal to all Israel, for a general good, in preventing the continual fires of dissensions and combustions in families: yea, it may be murders, poisons, adulteries, which that people, as the wisdom of God foresaw, was apt, out of the hardness of' their heart, to break out into, were it not for this preventing permission.

Hence, it was that for a further public good sake, and the public safety, David permitted Joab, a notorious malefactor, and Shimei and Adonijah, etc. And civil states and governors, in like cases, have and do permit and suffer what neither David nor any civil governors ought to do or have done, were it not to prevent the hazard of the whole, in the shedding of' much innocent blood, together with the nocent,[70] in civil combustions.

Peace. It may be said, Joab, Shimei, Adonijah, etc., were only, as it were, reprieved for a time, and proves only that a season ought to be attended for their punishment.

Truth. Answer. I answer, I produce not these instances to prove a permission of tares—anti-Christians, heretics—which other scriptures abundantly prove, but to make it clear, against the answerer's allegation that even in the civil state permission of notorious evil doers, even against

---

[69] Williams mistakenly cites Matthew 19:17-18.
[70] Harmful.

the civil state, is not disapproved by God himself and the wisest of his
servants in its season.

CHAPTER LV

Truth. I proceed. Hence, it is that some generals of armies, and
governors of cities, towns, etc., do, and, as those former instances prove,
lawfully permit some evil persons and practices. As for instance, in the
civil state, usury: for the preventing of a greater evil in the civil body, as
stealing, robbing, murdering, perishing of the poor, find the hindrance,
or stop, of commerce and dealing in the commonwealth. Just like
physician, wisely permitting noisome humors, and sometimes diseases,
when the cure or purging would prove more dangerous to the
destruction of the whole, a weak or crazy body, and specially at such a
time.

Thus, in many other instances, it pleased the Father of lights, the
God of Israel, to permit that people, especially in the matter of their
demand of a king, wherein he pleaded that himself as well as Samuel was
rejected.

This ground, to wit, for a common good of the whole, is the same
with that of the Lord Jesus commanding the tares to be permitted in the
world; because, otherwise, the good wheat should be endangered to be
rooted up out of the field or world also, as well as the tares. And
therefore, for the good sake, the tares, which are evil, were to be
permitted: yea, and for the general good of the whole world, the field
itself, which, for want of this obedience to that command of Christ,has
been and is laid waste and desolate with the fury and rage of civil war,
professedly raised and maintained, as all states profess, for the
maintenance of one true religion—after the pattern of that typical land of
Canaan—and to suppress and pluck up these tares of false prophets and
false professors, anti-Christians, heretics, etc., out of the world.

Hence *illae lachrymae*: hence Germany's, Ireland's, and now
England's, tears and dreadful desolations, which ought to have been, and
may be for the future,—by obedience to the command of the Lord Jesus,
concerning the permission of tares to live in the world, though not in the
church—I say, ought to have been, and may be mercifully prevented.

CHAPTER LVI

Peace. I pray descend now to the second evil which you observe in the answer's position, viz., that it would be evil to tolerate notorious evil doers, seducing teachers, etc.

Truth. I say, the evil is that he most improperly and confusedly joins and couples seducing teachers with scandalous livers.

Peace. But is it not true that the world is full of seducing teachers? And is it not true, that seducing teachers are notorious evil doers?

Truth. I answer, far be it from me to deny either. And yet in two things I shall discover the great evil of this joining and coupling seducing teacher and scandalous livers, as one adequate or proper object of the magistrates' care and work to suppress and punish.

First, it is not an homogeneal (as we speak), but an heterogeneal commixture or joining together of things most different in kinds and natures, as if they were both of one consideration.

For who knows not but that many seducing teachers, either of the paganish, Jewish, Turkish, or anti-Christian teachers, may be clear and free from scandalous offences in their life, as also from disobedience to the civil laws of a state? Yea, the answerer himself has elsewhere granted that if the laws of a civil state be not broken, the peace is not broken.

Again, who knows not that a seducing teacher properly sins against a church or spiritual estate and laws of it, and, therefore, ought most properly and only to be dealt withal in such a way, and by such weapons, as the Lord Jesus himself has appointed; gainsayers, opposites, and disobedients—either within his church or without—to be convinced, repelled, resisted, and slain withal?

Whereas, scandalous offenders against parents, against magistrates in the fifth command, and so against the life, chastity, goods, or good name in the rest, is properly transgression against the civil state and commonweal, or the worldly state of men: and, therefore, consequently, if the world, or civil state, ought to be preserved by civil government or governors, such scandalous offenders ought not to be tolerated, but suppressed, according to the wisdom and prudence of the said government.

Secondly, as there is a fallacious conjoining and confounding together persons of several kinds and natures, differing as much as spirit and flesh, heaven and earth, each from other: so is there a silent and implicit justification of all the unrighteous and cruel proceedings of Jews and

Gentiles against all the prophets of God, the Lord Jesus himself, and all his messengers and witnesses, whom their accusers have ever so coupled and mixed with notorious evil doers and scandalous livers.

Elijah was a troubler of the state; Jeremy weakened the hand of the people; yea, Moses made the people neglect their work; the Jews built the rebellious and bad city; the three worthies regarded not the command of the king; Christ Jesus deceived the people, was a conjuror and a traitor against Caesar in being king of the Jews—indeed he was so spiritually over the true Jew, the Christian—therefore, he was numbered with notorious evil doers, and nailed to the gallows between two malefactors.

Hence, Paul and all true messengers of Jesus Christ are esteemed seducing and seditious teachers and turners of the world upside down: yea, and to my knowledge –I speak with honorable respect to the answerer, so far as he has labored for many truths of Christ—the answerer himself has drunk of' this cup, to be esteemed a seducing teacher.

CHAPTER LVII

Peace. Yea, but he produces scriptures against such toleration, and for persecuting men for the cause of conscience: "Christ," says he, "had something against the angel of the church of Pergamos, for tolerating them that held the doctrine of' Balaam, and against the church of Thyatira, for tolerating Jezebel to teach and seduce." (Rev. 2:14, 20)

Truth. I may answer, with some admiration and astonishment, how it pleased the Father of lights and most jealous God to darken and veil the eye of so precious a man, as not to seek out and propose some scriptures in the proof of so weighty an assertion, as at least might have some color for, an influence of the civil magistrate in such cases: for,

First, he says not that Christ had aught against the city Pergamos, where Satan had his throne (Rev. 2[14, 20]), but against the church at Pergamos, in which was set up the throne of Christ.

Secondly, Christ's charge is not against the civil magistrate of Pergamos, but the messenger, or ministry, of the church in Pergamos.

Thirdly, I confess, so far as Balaam's or Jezebel's doctrine maintained a liberty of corporal fornication, it concerned the cities of Pergamos and Thyatira, and the angel or officers of those cities, to suppress not only such practices, but such doctrines also as the Roman emperor justly punished Ovid the poet, for teaching the wanton art of love, leading to and ushering on lasciviousness and uncleanness.

Fourthly, yet so far as Balaam's teachers, or Jezebel, did seduce the members of the church in Pergamos or Thyatira to the worship of the idolaters in Pergamos or Thyatira, which will appear to be the case—I say, so far I may well and properly answer, as himself answered before those scriptures, brought from Luke 11 and 2 Timothy 2, to prove patience and permission to men opposite, viz., "These scriptures," says he, "are directions to ministers of the gospel"; and in the end of that passage he adds, "Much less do they speak at all to civil magistrates."

Fifthly, either these churches and the angels thereof had power to suppress these doctrines of Balaam, and to suppress Jezebel from teaching, or they had not. That they had not cannot be affirmed, for Christ's authority is in the hands of his ministers and churches. (Matt. 16,18, and 1 Cor. 5)

If they had power, as must be granted, then, I conclude, sufficient power to suppress such persons, whoever they were that maintained Balaam's doctrine in the church at Pergamos, although the very magistrates themselves of the city of Pergamos (if Christians): and to have suppressed Jezebel from teaching and seducing in the church, had she been lady, queen, or empress, if there were no more but teaching without hostility. And if so, all power and authority of magistrates and governors of Pergamos and Thyatira, and all submitting or appealing to them in such cases, must needs fall, as none of Christ's appointment.

Lastly, from this perverse wresting of what is writ to the church and the officers thereof, as if it were written to the civil state and officers thereof, all may see how, since the apostasy of Antichrist, the Christian world (so called) has swallowed up Christianity; how the church and civil state, that is, the church and the world, are now become one flock of Jesus Christ; Christ's sheep, and the pastors or shepherds of them, all one with the several unconverted, wild, or tame beasts and cattle of the world, and the civil and earthly governors of them: the Christian church, or kingdom of the saints, that stone cut out of the mountain without hands (Dan. 2 [45]), now made all one with the mountain, or civil state, the

Roman empire, from whence it is cut or taken: Christ's lilies, garden, and love, all one with the thorns, the daughters, and wilderness of the world, out of' which the spouse or church of' Christ is called; and among whom, in civil things, for a while here below, she must necessarily be mingled and have converse, unless she will go out of the world before Christ Jesus, her Lord and husband, send for her home into the heavens. (1 Cor. 5:10)

CHAPTER LVIII

Peace. Having thus, by the help of Christ, examined those scriptures, or writings of truth, brought by the author against persecution, and cleared them from such veils and mists, wherewith Mr. Cotton has endeavored to obscure and darken their lights, I pray you, now, by the same gracious assistance, proceed to his answer to the second head of reasons, from the profession of famous princes against persecution for conscience, King James, Stephen of Poland, King of Bohemia, unto whom the answerer returns a treble answer.

"First," says he, "we willingly acknowledge that none is to be persecuted at all, no more than they may be oppressed for righteousness' sake.

"Again, we acknowledge that none is to be punished for his conscience, though misinformed, as has been said, unless his error be fundamental, or seditiously and turbulently promoted, and that after due conviction of his conscience, that it may appear he is not punished for his conscience, but for sinning against his conscience.

"Furthermore, we acknowledge, none is to be constrained to believe or profess the true religion, till he be convinced in judgment of the truth of it; but yet restrained he may be from blaspheming the truth, and from seducing any unto pernicious errors."

Truth. This first answer consists of a repetition and enumeration of such grounds or conclusions as Mr. Cotton in the entrance of this discourse laid down; and I believe that through the help of God, in such replies as I have made unto them, I have made it evident what weak foundations they have in the scriptures of truth, as also that when such conclusions, excepting the first, as grass and the flower of the grass shall fade, that holy word of the Lord, which the author against such persecution produces, and I have cleared, shall stand for ever, even when these heavens and earth are burnt.[71]

Peace. His second answer is this: "What princes profess and practice is not a rule of conscience. They many times tolerate that in point of state policy which cannot justly be tolerated in point of true Christianity.

"Again, princes many times tolerate offenders out of very necessity, when the offenders are either too many or too mighty for them to punish; in which respect David tolerated Joab and his murders, but against his will."

CHAPTER LIX

Unto those excellent and famous speeches of those princes, worthy to be written in golden letters, or rows of diamonds, upon all the gates of all the cities and palaces in the world, the answerer, without any particular reply, returns two things.

Truth. First, that princes' profession and practice is no rule of conscience: unto this, as all men will subscribe, so may they also observe how the answerer deals with princes.

One, while they are the nursing fathers of the church, not only to feed, but also to correct, and, therefore, consequently bound to judge what is true feeding and correcting: and, consequently, all men are bound to submit to their feeding and correcting.

Another, while, when princes cross Mr. Cotton's judgment and practice, then it matters not what the profession or practice of princes is: for, says he, their profession and practice is no rule to conscience.

I ask then, unto what magistrates or princes will themselves, or any so persuaded, submit, as unto keepers of both tables, as unto the antitypes of the kings of Israel and Judah, and nursing fathers and mothers of the church?

First, will it not evidently follow that by these tenents they ought not to submit to any magistrates in the world in these cases, but to magistrates just of their own conscience? And --

Secondly, that all other consciences in the world, except their own, must be persecuted by such their magistrates?

---

[71] "Isaiah 40:6; 2 Peter 2." (Williams's footnote)

And lastly, is not this to make magistrates but steps and stirrups to ascend and mount up into their rich and honorable seats and saddles; I mean great and settled maintenances, which neither the Lord Jesus, nor any of his first messengers, the true patterns, did ever know?

CHAPTER LX

Truth. In the second place, he says that princes out of state policy tolerate what suits not with Christianity, and out of state necessity tolerate (as David did Joab) against their wills.

To which I answer, first, that although with him, in the first, I confess that princes may tolerate that out of state policy which will not stand with Christianity, yet, in the second, he must acknowledge with me that there is a necessity sometimes of state toleration, as in the case of Joab, and so his former affirmation, generally laid down, viz., that it is evil to tolerate seducing teachers or scandalous livers, was not duly weighed in the balance of the sanctuary, and is too light.

Secondly, I affirm that that state policy and state necessity, which, for the peace of the state and preventing of rivers of civil blood, permit the consciences of men, will be found to agree most punctually with the rules of the best politician that ever the world saw, the King of kings, and Lord of lords, in comparison of whom Solomon himself had but a drop of wisdom compared to Christ's ocean, and was but a farthing candle compared with the all and ever glorious Sun of righteousness.[72]

That absolute rule of this great politician for the peace of the field which is the world, and for the good and peace of the saints who must have a civil being in the world, I have discoursed of in his command of permitting the tares, that is, anti-Christians, or false Christians, to be in the field of the world, growing up together with the true wheat, true Christians.

---

[72] "Christ Jesus the deepest politician that ever was, and yet he commanded a toleration of anti-Christians." (Williams's footnote)

CHAPTER LXI

Peace. His third answer is this: "For those three princes named by you, who tolerated religion, we can name you more and greater who have not tolerated heretics and schismatics, notwithstanding their pretence of conscience, and their arrogating the crown of martyrdom to their sufferings.

"Constantine the Great at the request of the general Council at Nicea, banished Arius, with some of his fellows. (Sozomen. *Ecclesiastical History, Book I,* chapters 19, 20)

"The same Constantine made a severe law against the   Donatists: and the like proceedings against them were used by Valentinian, Gratian, and Theodosius, as Augustine reports in Epistle 166. Only Julian the Apostate granted liberty to heretics as well as to pagans, that he might, by tolerating all weeds to grow, choke the vitals of Christianity: which was also the practice and sin of Valens the Arian.

"Queen Elizabeth, as famous for her government as most of the former, it is well known what laws she made and executed against papists. Yea, and King James, one of your own witnesses, though he was slow in proceeding against papists, as you say, for conscience' sake, yet you are not ignorant how sharply and severely he punished those whom the malignant world calls Puritans, men of more conscience and better faith than the papists whom he tolerated."

Truth. Unto this I answer: first, that for mine own part I would not use an argument from the number of princes, witnessing in profession of practice against persecution for cause of conscience; for the truth and faith of the Lord Jesus must not be received with respect of faces, be they never so high, princely and glorious.

Precious pearls and jewels, and far more precious truth, are found in muddy shells and places. The rich mines of golden truth lie hid under barren hills, and in obscure holes and corners.

The most high and glorious God has chosen the poor of the world, and the witnesses of truth (Rev. 11) are clothed in sackcloth, not in silk or satin, cloth of gold or tissue: and, therefore, I acknowledge, if the number of princes professing persecution be considered, it is rare to find a king, prince, or governor like Christ Jesus, the King of kings, and Prince of the princes of the earth, and who tread not in the steps of Herod the fox, or Nero the lion, openly or secretly persecuting the name of the Lord Jesus;

such were Saul, Jeroboam, Ahab, though under a mask or pretence of the name of the God of Israel.

To that purpose was it a noble speech of Buchanan,[73] who lying on his death-bed, sent this item to King James: "Remember my humble service to his majesty, and tell him that Buchanan is going to a place where few kings come."

CHAPTER LXII

Truth. Secondly, I observe how inconsiderately—I hope not willingly—he passes by the reasons and grounds urged by those three princes for their practices; for, as for the bare examples of kings or princes, they are but like shining sands, or gilded rocks, giving no solace to such as make woeful shipwreck on them.

In King James' speech, he passes by that golden maxim in divinity, "that God never loves to plant his church by blood."

Secondly, that civil obedience may be performed from the papists.

Thirdly, in his observation on Revelation 20, that true and certain note of a false church, to wit, persecution: "The wicked are besiegers, the faithful are besieged."

In King Stephen of Poland, his speech, he passes by the true difference between a civil and a spiritual government: "I am," said Stephen, "a civil magistrate over the bodies of men, not a spiritual over their souls."

Now to confound these is Babel; and Jewish it is to seek for Moses, and bring him from his grave (which no man shall find, for God buried him) in setting up a national state or church in a land of Canaan, which the great Messiah abolished at his coming.

Thirdly, he passes by, in the speech of the King of Bohemia, that foundation in grace and nature, to wit, "That conscience ought not to be violated or forced:" and indeed it is most true, that a soul or spiritual rape

---

[73] George Buchanan (1506-1582), Scotch historian, and tutor to James I, who corresponded with the reformer Theodore Beza and the astronomer Tycho Brahe. James repudiated his political ideas, which he considered too democratic. One account holds that the statement cited above was made when Buchanan was asked on his death-bed whether he repented for having written against the authority of kings.

is more abominable in God's eye than to force and ravish the bodies of all the women in the world.

Secondly, that most lamentably true experience of all ages, which that king observes, viz., "That persecution for cause of conscience has ever proved pernicious, being the cause all those wonderful innovations of, or changes in, the principallest and mightiest kingdoms of Christendom." He that reads the records of truth and time with an impartial eye shall find this to be the lancet that has pierced the veins of kings and kingdoms, of saints and sinners, and filled the streams and rivers with their blood.

Lastly, that king's observation of his own time, viz., "That persecution for cause of conscience was practiced most in England, and such places where popery reigned;" implying, as I conceive, that such practices commonly proceed from that great whore the church of Rome, whose daughters are like their mother, and all of a bloody nature, as most commonly all whores be.

CHAPTER LXIII

Now, thirdly, in that the answerer observes, "That among the Roman emperors, they that did not persecute were Julian the Apostate, and Valens the Arian; whereas the good emperors, Constantine, Gratian, Valentinian, and Theodosius, they did persecute the Arians, Donatists," etc.

Answer. It is no new thing for godly, and eminently godly men to perform ungodly actions: nor for ungodly persons, for wicked ends, to act what in itself is good and righteous.

Abraham, Jacob, David, Solomon, etc. (as well as Lamech, Saul, etc.) lived in constant transgression against the institution of so holy and so ratified a law of marriage,etc.; and this not against the light and checks of conscience (as other sins are wont to be recorded of them), but according to the dictate and persuasion of a resolved soul and conscience.

David, out of zeal to God, with thirty thousand of Israel and majestical solemnity, carries up the ark contrary to the order God was pleased to appoint: the issue was both God's and David's great offence. (2 Sam. 6)

David in his zeal would build a house to entertain his God! What more pious? And what more (in show) seriously consulted, when the prophet Nathan is admitted counselor? (2 Sam. 7)

And probable it is that his slaughter of Uriah was not without a good end, to wit, to prevent the dishonor of God's name in the discovery of his adultery with Bathsheba. Yet David was holy and precious to God still, though like a jewel fallen into the dirt. Whereas King Ahab, though acting his fasting and humiliation, was but Ahab still, though his act, in itself, was a duty, and found success with God.

CHAPTER LXIV

Peace. I have often heard that history reports, and I have heard that Mr. Cotton himself has affirmed it, that Christianity fell asleep in Constantine's bosom, and the laps and bosoms of those emperors professing the name of' Christ.

Truth. The unknowing zeal of Constantine and other emperors did more hurt to Christ Jesus' crown and kingdom than the raging fury of the most bloody Neros. In the persecutions of the latter, Christians were sweet and fragrant, like spice pounded and beaten in mortars. But these good emperors, persecuting some erroneous persons, Arius, etc., and advancing the professors of some truths of Christ—for there was no small number of truths lost in those times—and maintaining their religion by the material sword—I say, by this means Christianity was eclipsed, and the professors of it fell asleep. (Cant. 5 [2]) Babel, or confusion, was ushered in, and by degrees the gardens of the churches of saints were turned into the wilderness of whole nations, until the whole world became Christian, or Christendom. (Rev. 12, 13)

Doubtless those holy men, emperors and bishops, intended and aimed right to exalt Christ; but not attending to the command of Christ Jesus, to permit the tares to grow in the field of the world, they made the garden of the church and field of the world to be all one; and might not only sometimes, in their zealous mistakes, persecute good wheat instead of tares, but also pluck up thousands of those precious stalks by commotions and combustions about religion, as has been since practiced in the great and wonderful changes wrought by such wars in many great and mighty states and kingdoms, as we heard even now in the observation of the king of Bohemia.

CHAPTER LXV

Peace. Dear Truth, before you leave this passage concerning the emperors, I shall desire you to glance your eye on this not unworthy observation, to wit, how fully this worthy answerer has learned to speak the roaring language of lion-like persecution, far from the purity and peaceableness of Luke which he was wont to express in England. For thus he writes: "More and greater princes than these you mention," says he, "have not tolerated heretics and schismatics, notwithstanding their pretence of conscience, and their arrogating the crown of martyrdom to their sufferings."

Truth. Your tender ear and heart, sweet Peace, endure not such language. It is true that these terms, heretics (or willfully obstinate) and schismatics (or renders), are used in holy writ. It is true also that such pretend conscience, and challenge the crown of martyrdom to their suffering. Yet since, as King James spoke in his mark of a false church on Revelation 20, the wicked persecute and besiege, and the godly are persecuted and besieged, this is the common clamor of persecutors against the messengers and witnesses of Jesus in all ages, viz., you are heretics, schismatics, factious, seditious, rebellious. Have not all truth's witnesses heard such reproaches? You pretend conscience. You say you are persecuted for religion. You will say you are martyrs.

Oh! it is hard for God's children to fall to opinion and practice of persecution, without the ready learning the language thereof. And doubtless, that soul that can so readily speak Babel's language has cause to fear that he has not yet in point of worship left the gates or suburbs of it.

Peace. Again, in blaming Julian and Valens the Arian for tolerating "all weeds to grow," he notes their sinful end, that thereby they might "choke the vitals of Christianity"; and seems to consent, in this and other passages foregoing and following on a speech of Jerome, that the weeds of false religion tolerated in the world have a power to choke and kill true Christianity in the church.

Truth. I shall more fully answer to this on Jerome's speech, and show that if the weeds be kept out of the garden of the church, the roses and lilies therein will flourish, notwithstanding that weeds abound in the field of the civil state. When Christianity began to be choked, it was not when Christians lodged in cold prisons, but down-beds of ease, and persecuted others, etc.

CHAPTER LXVI

Peace. He ends this passage with approbation of Queen Elizabeth for persecuting the papists, and a reproof to King James for his persecuting the Puritans, etc.

Truth. I answer, if Queen Elizabeth, according to the answerer's tenent and conscience, did well to persecute according to her conscience, King James did not ill in persecuting according to his. For Mr. Cotton must grant that either King James was not fit to be a king, had not the essential qualifications of a king, in not being able rightly to judge who ought to be persecuted, and who not: or else he must confess that King James, and all magistrates, must persecute such whom in their conscience they judge worthy to be persecuted.

I say it again, though I neither approve Queen Elizabeth or King James in such their persecutions, yet such as hold this tenent of persecuting for conscience must also hold that civil magistrates are not essentially fitted and qualified for their function and office, except they can discern clearly the difference between such as are to be punished and persecuted, and such as are not.

Or else, if they be essentially qualified, without such a religious spirit of discerning, and yet must persecute the heretic, the schismatic, etc., must they not persecute according to their consciences and persuasion? And then doubtless, though he be excellent for civil government, may he easily, as Paul did ignorantly, persecute the Son of God instead of the son of perdition.

Therefore, lastly, according to Christ Jesus his command, magistrates are bound not to persecute, and to see that none of their subjects be persecuted and oppressed for their conscience and worship, being otherwise subject and peaceable in civil obedience.

CHAPTER LXVII

In the second place, I answer and ask, what glory to God, what good to the souls or bodies of their subjects do these princes bring in persecuting? etc.

Peace. Mr. Cotton tells us, in his discourse upon the third vial,[74] that Queen Elizabeth had almost fired the world in civil combustions by such her persecuting: for though he bring it in to another end, yet he confesses that it "raised all Christendom in combustion; raised the wars of 1588 and the Spanish Invasion;" and he adds, both concerning the English nation and the Dutch, "that if God had not borne witness to his people and their laws in defeating the intendments of their enemies against both the nations, it might have been the ruin of them both."

Truth. That those laws and practices of Queen Elizabeth raised those combustions in Christendom, I deny not: that they might likely have cost the ruin of England and Dutch, I grant.

That it was God's gracious work in defeating the intendments of their enemies, I thankfully acknowledge. But that God bore witness to such persecutions and laws for such persecutions, I deny. For,

First, event and success come alike to all, and are no arguments of love, or hatred, etc.

Secondly, the papists in their wars have ever yet had both in peace and war, victory and dominion; and therefore, if success be the measure, God has borne witness unto them.

It is most true, what Daniel in his eighth, and eleventh, and twelfth chapters, and John in his Revelation, eleventh, twelfth, and thirteenth chapters, write of the great success of Antichrist against Christ Jesus for a time appointed.

Success was various between Charles V and some German princes: Philip of Spain and the Low Countries; the French king and his Protestant subjects: sometimes losing, sometimes winning, interchangeably.

But most memorable is the famous history of the Waldenses and Albigenses, those famous witnesses of Jesus Christ, who rising from Waldo, at Lyons in France (1160), spread over France, Italy, Germany

---

[74] "The Pouring Out of the Seven Vials, or An Exposition of the Sixteenth Chapter of Revelation, with an Application of it to Our Times, By the Learned and Reverend John Cotton, B.D." London, 1642.

and almost all countries, into thousands and ten thousands, making separation from the pope and church of Rome. These fought many battles with various success, and had the assistance and protection of divers great princes against three succeeding popes and their armies; but after mutual slaughters and miseries to both sides, the final success of victory fell to the popedom and Romish church, in the utter extirpation of those famous Waldensian witnesses.

God's servants are all overcomers when they war with God's weapons, in God's cause and worship: and in Revelation second and third chapters, seven times it is recorded – to him that overcomes in Ephesus; to him that overcomes in Sardis, etc.; and Revelation 12, God's servants overcame the dragon, or devil, in the Roman emperors by three weapons—the blood of the Lamb, the word of their testimony, and the not loving of their lives unto the death.

CHAPTER LXVIII

Peace. The answerer, in the next place, descends to the third and last head of arguments produced by the author, taken from the judgment of ancient and later writers, yea, even of the papists themselves, who have condemned persecution for conscience' sake: some of which the answerer pleases to answer, and thus writes:

"You begin with Hilary, whose testimony without prejudice to the truth we may admit: for it is true, the Christian church does not persecute, but is persecuted.

'But to excommunicate a heretic, is not to persecute, that is, it is not to punish an innocent but a culpable and damnable person, and that not for conscience, but for persisting in error against light of conscience, whereof he has been convinced."

Truth. In this answer there are two things:

First, his confession of the same truth affirmed by Hilarius, to wit, that the Christian church does not persecute, but is persecuted: suiting with that foregoing observation of King James from Revelation 20.

Peace. Yet to this he adds a color thus: "Which," says he, "we may admit without prejudice to the truth."

Truth. I answer, if it be a mark of the church to be persecuted, and of the anti-Christian, or false church, to persecute, then those churches cannot be truly Christian, according to the first institution, which either actually themselves, or by the civil power of kings and princes given to them, or procured by them to fight for them, do persecute such as dissent from them, or be opposite against them.

Peace. Yea, but in the second place he adds, "that to excommunicate a heretic is not to persecute, but to punish him for sinning against the light of his own conscience," etc.

Truth. I answer, if this worthy answerer were thoroughly awaked from the spouse's spiritual slumber (Cant. 5 [3]), and had recovered from the drunkenness of the great whore who intoxicates the nations (Rev. 17 [2]), it is impossible that he should so answer: for

First, who questions whether to excommunicate a heretic, that is, all obstinate gainsayer, as we have opened the word upon Titus 3—I say, who questions whether that be to persecute?—excommunication being of a spiritual nature, a sentence denounced by the word of Christ Jesus, the spiritual King of his church; and a spiritual killing by the most sharp two-edged sword of the Spirit, in delivering up the person excommunicate to Satan. Therefore, who sees not that his answer comes not near our question?

Peace. In the answerer's second conclusion, in the entrance of this discourse, he proves persecution against a heretic for sinning against his conscience, and quotes Titus 3:10, which only proves, as I have there made it evident, a spiritual rejecting or excommunicating from the church of God, and so comes not near the question.

Here, again, he would prove churches charged to be false, because they persecute; I say, he would prove them not to be false, because they persecute not: for, says he, excommunication is not persecution. Whereas the question is, as the whole discourse, and Hilary's own amplification of the matter in this speech, and the practice of all ages testify, whether it be not a false church that does persecute other churches or members, opposing her in spiritual and church matters, not by excommunications, but by imprisonments, stocking, whipping, fining, banishing, hanging, burning, etc., notwithstanding that such persons in civil obedience and subjection are unreprovable.

Truth. I conclude this passage with Hilarius and the answerer, that the Christian church does not persecute; no more than a lily does scratch the thorns, or a lamb pursue and tear the wolves, or a turtle-dove hunt the hawks and eagles, or a chaste and modest virgin fight and scratch like whores and harlots.

And for punishing the heretic for sinning against his conscience after conviction—which is the second conclusion he affirms—to be by a civil sword, I have at large there answered.

CHAPTER LXIX

Peace. In the next place, he selects one passage out of Hilary—although there are many golden passages there expressed against the use of civil, earthly powers in the affairs of Christ. The passage is this:

"It is true also what he says, that neither the apostles nor we may propagate Christian religion by the sword; but if pagans cannot be won by the word, they are not to be compelled by the sword. Nevertheless, this hinders not," says he, "but if they or any other should blaspheme the true God and his true religion, they ought to be severely punished; and no less do they deserve, if they seduce from the truth to damnable heresy or idolatry."

Truth. In which answer I observe, first, his agreement with Hilary, that the Christian religion may not be propagated by the civil sword.

Unto which I reply and ask, then what means this passage in his first answer to the former speeches of the king, viz., "We acknowledge that none is to be constrained to believe or profess the true religion, till he be convinced in judgment of the truth of it?" implying two things.

First, that the civil magistrate, who is to constrain with the civil sword, must judge all the consciences of their subjects, whether they be convinced or no.

Secondly, when the civil magistrate discerns that his subjects' consciences are convinced, then he may constrain them *vi et arms* hostilely.

And accordingly, the civil state and magistracy judging in spiritual things, who knows not what constraint lies upon all consciences in Old and New England to come to church, and pay church duties, which is upon the point—though with a sword of a finer gilt and trim in New England—nothing else but that which he confesses Hilary says true should not be done, to wit, a propagation of religion by the sword.

Again, although he confesses that propagation of religion ought not to be by the sword, yet he maintains the use of the sword, when persons, in the judgment of the civil state, for that is implied, blaspheme the true God, and the true religion, and also seduce others to damnable heresy and idolatry. Which, because he barely affirms in this place, I shall defer my answer unto the after reasons of Mr. Cotton and the elders of New English churches; where scriptures are alleged, and in that place, by God's assistance, they shall be examined and answered.

CHAPTER LXX

Peace. The answerer thus proceeds: "Your next writer is Tertullian, who speaks to the same purpose in the place alleged by you. His intent is only to restrain Scapula, the Roman governor of Africa, from persecuting the Christians for not offering sacrifice to their gods: and for that end, fetched an argument from the law of natural equity, not to compel any to any religion, but permit them to believe, or not to believe at all.

"Which we acknowledge; and accordingly we judge, the English may permit the Indians to continue in their unbelief. Nevertheless, it will not therefore be lawful to tolerate the worship of devils or idols, to the seduction of any from the truth."

Truth. Answer. In this passage he agrees with Tertullian, and gives instance in America of' the English permitting the Indians to continue in their unbelief: yet withal he affirms it not lawful to tolerate worshipping of devils, or seduction from the truth.

I answer, that in New England it is well known that they not only permit the Indians to continue in their unbelief, which neither they nor all the ministers of Christ on earth, nor angels in heaven, can help, not being able to work belief: but they also permit or tolerate them in their paganish worship, which cannot be denied to be a worshipping of devils, as all false worship is.

And therefore, consequently, according to the same practice, did they walk by rule and impartially, not only the Indians, but their countrymen, French, Dutch, Spanish, Persians, Turks, Jews, etc., should also be permitted in their worships, if correspondent in civil obedience.

Peace. He adds further, "When Tertullian says, 'That another man's religion neither hurts nor profits any;' it must be understood of private worship and religion professed in private—otherwise a false religion professed by the members of the church, or by such as have given their names to Christ, will be the ruin and desolation of the church, as appears by the threats of Christ to the churches." (Rev. 2)

Truth. I answer, passing by that unsound distinction of members of the church, or those that have given their names to Christ, which in point of visible profession and worship will appear to be all one, it is plain,

First, that Tertullian does not there speak of private, but of public worship and religion.

Secondly, although it be true in a church of Christ that a false religion or worship permitted will hurt, according to those threats of Christ (Rev. 2), yet in two cases a false religion will not hurt – which is most like to have been Tertullian's meaning.

First, a false religion out of the church will not hurt the church, no more than weeds in the wilderness hurt the enclosed garden, or poison hurt the body when it is not touched or taken, yea, and antidotes are received against it.

Secondly, a false religion and worship will not hurt the civil state in case the worshippers break no civil law: and the answerer elsewhere acknowledges that the civil laws not being broken, civil peace is not broken: and this only is the point in question.

CHAPTER LXXI

Peace. "Your next author," says he, "Jerome, crosses not the truth, nor advantages your cause; for we grant what he says, that heresy must be cut off with the sword of the Spirit: but this hinders not, but being so cut down, if the heretic will persist in his heresy to the seduction of others, he may be cut off also by the civil sword, to prevent the perdition of others. And that to be Jerome's meaning appears by his note upon that of the apostle, *A little leaven leaveneth the whole lump.* Therefore, says he, a spark as soon as it appears, is to be extinguished, and the leaven to be removed from the rest of the dough; rotten pieces of flesh are to be cut off, and a scabbed beast is to be driven from the sheepfold; lest the whole house, body, mass of dough, and flock, be set on fire with the spark, be putrefied with the rotten flesh, soured with the leaven, perish by the scabbed beast.

Truth. I answer, first, he grants to Jerome[75] that heresy must be cut off with the sword of the Spirit; yet, withal he maintains a cutting off by a second sword, the sword of the magistrate; and conceives that Jerome so means, because he quotes that of the apostle, *A little leaven leaveneth the whole lump.*

Answer. It is no argument to prove that Jerome meant a civil sword by alleging I Corinthians 5 [6], or Galatians 5 [9], which properly and only approve a cutting off by the sword of the Spirit in the church, and the purging out of the leaven in the church, in the cities of Corinth and Galatia.

And if Jerome should so mean as himself does, yet, first, that grant of his, that heresy must be cut off with the sword of the Spirit, implies an absolute sufficiency in the sword of the Spirit to cut it down, according to that mighty operation of scriptural weapons (2 Cor. 10:4), powerfully sufficient, either to convert the heretic to God, and subdue his very thoughts into subjection to Christ, or else spiritually to slay and execute him.

Secondly, it is clear to be the meaning of the apostle, and of the Spirit of God, not there to speak to the church in Corinth or Galatia, or any other church, concerning any other dough, or house, or body, or flock, but the dough, the body, the house, the flock of Christ, his church: out of which such sparks, such leaven, such rotten flesh, and scabbed sheep, are to be avoided.

Nor could the eye of this worthy answerer ever be so obscured as to run to a smith's shop for a sword of iron and steel to help the sword of the Spirit, if the Sun of Righteousness had once been pleased to show him that a national church, which elsewhere he professes against, a state-church, whether explicit, as in old England, or implicit, as in New, is not the institution of the Lord Jesus Christ.

The national, typical state-church of the Jews, necessarily called for such weapons; but the particular churches of Christ in all parts of the world, consisting of Jews or Gentiles, is powerfully able, by the sword of the Spirit to defend itself, and offend men or devils, although the state or kingdom, wherein such a church or churches of Christ are gathered, have

---

[75] Williams mistakenly wrote Tertullian when he clearly intended Jerome. Underhill, in the 1848 edition, corrected the error in the text.

neither carnal spear nor sword, etc.; as once it was in the national church of the land of Canaan.[76]

CHAPTER LXXII

Peace. "Brentius, whom you next quote," says he, "speaks not to your cause. We willingly grant you, that man has no power to make laws to bind conscience; but this hinders not, but men may see the laws of God observed which do bind conscience."

Truth. I answer, in granting with Brentius that man has not power to make laws to bind conscience, he overthrows such his tenent and practice as restrain men from their worship according to their conscience and belief, and constrain them to such worships, though it be out of a pretence that they are convinced, which their own souls tell them they have no satisfaction nor faith in.

Secondly, whereas he affirms that men may make laws to see the laws of God observed:

I answer, as God needs not the help of a material sword of steel to assist the sword of the Spirit in the affairs of conscience, so those men, those magistrates, yea, that commonwealth which makes such magistrates, must needs have power and authority from Christ Jesus to sit as judge, and to determine in all the great controversies concerning doctrine, discipline, government, etc.

And then I ask whether upon this ground it must not evidently follow, that either there is no lawful commonwealth, nor civil state of men in the world, which is not qualified with this spiritual discerning: and then also, that the very commonweal has more light concerning the church of Christ than the church itself, or, that the commonweal and magistrates thereof, must judge and punish as they are persuaded in their own belief and conscience, be their conscience paganish, Turkish, or anti-Christian. What is this but to confound heaven and earth together, and not only to take away the being of Christianity out of the world, but to take away all civility, and the world out of the world, and to lay all upon heaps of confusion?

---

[76] "1 Samuel 13." (Williams's footnote)

CHAPTER LXXIII

Peace. "The like answer," says he, "may be returned testimony to Luther, whom you next allege.

"First, that the government of the civil magistrate extends no further than over the bodies and goods of their subjects, not over their souls; and, therefore, they may not undertake to give laws unto the souls and consciences of men.

"Secondly, that the church of Christ does not use the arm of secular power to compel men to the true profession of the truth, for this is to be done with spiritual weapons, whereby Christians are to be exhorted, not compelled. But this," says he, "hinders not that Christians sinning against light of faith and conscience may justly be censured by the church with excommunication, and by the civil sword also, in case they shall corrupt others to the perdition of their souls."

Truth. I answer, in this joint confession of the answerer with Luther, to wit, that the government of the civil magistrate extends no further than over the bodies and goods of their subjects, not over their souls: who sees not what a clear testimony from his own mouth and pen is given, to wit, that either the spiritual and church estate, the preaching of the word, and the gathering of the church, the baptism of it, the ministry, government, and administrations thereof, belong to the civil body of the commonweal, that is, to the bodies and goods of men, which seems monstrous to imagine? Or else that the civil magistrate cannot, without exceeding the bounds of his office, meddle with those spiritual affairs?

Again, necessarily must it follow that these two are contradictory to themselves, to wit, the magistrates' power extends no further than the bodies and goods of the subject, and yet the magistrate must punish Christians for sinning against the light of faith and conscience, and for corrupting the souls of men.

The Father of lights make this worthy answerer, and all that fear him, to see their wandering in this case: not only from his fear, but also from the light of reason itself, their own convictions and confessions.

Secondly, in his joint confession with Luther, that the church does not use the secular power to compel men to the faith and profession of the truth, he condemns, as before I have observed,

First, his former implication, viz., that they may be compelled when they are convinced of the truth of it.

Secondly, their own practice who suffer no man of any different conscience and worship to live in their jurisdiction, except that he depart from his own exercise of religion and worship, differing from the worship allowed of in the civil state, yea, and also actually submit to come to their church.

Which, however it is colored over with this varnish, viz., that men are compelled no further than unto the hearing of the word, unto which all men are bound, yet it will appear that teaching and being taught in a church estate is a church worship, as true and proper a church worship as the supper of the Lord. (Acts 2:46)

Secondly, all persons, papist and Protestant, that are conscientious, have always suffered upon this ground especially, that they have refused to come to each other's church or meeting.

CHAPTER LXXIV

Peace. The next passage in the author which the answerer descends unto is the testimony of the papists themselves, a lively and shining testimony from scriptures alleged both against themselves and all that associate with them (as power is in their hand) in such unchristian and bloody both tenents and practices.

"As for the testimony of the popish book," says he, "we weight it not, as knowing whatever they speak for toleration of religion where themselves are under hatches, when they come to sit at stern they judge and practice quite contrary, as both their writings and judicial proceedings have testified to the world these many years."

Truth. I answer, although both writings and practices have been such, yet the scriptures and expressions of truth alleged and uttered by them, speak loud and fully for them when they are under the hatches, that for their conscience and religion they should not there be choked and smothered, but suffered to breathe and walk upon the decks, in the air of civil liberty and conversation, in the ship of the commonwealth, upon good assurance given of civil obedience to the civil state.

Again, if this practice be so abominable in his eyes from the papists, viz., that they are so partial as to persecute when they sit at helm, and yet cry out against persecution when they are under the hatches, I shall beseech the righteous Judge of the whole world to present, as in a water or glass where face answers to face, the faces of the papist to the Protestant, answering to each other in the sameness of partiality, both of this doctrine and practice.

When Mr. Cotton and others have formerly been under hatches, what sad and true complaints have they abundantly poured forth against persecution! How have they opened that heavenly scripture, Canticles 4:8, where Christ Jesus calls his tender wife and spouse from the fellowship with persecutors in their dens of lions and mountains of leopards?

But coming to the helm, as he speaks of the papists how, both by preaching, writing, printing, practice, do they themselves—I hope in their persons lambs—unnaturally and partially express towards others the cruel nature of such lions and leopards?

Oh! that the God of heaven might please to tell them how abominable in his eyes are a weight and a weight, a stone and a stone, in the bag of weights, one weight for themselves when they are under hatches, and another for others when they come to helm.

Nor shall their confidence of their being in the truth, which they judge the papists and others are not in, no, nor the truth itself, privilege them to persecute others, and to exempt themselves from persecution, because (as formerly)—

First, it is against the nature of true sheep to persecute, or hunt the beasts of the forest: no, not the same wolves who formerly have persecuted themselves.

Secondly, if it be a duty and charge upon all magistrates, in all parts of the world, to judge and persecute in and for spiritual causes, then either they are no magistrates who are not able to judge in such cases, or else they must judge according to their consciences, whether pagan, Turkish, or anti-Christian.

Lastly,[77] notwithstanding their confidence of the truth of their own way, yet the experience of our fathers' errors, our own mistakes and ignorance, the sense of our own weaknesses and blindness in the depths of the prophecies and mysteries of the kingdom of Christ, and the great professed expectation of light to come which we are not now able to comprehend, may abate the edge, yea, sheath up the sword of persecution toward any, especially such as differ not from them in doctrines of

---

[77] "Pills to purge out the spirit of persecution." (Williams's footnote)

repentance, or faith, or holiness of heart and life, and hope of glorious and eternal union to come, but only in the way and manner of the administrations of Jesus Christ.

CHAPTER LXXV

Peace. To close this head of the testimony of writers, it pleases the answerer to produce a contrary testimony of Austin,[78] Opatus, etc.

Truth. I readily acknowledge, as formerly I did concerning the testimony of princes, that Antichrist is too hard for Christ at votes and numbers; yea, and believe that in many points, wherein the servants of God these many hundred years have been fast asleep, superstition and persecution have had more suffrages and votes from God's own people, than has either been honorable to the Lord, or peaceable to their own or the souls of others: therefore, not to derogate from the precious memory of any of them, let us briefly consider what they have in this point affirmed.

To begin with Austin: "They murder," says he, "souls, and themselves are afflicted in body, and they put men to everlasting death, and yet they complain when themselves are put to temporal death."

I answer, this rhetorical persuasion of human wisdom seems very reasonable in the eye of flesh and blood; but one scripture more prevails with faithful and obedient souls than thousands of plausible and eloquent speeches: in particular,

First, the scripture uses soul-killing in a large sense, not only for the teaching of false prophets and seducers, but even for the offensive walking of Christians: in which respect (1 Cor. 8 [9]) a true Christian may be guilty of destroying a soul for whom Christ died, and therefore by this rule ought to be hanged, burned, etc.

Secondly, that plausible similitude will not prove that every false teaching or false practice actually kills the soul, as the body is slain, and slain but once; for souls infected or bewitched may again recover. (1 Cor. 5; Gal. 5; 2 Tim. 2, etc.)

Thirdly, for soul-killings, yea, also for soul-woundings and grievings, Christ Jesus has appointed remedies sufficient in his church. There comes

---

[78] Augustine.

forth a two-edged sword out of his month (Rev. 1, 2), able to cut down heresy, as is confessed: yea, and to kill the heretic: yea, and to punish his soul everlastingly, which no sword of steel can reach unto in any punishment comparable or imaginable. And therefore, in this case, we may say of this spiritual soul-killing by the sword of Christ's mouth, as Paul concerning the incestuous person (2 Cor. 2 [6]), *Sufficient is this punishment,* etc.

Fourthly, although no soul-killers, nor soul-grievers may be suffered in the spiritual state, or kingdom of Christ, the church; yet he has commanded that such should be suffered and permitted to be and live in the world, as I have proved on Matthew 13: otherwise thousands and millions of souls and bodies both must be murdered and cut off by civil combustions and bloody wars about religion.

Fifthly, I argue thus: the souls of all men in the world are either naturally dead in sin, or alive in Christ. If dead in sin, no man can kill them, no more than he can kill a dead man: nor is it a false teacher, or false religion, that can so much prevent the means of spiritual life as one of these two: either the force of a material sword, imprisoning the souls of men in a state or national religion, ministry, or worship, or, secondly, civil wars and combustions for religion's sake, whereby men are immediately cut off without any longer means of repentance.

Now again, for the souls that are alive in Christ he has graciously appointed ordinances powerfully sufficient to maintain and cherish that life—armor of proof able to defend them against men and devils.

Secondly, the soul once alive in Christ, is like Christ himself (Rev. 1[18]), alive forever (Rom. 6:8); and cannot die a spiritual death.

Lastly, grant a man to be a false teacher, a heretic, a Balaam, a spiritual witch, a wolf, a persecutor, breathing out blasphemies against Christ and slaughters against his followers, as Paul did (Acts 9 [1]), I say, these who appear soul-killers today, by the grace of Christ may prove, as Paul, soul-savers tomorrow: and says Paul to Timothy (1 Tim. 4[16], *Thou shalt save thyself and them that hear thee:* which all must necessarily be prevented, if all that comes within the sense of these soul-killers must, as guilty of blood, be corporally killed and put to death.

CHAPTER LXXVI[79]

Peace. Dear Truth, your answers are so satisfactory to Austin's speech, that if Austin himself were now living, methinks he should be of your mind. I pray descend to Optatus, "who," says the answerer, "justifies Macarius for putting some heretics to death, affirming that he had done no more herein than what Moses, Phineas, and Elias had done before him."

Truth. These are shafts usually drawn from the quiver of the ceremonial and typical state of the national church of the Jews, whose shadowish and figurative state vanished at the appearing of the body and substance, the Sun of righteousness, who set up another kingdom, or church (Heb. 12 [27], ministry and worship, in which we find no such ordinance, precept, or precedent of killing men by material swords for religion sake.

More particularly concerning Moses, I query what commandment, or practice of Moses, either Optatus, or the answerer here intend? Probably that passage of Deuteronomy 13[15] wherein Moses appointed a slaughter, either of a person or a city, that should depart from the God of Israel, with whom that national church was in covenant. And if so, I shall particularly reply to that place in my answer to the reasons hereunder mentioned.

Concerning Phineas's zealous act:

First, his slaying of the Israelitish man and woman of Midian, was not for spiritual but corporal filthiness.

Secondly, no man will produce his fact as precedential to any minister of the gospel so to act in any civil state or commonwealth; although I believe in the church of God it is precedential for either minister or people to kill and slay with the two-edged sword of the Spirit of God, any such bold and open presumptuous sinners as these were.

Lastly, concerning Elijah: there were two famous acts of Elijah of a killing nature:

First, that of slaying eight hundred and fifty of Baal's prophets (1 Kgs 18[40]).

Secondly, of the two captains and their fifties, by fire, etc.

---

[79] Misnumbered LXVI in the first edition.

For the first of these, it cannot figure, or type out, any material slaughter of the many thousands of false prophets in the world by any material sword of iron or steel: for as that passage was miraculous, so find we not any such commission given by the Lord Jesus to the ministers of the Gospel. And lastly, such a slaughter must not only extend to all the false prophets in the world, but, according to the answerer's grounds, to the many thousands of thousands of idolaters and false worshippers in the kingdoms and nations of the world.

For the second act of Elijah, as it was also of a miraculous nature, so, secondly, when the followers of the Lord Jesus (Luke 9 [64]) proposed such a practice to the Lord Jesus, for injury offered to his own person, he disclaimed it with a mild check to their angry spirits, telling them plainly they knew not what spirits they were of: and adds that gentle and merciful conclusion, that he came not to destroy the bodies of' men, as contrarily Antichrist does—alleging these instances from the Old Testament, as also Peter's killing Ananias (Acts 5:5) and Peter's vision and voice, *Arise, Peter, kill and eat.* (Acts 10 [13])

CHAPTER LXXVII

Peace. You have so satisfied these instances brought by Optatus that methinks Optatus and the answerer himself might rest satisfied.

I will not trouble you with Bernard's argument from Romans 13, which you have already on that scripture so largely answered.

But what think you, lastly, of Calvin, Beza, and Aretius?

Truth. Answer. Since matters of fact and opinion are barely related by the answerer without their grounds, whose grounds, notwithstanding, in this discourse are answered—I answer, if Paul himself were joined with them, yea, or an angel from heaven bringing any other rule than what the Lord Jesus has once delivered, we have Paul's conclusion and resolution, peremptory and dreadful. (Gal. 1:8)

Peace. This passage finished, let me finish the whole by proposing one conclusion of the author of the arguments, viz., "It is no prejudice to the commonwealth if liberty of conscience were suffered to such as fear God indeed: Abrabam abode a long time among the Canaanites, yet contrary to them in religion. (Gen. 13:7; 16:13) Again, he sojourned in

Gerar, and King Abimelech gave him leave to abide in his land. (Gen. 20, 21, 23, 24)

"Isaac also dwelt in the same land, yet contrary in religion." (Gen. 26)

"Jacob lived twenty years in one house with his uncle Laban, yet different in religion." (Gen. 31)

"The people of Israel were about four hundred and thirty years in that infamous land of Egypt, and afterwards seventy years in Babylon, all which times they differed in religion from the states." (Exod. 12; 2 Chr. 36)

"Come to the time of Christ, where Israel was under the Romans, where lived divers sects of religion, as Herodians, Scribes, and Pharisees, Sadducces and Libertines, Theudaeans and Samaritans, beside the common religion of the Jews, and Christ and his apostles. All which differed from the common religion of the state, which was like the worship of Diana, which almost the whole world then worshipped. (Acts 19,20)

"All these lived under the government of Caesar, being nothing hurtful unto the commonwealth, giving unto Caesar that which was his. And for their religion and consciences towards God, he left them to themselves, as having no dominion over their souls and consciences: and when the enemies of the truth raised up any tumults, the wisdom of the magistrate most wisely appeased them." (Acts 18:14; 19:35)

Unto this the answerer returns thus much:

"It is true, that without prejudice to the commonwealth, liberty of conscience may be suffered to such as fear God indeed, as knowing they will not persist in heresy or turbulent schism when they are convinced in conscience of the sinfulness thereof. But the question is, whether a heretic, after once or twice admonition, and so after conviction, and any other scandalous and heinous offender, may be tolerated either in the church without excommunication, or in the commonweal without such punishment as may preserve others from dangerous and damnable infection."

CHAPTER LXXIXA[80]

Truth. I here observe the answerer's partiality, that none but such as truly fear God should enjoy liberty of conscience; whence the inhabitants of the world must either come into the estate of men fearing God, or else dissemble a religion in hypocrisy, or else be driven out of the world. One must follow. The first is only the gift of God; the second and third are too commonly practiced upon this ground.

Again, since there is so much controversy in the world where the name of Christ is taken up, concerning the true church, the ministry, and worship, and who are those that truly fear God; I ask, who shall judge in this case, who be they that fear God?

It must needs be granted that such as have the power of suffering, or not suffering such consciences, must judge: and then must it follow, as before I intimated, that the civil state must judge of the truth of the spiritual; and then magistrates fearing or not fearing God, must judge of the fear of God; also, that their judgment or sentence must be according to their conscience, of what religion soever: or that there is no lawful magistrate, who is not able to judge in such cases. And lastly, that since the sovereign power of all civil authority is founded in the consent of the people, that every commonweal has radically and fundamentally in it a power of true discerning the true fear of God, which they transfer to their magistrates and officers: or else, that there are no lawful kingdoms, cities, or towns in the world in which a man may live, and unto whose civil government he may submit: and then, as I said before, there must be no world, nor is it lawful to live in it, because it has not a true discerning spirit to judge them that fear or not fear God.

Lastly, although this worthy answerer so readily grants that liberty of conscience should be suffered to them that fear God indeed: yet we know what the ministers of the churches of New England wrote in answer to the [thirty-first] question[81] sent to them by some ministers of the church

---

[80] In the first edition there are two chapters titled LXXIX; there is no chapter LXXVIII.

[81] The first edition says "to the 3 question," though it was changed to "thirty-first question" in the errata. Both Underhill and Caldwell assume that Williams referred to the "thirty-two questions" (see footnote below), but left the number incomplete and the word "question" singular. It may be that Williams referred to the thirty-first question: "Whether would you permit any company of ministers and people (being otherwise in

of Old England,[82] viz., that although they confessed them to be such persons whom they approved of far above themselves, yea, who were in their hearts to live and die together; yet if they, and other godly people with them, coming over to them, should differ in church constitution, they then could not approve their civil cohabitation with them, and, consequently, could not advise the magistrates to suffer them to enjoy a civil being within their jurisdiction.

Hear, 0 heavens! and give ear, O, earth! [Isaiah 1:2] yea, let the heavens be astonished, and the earth tremble [Jeremiah 2:12], at such an answer as this from such excellent men to such whom they esteem for godliness above themselves!

CHAPTER LXXIX

Peace. Yea, but they say, they doubt not if they were there but they should agree; for, say they, either you will come to us, or you may show us light to come to you, for we are but weak men, and dream not of perfection in this life.

Truth. Alas, who knows not what lamentable differences have been between the same ministers of the church of England, some conforming, others leaving their livings, friends, country, life, rather than conform; when others again, of whose personal godliness it is not questioned, have succeeded by conformity unto such forsaken (so-called) livings? How great the present differences, even among them that fear God, concerning faith, justification, and the evidence of it, concerning repentance and godly sorrow, as also and mainly concerning the church, the matter, form, administrations, and government of it?[83]

Let none now think that the passage to New England by sea, or the nature of the country, can do what only the key of David can do, to wit, open and shut the consciences of men.

---

some measure approvable) to sit down by you, and set up and practice another form of discipline, enjoying like liberty with yourselves in the Commonwealth, and accepted as a sister church by the rest of your churches."

[82] "Church Government and Church Covenant discussed in an answer of the Elders of the Several Churches in New England to thirty-two questions sent over to them by divers Ministers in England to declare their judgment therein." London, 1643.

[83] "Between the Presbyterians and the Independents, Covenanters and Non-covenanters, of both which many are truly godly in their persons." (Williams's footnote)

Beside, how can this be a faithful and upright acknowledgment of their weakness and imperfection, when they preach, print, and practice such violence to the souls and bodies of others, and by their rules and grounds ought to proceed even to the killing of those whom they judge so dear unto them, and in respect of godliness far above themselves?

CHAPTER LXXX

Peace. Yea, but, say they, the godly will not persist in heresy, or turbulent schism, when they are convinced in conscience, etc.

Truth. Sweet Peace, if the civil court and magistracy must judge, as before I have written, and those civil courts are as lawful, consisting of natural men as of godly persons, then what consequences necessarily will follow I have before mentioned. And I add, according to this conclusion it must follow, that, if the most godly persons yield not to once or twice admonition, as is maintained by the answerer, they must necessarily be esteemed obstinate persons; for if they were godly, says he, they would yield.[84] Must it not then be said, as it was by one passing sentence of banishment upon some whose godliness was acknowledged, that he that commanded the judge not to respect the poor in the cause of judgment, commands him not to respect the holy or the godly person?

Hence, I could name the place and time when a godly man, a most desirable person for his trade, etc., yet something different in conscience, propounded his willingness and desire to come to dwell in a certain town in New England; it was answered by a chief of the place, This man differs from us, and we desire not to be troubled. So that in conclusion, for no other reason in the world, the poor man, though godly, useful, and peaceable, could not be admitted to a civil being and habitation on the common earth, in that wilderness, among them.

The latter part of the answer, concerning the heretic, or obstinate person, to be excommunicated, and the scandalous offender to be punished in the commonweal, which neither of both come near our question: I have spoken I fear too largely already.

---

[84] "The doctrine of persecution necessarily and most commonly falls heavily upon the most godly persons." (Williams's footnote)

Peace. Mr. Cotton concludes with a confident persuasion of having removed the grounds of that great error, viz., that persons are not to be persecuted for cause of' conscience.

Truth. And I believe, dear Peace, it shall appear to them that with fear and trembling at the word of the Lord examine these passages, that the charge of' error rebound back, even such an error as may well be called the bloody tenent—so directly contradicting the spirit, and mind, and practice of the Prince of Peace; so deeply guilty of the blood of souls, compelled and forced to hypocrisy in a spiritual and soul-rape; so deeply guilty of the blood of the souls under the altar, persecuted in all ages for the cause of conscience, and so destructive to the civil peace and welfare of all kingdoms, countries, and commonwealths.

CHAPTER LXXXI

Peace. To this conclusion, dear Truth, I heartily subscribe, and know the God, the Spirit, the Prince, the angels, and all the true awaked sons of peace, will call you blessed.

Truth. How sweet and precious are these contemplations, but oh! how sweet the actions and fruitions!

Peace. Thy lips drop as the honey-comb, honey and milk are under thy tongue; oh! that these drops, these streams, might flow without a stop or interruption!

Truth. The glorious white troopers (Rev. 19) shall in time be mounted, and he that is the most high Prince of princes, and Lord General of generals mounted upon the word of truth and meekness (Ps. 45) shall triumph gloriously, and renew our meetings. But hark, what noise is this?

Peace. These are the doleful drums, and shrill-sounding trumpets, the roaring, murdering cannons, the shouts of conquerors, the groans of wounded, dying, slaughtered righteous with the wicked. Dear Truth, how long? How long these dreadful sounds and direful sights? How long before my glad return and restitution?

Truth. Sweet Peace, who will believe my true report? Yet true it is, if I were once believed, blessed truth and peace should not so soon be parted.

Peace. Dear Truth, what welcome have you found of late beyond your former times, or present expectations?

Truth. Alas! my welcome changes as the times, and strongest swords and arms prevail: were I believed in this, that Christ is not delighted with the blood of men, but shed his own for his bloodiest enemies, that by the word of Christ no man for gainsaying Christ, or joining with the enemy Antichrist, should be molested with the civil sword; were this foundation laid as the Magna Charta of highest liberties, and good security given on all hands for the preservation of it, how soon should every brow and house be stuck with olive branches?

Peace. This heavenly invitation makes me bold once more to crave thy patient ear and holy tongue. Error's impatient and soon tired, but you are light, and like the Father of lights, unwearied in your shinings. Lo here! what once again I present to your impartial censure.

A MODEL OF CHURCH AND CIVIL POWER
COMPOSED BY
MR. COTTON AND THE MINISTERS OF NEW ENGLAND,
AND SENT TO THE CHURCH AT SALEM, AS A FURTHER
CONFIRMATION
OF THE BLOODY DOCTRINE OF PERSECUTION FOR
CAUSE OF CONSCIENCE,
EXAMINED AND ANSWERED[85]

CHAPTER LXXXII A[86]

Truth. What have you there?

Peace. Here is a combination of your own children against your very life and mine: here is a model, framed by many able, learned, and godly hands, of such a church and commonweal as awakens Moses from his unknown grave, and denies Jesus yet to have seen the earth.

Truth. Begin, sweet Peace, read and propound. My hand shall not be tired with holding the balances of the sanctuary. Do thou put in, and I shall weigh as in the presence of Him whose pure eyes cannot behold iniquity.

---

[85] Williams added to the title "Composed by Mr. Cotton and the Ministers of New England, and sent to the Church at Salem." Cotton denied "that he was none of them that composed it." Further, "however this model came to Salem, the Ministers say it was not sent by them." In *The Bloody Tenent Yet More Bloody* Williams maintained his position. Caldwell notes that Richard Mather, Ralph Partridge, and John Cotton, were assigned to "draw up a scriptural model of church government, unto the end that out of those there might be one educed, which the synod might after the most filling thoughts upon it, send abroad." He suggests that this document developed from the work of one or more of these men.

[86] In the first edition there were two chapters numbered LXXXII, here designated A and B.

Peace. Thus, then, speaks the preface or entrance: "Seeing God has given a distinct power to church and commonweal, the one spiritual (called the power of the keys), the other civil (called the power of the sword), and has made the members of both societies subject to both authorities, so that every soul in the church is subject to the higher powers in the commonweal, and every member of the commonweal, being a member of the church, is subject to the laws of Christ's kingdom, and in him to the censures of the church:—the question is how the civil state and the church may dispense their several governments without infringement and impeachment of the power and honor of the one or of the other, and what bounds and limits the Lord has set between both the administrations."[87]

Truth. From that conclusion, dear Peace, that "every member of the commonweal, being a member of the church, is subject to the laws of Christ's kingdom, and in Him to the censures of the church," I observe that they grant the church of Christ in spiritual causes to be superior and over the highest magistrates in the world, if members of the church.

Hence therefore I infer, may she refuse to receive, and may also cast forth any, yea, even the highest, if obstinate in sin, out of her spiritual society.

Hence, in this spiritual society, that soul who has most of Christ, most of his Spirit, is most (spiritually) honorable, according to the scriptures quoted. (Acts 15:20; Isaiah 49: 23; Galatians 3:28)

And if so, how can this stand with their common tenent that the civil magistrate must keep the first table: set up, reform the church, and be judge and governor in all ecclesiastical as well as civil causes?

Secondly, I observe the lamentable wresting of this one scripture, Isaiah 49:23. Sometimes this scripture must prove the power of the civil magistrates, kings, and governors over the church in spiritual causes, etc. Yet here this scripture is produced to prove kings and magistrates (in spiritual causes) to be censured and corrected by the same church. It is true in several respects, he that is a governor may be a subject; but in one and same respect to judge and to be judged, to sit on the bench and stand at the bar of Christ Jesus, is as impossible as to reconcile the east and west together.

---

[87] "Matthew 10:19, 16:19; John 20:23; Romans 13:1; Titus 3:1; Isaiah 49:23; Galatians 3:28." (Williams's footnote)

CHAPTER LXXXII B

The first head, that both jurisdictions may stand together.

Peace. "Whereas divers affecting transcending power to themselves over the church, have persuaded the princes of the world that the kingdom of Christ in his church cannot rise or stand without the falls of those commonweals wherein it is set up, we do believe and profess the contrary to this suggestion; the government of the one being of this world, the other not; the church helping forward the prosperity of the commonweal by means only ecclesiastical and spiritual, the commonweal helping forward her own and the church's felicity by means political or temporal:—the falls of commonweals being known to arise from their scattering and diminishing the power of the church, and the flourishing of commonweals with the well ordering of the people, even in moral and civil virtues, being observed to arise from the vigilant administration of the holy discipline of the church, as Bodin, a man not partial to church discipline, plainly testifies.[88] The vices in the free estate of Geneva, *quae legibus nusquam vindicantur,* by means of church discipline, *sine vi et tumultu coercentur,* the Christian liberty not freeing us from subjection to authority, but from enthrallment and bondage unto sin."[89]

Truth. Answer. From this confession, that the church, or kingdom of Christ, may be set up without prejudice of the commonweal, according to John 18:36, *My kingdom is not of this world,* etc., I observe that although the kingdom of Christ, the church, and the civil kingdom or government be not inconsistent, but that both may stand together; yet that they are independent according to that scripture, and that therefore there may be, as formerly I have proved, flourishing commonweals and societies of men, where no church of Christ abides. And, secondly, the commonweal may be in perfect peace and quiet, notwithstanding the church, the commonweal of Christ, be in distractions and spiritual oppositions, both against their religions and sometimes among

---

[88] Jean Bodin (1530-1596), French political philosopher who proposed as the ideal government a democratic monarchy that balanced king and parliament, with legislative authority based on divine right, limited by natural law. His chief work was *Six Books of a Commonweal* (1606). Williams's comment that Bodin was "a man not partial to church discipline" may refer to the fact that in 1551 Bodin was released from his vows as a priest under circumstances that were unclear.

[89] "John 17:36; Rom. 1:2-3; 1 Tim. 2:2; Jer. 29:7; Ezra 7:23." (Williams's footnote)

themselves, as the church of Christ in Corinth troubled with divisions, contentions, etc.

Secondly, I observe, it is true the church helps forward the prosperity of the commonweal by spiritual means. (Jer. 29:7) The prayers of God's people procure the peace of the city where they abide; yet, that Christ's ordinances and administrations of worship are appointed and given by Christ to any civil state, town, or city, as is implied by the instance of Geneva, that I confidently deny.

The ordinances and discipline of Christ Jesus, though wrongfully and profanely applied to natural and unregenerate men, may cast a blush of civility and morality upon them, as in Geneva and other places—for the shining brightness of' the very shadow of Christ's ordinances casts a shame upon barbarism and incivility—yet withal, I affirm, that the misapplication of ordinances to unregenerate and unrepentant persons hardens up their souls in a dreadful sleep and dream of' their own blessed estate, and sends millions of souls to hell in a secure expectation of a false salvation.[90]

CHAPTER LXXXIV

The second head, concerning superiority of each power.

Peace. "Because contention may arise in future times which of these powers under Christ is the greatest, as it has been under Antichrist, we conceive, first, that the power of the civil magistrate is superior to the church policy in place, honors, dignity, earthly power in the world; and the church superior to him, being a member of' the church, ecclesiastically; that is, in a church way, ruling and ordering him by spiritual ordinances according to God for his soul's health, as any other member. So that all the power the magistrate has over the church is temporal, not spiritual; and all the power the church has over the magistrate is spiritual, not temporal. And as the church has no temporal power over the magistrate, *in ordine ad bonum spirituale,* so the

---

[90] "Christ's ordinances put upon the whole city or nation may more civilize and moralize, but never Christianize them." (Williams's footnote)

magistrate has no spiritual power over the church *in ordine ad bonum temporale*.[91]

"Secondly, the delinquency of either party calls for the exercise of the power of terror from the other part; for no rulers ordained of God are a terror to good works, but to evil. (Romans 13:3) So that if the church offend, the offence of the church calls upon the civil magistrate, either to seek the healing thereof as a nursing father, by his own grave advice and the advice of other churches; or else, if he cannot so prevail, to put forth and exercise the superiority of his power in redressing what is amiss, according to the quality of the offence, by the course of civil justice.

"On the other side, if the magistrate being a member of the church shall offend, the offence calls upon the church either to seek the healing thereof in a brotherly way, by conviction of his sin; or else, if they cannot prevail, then to exercise the superiority of their power in removing of the offence, and recovering of the offender, by church censures."

Truth. If the end of spiritual or church power is *bonum spirituale*, a spiritual good, and the end of civil or state power is *bonum temporale*, a temporal good; and secondly, if the magistrate have no spiritual power to attain to his temporal end, no more than a church has any temporal power to attain to her spiritual end, as is confessed:—I demand, if this be not a contradiction against their own disputes, tenents, and practices, touching that question of persecution for cause of conscience. For if the magistrate be supreme judge, and so, consequently, give supreme judgment, sentence, and determination, in matters of the first table and of the church, and be *custos utriusque tabula*, keeper of both tables (as they speak), and yet have no spiritual power as is affirmed—how can he determine what the true church and ordinances are, and then set them up with the power of the sword? How can he give judgment of a false church, a false ministry, a false doctrine, false ordinances, and with a civil sword pull them down, if he have no spiritual power, authority, or commission from Christ Jesus for these ends and purposes?

Further, I argue thus: If the civil officer of state must determine, judge, and punish in spiritual causes, his power, authority, and commission must be either spiritual or civil, or else he has none at all: and so acts without a commission and warrant from the Lord Jesus; and

---

[91] "Romans 13:1,5,6; Isaiah 49:23; Luke 12:14; John 8:11. And that *judicium* of the church in lawsuits, 1 Corinthians 6:2, is only *arbitrarium*, not *coactivum*." (Williams's footnote)

so, consequently, stands guilty at the bar of Christ Jesus, to answer for such his practice as a transcendent delinquent.

Now for civil power, these worthy authors confess that the government of the civil magistrate extends no further than over the bodies and goods of the subject, and therefore has no civil power over the soul, and therefore, say I, not in soul-causes.

Secondly, it is here confessed, in this passage, that to attain his civil end, or *bonum temporale*, he has no spiritual power; and therefore, of necessity, out of their own mouths must they be judged for provoking the magistrate, without either civil or spiritual power, to judge, punish, and persecute in spiritual causes; and to fear and tremble, lest they come near those frogs which proceed out of the mouth of the dragon, and beast, and false prophet [Rev. 16:13], who, by the same arguments which the authors here use, stir up the kings of the earth to make war against the Lamb, Christ Jesus, and his followers. (Rev. 17 [14])

CHAPTER LXXXV

In the next place, I observe upon the point of delinquency, such a conclusion as heaven and earth may stand amazed at. If the church offend, say they, after advice refused, in conclusion the magistrate must redress, that is, punish the church (that is, in church offences and cases) by a course of civil justice.

On the other side, if the civil magistrate offend after admonition used, and not prevailing, in conclusion the church proceeds to censure, that is to excommunication, as is afterward more largely proved by them.

Now I demand, if the church be a delinquent, who shall judge? It is answered, the magistrate. Again, if magistrate be a delinquent, I ask who shall judge? It is answered, the church. Whence I observe—which is monstrous in all cases in the world—that one person, to wit, the church or magistrate, shall be at one time the delinquent at the bar and the judge upon the bench. This is clear thus: the church must judge when the magistrate offends; and yet the magistrate must judge when the church offends. And so, consequently, in this case must judge whether she contemn civil authority in the second table, for thus dealing with him: or whether she have broken the rules of the first table, of which (say they) God has made him keeper and conserver. And therefore, though the church make him a delinquent at the bar, yet by their confession God has made him a judge on the bench. What blood, what tumults, have been and must be spilt upon these grounds?

Peace. Dear Truth, no question but the church may punish the magistrate spiritually in spiritual cases; and the magistrate may punish the church civilly in civil cases; but that for one and the same cause the church must punish the magistrate, and the magistrate the church, this seems monstrous, and needs explication.

Truth. Sweet Peace, I illustrate with this instance. A true church of Christ, of which, according to the authors' supposition, the magistrate is a member, chooses and calls one of her members to office. The magistrate opposes. The church, persuaded that the magistrate's exceptions are insufficient—according to her privilege, which these authors maintain against the magistrate's prohibition—proceeds to ordain her officer. The magistrate charges the church to have made an unfit and unworthy choice, and, therefore, according to his place and power, and according to his conscience and judgment, he suppresses such an officer, and makes void the church's choice. Upon this the church complains against the magistrate's violation of her privileges given her by Christ Jesus, and cries out that the magistrate is turned persecutor, and, not prevailing with admonition, she proceeds to excommunication against him. The magistrate, according to his conscience, endures not such profanation of ordinances as he conceives; and therefore, if no advice and admonition prevail, he proceeds against such obstinate abusers of Christ's holy ordinances (as the authors grant he may) in civil court of justice, yea, and—I add according to the pattern of Israel—cuts them off by the sword, as obstinate usurpers and profaners of the holy things of Christ.

I demand what help has any poor church of Christ in this case by maintaining this power of the magistrate to punish the church of Christ, I mean in spiritual and soul-cases? For otherwise I question not but he may put all the members of the church to death justly, if they commit crimes worthy thereof, as Paul spoke. (Acts 25 [11])

Shall the church here fly to the pope's sanctuary against emperors and princes excommunicate, to wit, give away their crowns, kingdoms, or dominions, and invite foreign princes to make war upon them and their territories? The authors surely will disclaim this; and yet I shall prove their tenents tend directly unto such a practice.

Or secondly, shall she say the magistrate is not a true magistrate, because not able to judge and determine in such cases? This their confession will not give them leave to say, because they cannot deny unbelievers to be lawful magistrates: and yet it shall appear, notwithstanding their confession to the contrary, their tenents imply that none but a magistrate after their own conscience is a lawful magistrate.

Therefore, thirdly, they must ingenuously and honestly confess that if it be the duty of the magistrate to punish the church in spiritual cases, he must then judge according to his conscience and persuasion, whatever his conscience be: and then let all men judge into what a woeful state they bring both the civil magistrate and church of Christ, by such a church-destroying and state-destroying doctrine.

Peace. Some will here say, in such a case either the magistrate or the church must judge; either the spiritual or civil state must be supreme.

I answer, if the magistrate be of another religion, --

First, what has the church to judge him being without? (1 Cor. 5 [12, 13]

Secondly, if he be a member of the church, doubtless the church has power to judge, in spiritual and soul-cases, with spiritual and church censures, all that are within. (1 Cor. 5:1-11)

Thirdly, if the church offend against the civil peace of the state by wronging the bodies or goods of any, the magistrate *bears not the sword in vain* (Rom. 13 [4]) to correct any or all the members of the church. And this I conceive to be the only way of the God of peace.

CHAPTER LXXXVI

The third head concerns the end of both these powers.

"First, the common and last end of both is God's glory, and man's eternal felicity.

"Secondly, the proper ends—

"First, of commonwealth, is the procuring, preserving, increasing of external and temporal peace and felicity of the state, in all godliness and honesty. (1 Tim. 2:1,2)

"Secondly, of the church, a begetting, preserving, increasing of internal and spiritual peace and felicity of the church, in all godliness and honesty. (Isa. 2:3,4; 9:7) So that magistrates have power given them from

Christ in matters of religion, because they are bound to see that outward peace be preserved, not in all ungodliness and dishonesty, for such peace is Satanical; but in all godliness and honesty, for such peace God aims at. And hence the magistrate is *custos* of both the tables of godliness, in the first of honesty, in the second for peace's sake. He must see that honesty be preserved within his jurisdiction, or else the subject will not be *bonus cives*. He must see that godliness as well as honesty be preserved, else the subject will not be *bonus vir*, who is the best *bonus cives*. He must see that godliness and honesty be preserved, or else himself will not be *bonu magistratus*."[92]

Truth. In this passage here are divers particulars affirmed, marvelous destructive both to godliness and honesty, though under a fair mask and color of both.

First, it will appear that in spiritual things they make the garden and the wilderness, as often I have intimated—I say, the garden and the wilderness, the church and the world, are all one: for thus,

If the powers of the world, or civil state are bound to propose external peace in all godliness for their end, and the end of the church be to preserve internal peace in all godliness, I demand, if their end (godliness) be the same, is not their power and state the same also? Unless they make the church subordinate to the commonwealth's end, or the commonweal subordinate to the church's end, which—being the governor and setter up of it, and so consequently the judge of it—it cannot be.

Now, if godliness be the worshipping and walking with God in Christ, is not the magistrate and commonweal charged more by this tenent with the worship and ordinances of God, than the church? For the magistrate they charge with the external peace in godliness, and the church but with the internal.

I ask further, what is this internal peace in all godliness? Whether intend they internal, within the soul, which only the eye of God can see, opposed to external, or visible, which man also can discern, or else, whether they mean internal, that is spiritual, soul-matters, matters of

---

[92] "Carmier. De Eccles. p. 376. Park. part. polit. lib. I. cap. 1" (Williams's footnote) Daniel Charmier, French Protestant polemic, whose principal work was *Panstrateiae Catholicae* (1626). "Park. part. polit." refers to *De Politeia Ecclesiasticu hierarchia opposita* by Robert Parker.

God's worship? And then I say, that peace, to wit, of godliness or God's worship, they had before granted to the civil state.

Peace. The truth is, as I now perceive, the best and most godly of that judgment declare themselves never to have seen a true difference between the church and the world, and the spiritual and civil state; and howsoever these worthy authors seem to make a kind of separation from the world, and profess that the church must consist of spiritual and living stones, saints, regenerate persons, and so make some peculiar enclosed ordinances, as the Supper of the Lord, which none, say they, but godly persons must taste of; yet, by compelling all within their jurisdiction to an outward conformity of the church worship, of the word and prayer, and maintenance of the ministry thereof, they evidently declare that they still lodge and dwell in the confused mixtures of the unclean and clean, of the flock of Christ and herds of the world together—I mean, in spiritual and religious worship.

Truth. For a more full and clear discussion of this scripture (1 Tim. 2:1,2) on which is weakly built such a mighty building, I shall propose and resolve these four queries.

CHAPTER LXXXVII

First, what is meant by godliness and honesty in this place ?

Secondly, what may the scope of the Holy Spirit of God be in this place?

Thirdly, whether the civil magistrate was then *custos utriusque tabulae*, keeper of both tables? etc.

Fourthly, whether a church, or congregation of Christians, may not live in godliness and honesty, although the civil magistrate be of another conscience and worship, and the whole state and country with him?

To the first, what is here meant by godliness and honesty?

Answer. I find not that the Spirit of God here intended the first and second table.

For, however the word ευσεβια signify godliness, or the worship of God, yet the second word σεμνοτης, I find not that it signifies such an honesty as comprises the duties of the second table, but such an honesty as signifies solemnity, gravity; and so it is turned by the translator (Titus 2:7), σεμνοτης εν τη διδασκαλια αδιαφθοριανσεμνοτητα, that is, *in doctrine incorruptness, gravity,* which doctrine cannot there be taken for the doctrine of the civil state, or second table, but the gravity, majesty, and solemnity of the spiritual doctrine of Christianity. So that, according to the translators' own rendering of that word in Titus, this place of Timothy should be thus rendered, *in all godliness,* or worshipping of' God, *and gravity;* that is, a solemn or grave profession of the worship of' God. And yet this mistaken and misinterpreted scripture is that great castle and stronghold which so many fly unto concerning the magistrates' charge over the two tables.

Secondly, what is the scope of the Spirit of God in this place?

I answer, first, negatively; the scope is not to speak of the duties of the first and second table.

Nor, secondly, is the scope to charge the magistrate with forcing the people, who have chosen him, to godliness, or God's worship, according to his conscience—the magistrate keeping the peace of external godliness, and the church of internal, as is affirmed; but,

Secondly, positively; I say the Spirit of God by Paul in this place provokes Timothy and the church at Ephesus, and so consequently all the ministers of Christ's churches, and Christians, to pray for two things:

First, for the peaceable and quiet state of the countries and places of their abode; that is implied in their praying, as Paul directs them, for a quiet and peaceable condition, and suits sweetly with the command of the Lord to his people, even in Babel (Jeremiah 29:7), *Pray for the peace of the city, and seek the good of it; for in the peace thereof it shall go well with you.* Which rule will hold in any pagan or popish city, and therefore consequently are God's people to pray against wars, famines, pestilences, and especially to be far from kindling coals of war, and endeavor the bringing in and advancing their conscience by the sword.

Secondly, they are here commanded to pray for the salvation of' all men; that all men, and especially kings and magistrates, might be saved, and come to the knowledge of the truth; implying that the grave—or solemn and shining—profession of godliness, or God's worship, according to Christ Jesus, is a blessed means to cause all sorts of men to be affected with the Christian profession, and to come to the same knowledge of that one God and one Mediator, Christ Jesus. All which tends directly against what it is brought for, to wit, the magistrates forcing all men to godliness, or the worshipping of God, which in truth causes the greatest breach of peace, and the greatest distractions in the world, and the setting up that for godliness or worship which is no more than Nebuchadnezzar's golden image, a state-worship, and in some places the worship of the beast and his image. (Dan. 3; Rev. 13)

CHAPTER LXXXVIII

Thirdly, I query, whether the civil magistrate, which was then the Roman emperor, was keeper or guardian of both tables, as is affirmed?

Scripture and all history tell us that those Caesars were not only ignorant, without God, without Christ, etc.; but professed worshippers, or maintainers, of the Roman gods or devils; as also notorious for all sorts of wickedness; and, lastly, cruel and bloody lions and tigers toward the Christians for many hundred years.

Hence, I argue from the wisdom, love, and faithfulness of the Lord Jesus in his house, it was impossible that he should appoint such ignorant, such idolatrous, such wicked, and such cruel persons to be his chief officers and deputy lieutenants under himself to keep the worship of God, to guard his church, his wife. No wise and loving father was ever known to put his child, no, not his beasts, dogs, or swine, but unto fitting keepers.

Men judge it matter of high complaint that the records of parliament, the king's children, the Tower of London, the great seal, should be committed to unworthy keepers! And can it be, without high blasphemy, conceived that the Lord Jesus should commit his sheep, his children, yea, his spouse, his thousand shields and bucklers in the tower of his church, and lastly, his great and glorious broad seals of baptism and his supper, to be preserved pure in their administrations—I say, that the Lord Jesus, who is wisdom and faithfulness itself, should deliver these to such keepers?

Peace. Some will say, it is one thing what persons are in fact and practice; another what they ought to be by right and office.

Truth. In such cases as I have mentioned, no man does in the common eye of reason deliver such matters of charge and trust to such as declare themselves and sins (like Sodom) at the very time of this great charge and trust to be committed to them.

Peace. It will further be said that many of the kings of Judah, who had the charge of establishing, reforming—and so, consequently, of keeping the first table—the church, God's worship, etc., were notoriously wicked, idolatrous, etc.

Truth. I must then say, the case is not alike; for when the Lord appointed the government of Israel, after the rejection of Saul, to establish a covenant of succession in the type unto Christ, let it be minded what pattern and precedent it pleased the Lord to set for the after kings of Israel and Judah, in David, the man after his own heart.

But now the Lord Jesus being come himself, and having fulfilled the former types, and dissolved the national state of the church, and established a more spiritual way of worship all the world over, and appointed a spiritual government and governors, it is well known what the Roman Caesars were, under whom both Christ Jesus himself and his servants after him lived and suffered; so that if the Lord Jesus had appointed any such deputies—as we find not a tittle to that purpose, nor have a shadow of true reason so to think—he must, I say, in the very first institution, have pitched upon such persons for these *custodes utriusque tabula*, keepers of both tables, as no man wise, or faithful, or loving, would have chosen in any of the former instances, or cases of a more inferior nature.

Beside, to that great pretence of Israel, I have largely spoken to.

Secondly, I ask, how could the Roman Caesars, or any civil magistrates, be *custodes*, keepers of the church and worship of God, when, as the authors of these positions acknowledge, that their civil power extends but to bodies and goods?

And for spiritual power they say they have none, *adbonum temporale* (to a temporal good), which is their proper end; and then, having neither civil nor spiritual power from the Lord Jesus to this purpose, how come they to be such keepers as is pretended?

Thirdly, if the Roman emperors were keepers, what keepers were the apostles, unto whom the Lord Jesus gave the care and charge of the churches, and by whom the Lord Jesus charged Timothy (1 Tim. 6 [14]) to keep those commands of the Lord Jesus without spot until his coming?

These keepers were called the foundation of the church (Eph. 2:20) and made up the crown of twelve stars about the head of the woman (Rev. 12 [1]); whose names were also written in the twelve foundations of New Jerusalem. (Rev. 21 [14])

Yea, what keepers then are the ordinary officers of the church, appointed to be the shepherds or keepers of the flock of Christ; appointed to be the porters or door keepers, and to watch in the absence of Christ? (Mark 13:34; Acts 20 [28-31])

Yea, what charge has the whole church itself, which is the pillar and ground of the truth (1 Tim. 2), in the midst of which Christ is present with his power (1 Cor. 5 [4]) to keep out or cast out the impenitent and obstinate, even kings and emperors themselves, from their spiritual society? (1 Cor. 5; James 3:1; Gal. 3:28)

Fourthly, I ask, whether in the time of the kings of Israel and Judah—whom I confess in the typical and national state to be charged with both tables—I ask, whether the kings of the Assyrians, the kings of the Ammonites, Moabites, Philistines, were also constituted and ordained keepers of the worship of God as the kings of Judah were, for they were also lawful magistrates in their dominions? Or, whether the Roman emperors were *custodes*, or keepers, more than they? Or more than the king of Babylon, Nebuchadnezzar, under whose civil government God's people lived, and in his own land and city? (Jer. 29)

CHAPTER LXXXIX

Peace. You remember, dear Truth, that Constantine, Theodosius, and others, were made to believe that they were the antitypes of the kings of Judah, the church of God; and Henry VIII was told that that title, *Defensor fidei,* defender of the faith, though sent him by the pope for writing against Luther, was his own diadem, due unto him from heaven. So likewise since, the kings and queens of England have been instructed.

Truth. But it was not so from the beginning, as that very difference between the national state of the church of God then, and other kings and magistrates of the world, not so charged, does clearly evince, and leads us to the spiritual king of the church, Christ Jesus, the king of Israel, and his spiritual government and governors therein.

Fifthly, I ask, whether had the Roman Caesars more charge to see all their subjects observe and submit to the worship of God in their dominion of the world than a master, father, or husband now, under the gospel, in his family?

Families are the foundations of government; for what is a commonweal but a commonweal of families, agreeing to live together for common good?

Now in families, suppose a believing Christian husband has an unbelieving, anti-Christian wife. What other charge in this respect is given to a husband (1 Cor. 7 [12-15]), but to dwell with her as a husband, if she be pleased to dwell with him, but, to be so far from forcing her from her conscience unto his, as that if for his conscience' sake she would depart, he was not to force her to tarry with him. (1 Cor. 7) Consequently, the father or husband of the state differing from the commonweal in religion, ought not to force the commonweal nor to be forced by it, yet is he to continue a civil husband's care, if the commonweal will live with him, and abide in civil covenant.

Now as a husband by his love to the truth, and holy conversation in it, and seasonable exhortations, ought to endeavor to save his wife, yet abhorring to use corporal compulsion, yea, in this case to child or servant: so ought the father, husband, governor of the commonweal, endeavor to win and save whom possibly he may, yet far from the appearance of civil violence.

Sixthly, if the Roman emperors were charged by Christ with his worship in their dominion, and their dominion was over the world, as was the dominion of the Grecian, Persian, and Babylonian monarchy before them, who sees not, if the whole world be forced to turn Christian—as afterward and since it has pretended to do—who sees not then that the world, for whom Christ Jesus would not pray, and the god of it, are reconciled to Jesus Christ, and the whole field of the world become his enclosed garden?

Seventhly, if the Roman emperors ought to have been by Christ's appointment keepers of both tables, antitypes of Israel and Judah's kings; how many millions of idolaters and blasphemers against Christ Jesus and his worship, ought they to have put to death, according to Israel's pattern.

Lastly, I ask, if the Lord Jesus had delivered his sheep to these wolves, his wife and spouse to such adulterers, his precious jewels to such great thieves and robbers of the world, as the Roman emperors were, what is the reason that he has never pleased to send any of his servants to their gates to crave their help and assistance in this his work, to put them in mind of' their office, to challenge and claim such a service from them, according to their office, as it pleased God always to send to the kings of Israel and Judah in the like case?

Peace. Some will here object Paul's appealing to Caesar.

Truth. And I must refer them to what I formerly answered to that objection. Paul never appealed to Caesar as a judge appointed by Christ Jesus to give definitive sentence in any spiritual or church controversy; but against the civil violence and murder which the Jews intended against him, Paul justly appealed. For otherwise, if in a spiritual cause he should have appealed, he should have overthrown his own apostleship and power given him by Christ Jesus in spiritual things, above the highest kings or emperors of the world beside.

CHAPTER XC

Peace. Blessed Truth, I shall now remember you of the fourth query upon this place of Timothy; to wit, whether a church of Christ Jesus may not live in God's worship and comeliness, notwithstanding that the civil magistrate profess not the same but a contrary religion and worship in his own person and the country with him.

Truth. I answer; the churches of Christ under the Roman emperors did live in all godliness and Christian gravity, as appears by all their holy and glorious practices, which the scripture abundantly testifies.

Secondly, this flows from an institution or appointment of such a power and authority, left by the Lord Jesus to his apostles and churches, that no ungodliness or dishonesty, in the first appearance of it, was to be suffered, but suppressed and cast out from the churches of Christ, even the little leaven of doctrine or practice. (1 Cor. 5; Gal. 5)

Lastly, I add, that although sometimes it pleases the Lord to vouchsafe his servants peace and quietness, and to command them here in Timothy to pray for it, for those good ends and purposes for which God has appointed civil magistracy in the world, to keep the world in peace and quietness: yet God's people have used most to abound with godliness and honesty when they have enjoyed least peace and quietness. Then, like those spices (Cant. 4:14), myrrh, frankincense, saffron, calamus, etc., they have yielded the sweetest savor to God and man when they were pounded and burnt in cruel persecution of the Roman censors. Then are they, as God's venison, most sweet when most hunted: God's stars shining brightest in the darkest night: more heavenly in conversation, more mortified, more abounding in love each to other, more longing to be with God, when the inhospitable and savage world

has used them like strangers, and forced them to hasten home to another
country which they profess to seek.

CHAPTER XCI

Peace. Dear Truth, it seems not to be unreasonable to close up this
passage with a short descant upon the assertion, viz., "A subject without
godliness will not be *bonus vir*, a good man, nor a magistrate, except he
see godliness preserved, will not be *bonus magistratus.*"

Truth. I confess that without godliness, or a true worshipping of
God with an upright heart, according to God's ordinances, neither
subjects nor magistrates can please God in Christ Jesus, and so be
spiritually or Christianly good; which few magistrates and few men either
come to, or are ordained unto: God having chosen a little flock out of the
world, and those generally poor and mean. (1 Cor. 1:26; James 2:5) Yet
this I must remember you of, that when the most high God created all
things of nothing, he saw and acknowledged divers sorts of goodness,
which must still be acknowledged in their distinct kinds: a good air, a
good ground, a good tree, a good sheep, etc.

I say the same in artificials, a good garment, a good house, a good
sword, a good ship.

I also add, a good city, a good company or corporation, a good
husband, father, master.

Hence also we say, a good physician, a good lawyer, a good seaman,
a good merchant, a good pilot for such or such a shore or harbor: that is,
morally, civilly good, in their several civil respects and employments.

Hence (Ps. 122), the church, or city of God, is compared to a city
compact within itself; which compactness may be found in many towns
and cities of the world, where yet has not shined any spiritual or
supernatural goodness. Hence, the Lord Jesus (Matt. 12[25]) describes an
ill state of a house or kingdom, viz., to be divided against itself, which
cannot stand.

These I observe to prove, that a subject, a magistrate, may be a good
subject, a good magistrate, in respect of civil or moral goodness, which
thousands want; and where it is, it is commendable and beautiful, though
godliness, which is infinitely more beautiful, be wanting, and which is

only proper to the Christian state, the commonweal of Israel, the true church, the holy nation. (Eph. 2; 1 Pet. 2)

Lastly, however the authors deny that there can be *bonus magistratus*, a good magistrate, except he see all godliness preserved; yet themselves confess that civil honesty is sufficient to make a good subject, in these words, viz., "he must see that honesty be preserved within his jurisdiction, else the subject will not be *bonus cives*, a good citizen;" and doubtless, if the law of relations hold true, that civil honesty which makes a good citizen, must also, together with qualifications fit for a commander, make also a good magistrate.

CHAPTER XCII

Peace. The fourth head is, the proper means of both these powers to attain their ends.

"First, the proper means whereby the civil power may and should attain its end are only political, and principally these five.

"First, the erecting and establishing what form of civil government may seem in wisdom most meet, according to general rules of the word, and state of the people.

"Secondly, the making, publishing, and establishing of wholesome civil laws, not only such as concern civil justice, but also the free passage of true religion: for outward civil peace arises and is maintained from them both, from the latter as well as from the former.

"Civil peace cannot stand entire where religion is corrupted. (2 Chr. 15:3,5,6; Jud. 8). And yet such laws, though conversant about religion, may still be counted civil laws: as on the contrary, an oath does still remain religious, though conversant about civil matters.

"Thirdly, election and appointment of civil officers, to see execution of those laws.

"Fourthly, civil punishments and rewards of transgressors and observers of these laws.

"Fifthly, taking up arms against the enemies of civil peace.

"Secondly, the means whereby the church may and should attain her ends, are only ecclesiastical, which are chiefly five.

"First, setting up that form of church government only of which Christ has given them a pattern in his word.

"Secondly, acknowledging and admitting of no lawgiver in the church but Christ, and the publishing of his laws.

"Thirdly, electing and ordaining of such officers only as Christ has appointed in his word.

"Fourthly, to receive into their fellowship them that are approved, and inflicting spiritual censures against them that offend.

"Fifthly, prayer and patience in suffering any evil from them that be without, who disturb their peace.

"So that magistrates, as magistrates, have no power of setting up the form of church government, electing church officers, punishing with church censures; but to see that the church does her duty herein. And on the other side, the churches, as churches, have no power, though as members of the commonweal they may have power, of erecting or altering forms of' civil government, electing of civil officers, inflicting civil punishments—no, not on persons excommunicated—as by deposing magistrates from their civil authority, or withdrawing the hearts of the people against them, to their laws, no more than to discharge wives, or children, or servants, from due obedience to their husbands, parents, or masters: or by taking up arms against their magistrates, though they persecute them for conscience: for though members of churches who are public officers also of the civil state may suppress by force the violence of usurpers, as Jehoiada did Athaliah, yet this they do not as members of the church, but as officers of the civil state."

Truth. Here are divers considerable passages which I shall briefly examine so far as concerns our controversy.

First, whereas they say that the civil power may erect and establish what form of civil government may seem in wisdom most meet, I acknowledge the proposition to be most true, both in itself, and also considered with the end of it, that a civil government is an ordinance of God, to conserve the civil peace of people so far as concerns their bodies and goods, as formerly has been said.

But from this grant I infer, as before has been touched, that the sovereign, original, and foundation of civil power lies in the people—whom they must needs mean by the civil power distinct from the government set up: and if so, that a people may erect and establish what form of government seems to them most meet for their civil condition. It is evident that such governments as are by them erected and established have no more power, nor for no longer time, than the civil power, or people consenting and agreeing, shall betrust them with. This is clear not only in reason, but in the experience of all commonweals, where the people are not deprived of their natural freedom by the power of tyrants.

And if so—that the magistrates receive their power of governing the church from the people—undeniably it follows that a people, as a people, naturally considered, of what nature or nation soever in Europe, Asia, Africa, or America, have fundamentally and originally, as men, a power to govern the church, to see her do her duty, to correct her, to redress, reform, establish, etc. And if this be not to pull God, and Christ, and Spirit out of heaven, and subject them unto natural, sinful, inconstant men, and so consequently to Satan himself, by whom all peoples naturally are guided, let heaven and earth judge.

Peace. It cannot, by their own grant, be denied, but that the wildest Indians in America ought (and in their kind and several degrees do) to agree upon some forms of government, some more civil compact in towns, etc., some less. As also, that their civil and earthly governments be as lawful and true as any governments in the world, and therefore consequently their governors are keepers of the church, or both tables, if any church of Christ should arise or be among them: and therefore, lastly, if Christ have betrusted and charged the civil power with his church, they must judge according to their Indian or American consciences, for other consciences it cannot be supposed they should have.

CHAPTER XCIII

Truth. Again, whereas they say that outward civil peace cannot stand where religion is corrupted; and quote for it 2 Chronicles 15:3, 5, 6, and Judges 8.

I answer, with admiration, how such excellent spirits as these authors are furnished with, not only in heavenly but earthly affairs, should so forget, and be so fast asleep in things so palpably evident, as to say that outward civil peace cannot stand where religion is corrupt. When so many stately kingdoms and governments in the world have long and long enjoyed civil peace and quiet, not withstanding their religion is so corrupt as that there is not the very name of Jesus Christ among them.

And this every historian, merchant, traveler, in Europe, Asia, Africa, America, can testify: for so spoke the Lord Jesus himself'. (John 16 [20]) *The world shall* sing and *rejoice.*

Secondly, for that scripture (2 Chr. 15:3), relating the miseries of Israel and Judah, and God's plagues upon that people for corruption of their religion, it must still have reference to that peculiar state unto which God called the seed of one man, Abraham, in a figure, dealing so with them as he dealt not with any nation in the world. (Ps. 147; Rom. 9)

The antitype to this state I have proved to be the Christian church, which consequently has been and is afflicted with spiritual plagues, desolations, and captivities, for corrupting of that religion which has been revealed unto them. This appears by the seven churches; and the people of God, now so many hundred years in woeful bondage and slavery to the mystical Babel, until the time of their joyful deliverance.

Peace. Yea; but they say that "such laws as are conversant about religion may still be accounted civil laws, as on the contrary an oath does still remain religious, though conversant about civil matters."

Truth. Laws respecting religion are twofold.

First, such as concern the acts of worship and the worship itself, the ministers of it, their fitness or unfitness, to be suppressed or established: and for such laws we find no footing in the New Testament of Jesus Christ.

Secondly, laws respecting religion may be as merely concern the civil state, bodies, and goods of such and such persons, professing these and these religions; viz., that such and such persons, notorious for mutinies, treasons, rebellions, massacres, be disarmed: again, that no persons, papists, Jews, Turks, or Indians, be disturbed at their worship, a thing which the very Indians abhor to practice toward any. Also, that immunity and freedom from tax and toll may be granted unto the people of' such and such religion, as the magistrate pleases. (Ezra 7 [24])

These and such as are of this nature, concerning only the bodies and goods of such and such religious persons, I confess are merely civil.

But now, on the other hand, that laws restraining persons from such and such a worship, because the civil state judges it to be false:

That laws constraining to such and such a worship, because the civil state judges this to be the only true way of worshipping God:

That such and such a reformation of worship be submitted unto by all subjects in such a jurisdiction:

That such and such churches, ministers, ministries, be pulled down, and such and such churches, ministries, and ministrations, set up:

That such laws properly concerning religion, God, the souls of men, should be civil laws and constitutions, is as far from reason as that the commandments of Paul, which he gave the churches concerning Christ's worship (1 Cor. 11,14), were civil and earthly constitutions: or that the canons and constitutions of either ecumenical or national synods, concerning religion, should be civil and state conclusions and arguments.

To that instance of an oath remaining religious, though conversant about civil things; I answer and acknowledge, an oath may be spiritual, though taken about earthly business; and accordingly it will prove, and only prove, what before I have said, that a law may be civil though it concern persons of this and of that religion, that is, as the persons professing it are concerned in civil respects of bodies or goods, as I have opened; whereas if it concern the souls and religions of men, simply so considered in reference to God, it must of necessity put on the nature of a religious or spiritual ordinance or constitution.

Beside, it is a most improper and fallacious instance; for an oath, being an invocation of a true or false God to judge in a case, is an action of a spiritual and religious nature, whatever the subject matter be about which it is taken, whether civil or religious: but a law or constitution may be civil or religious, as the subject about which it is conversant is either civil (merely concerning bodies, or goods) or religious, concerning soul and worship.

CHAPTER XCIV

Peace. Their fifth head is concerning the magistrates' power in making of laws.

"First, they have power to publish and apply such civil laws in a state, as either are expressed in the word of God in Moses' judicials—to wit, so far as they are of general and moral equity, and so binding all nations in all ages—to be deducted by way of general consequence and proportion from the word of God.

"For in a free state no magistrate has power over the bodies, goods, lands, liberties of a free people, but by their free consents. And because free men are not free lords of their own estates, but are only stewards unto God, therefore they may not give their free consents to any magistrate to dispose of their bodies, goods, lands, liberties, at large as themselves please, but as God, the sovereign Lord of all, alone. And because the word is a perfect rule, as well of righteousness as of holiness, it will be therefore necessary that neither the people give consent, nor that the magistrate take power to dispose of the bodies, goods, lands, liberties of the people, but according to the laws and rules of the word of God.

"Secondly, in making laws about civil and indifferent things about the commonweal.

"First, he has no power given him of God to make what laws he please, either in restraining from or constraining to the use of indifferent things; because that which is indifferent in its nature, may sometimes be inexpedient in its use, and consequently unlawful (1 Cor. 2:5), it having been long since defended upon good ground, *Quicquid non expedit, quatenus non expedit, non licet.*

"Secondly, he has no power to make any such laws about indifferent things, wherein nothing good or evil is shown to the people, but only or principally the mere authority or will of the imposer, for the observance of them. (Col. 2:21,22; 1 Cor. 7:23, compared with Eph. 6:6)

"It is a prerogative proper to God to require obedience of the sons of men, because of his authority and will.

"The will of no man is *regula recti*, unless first it be *regula recta.*

"It is an evil speech of some, that in some things the will of the law, not the *ratio* of it, must be the rule of conscience to walk by; and that princes may forbid men to seek any other reason but their authority, yea, when they command *frivola et dura.* And therefore it is the duty of the magistrate, in all laws about indifferent things, to show the reasons, not only the will: to allow the expediency as well as the indifferency of things of that nature.

"For we conceive in laws of this nature, it is not the will of the lawgiver only, but the reason of the law which binds. *Ratio est rex legis, et lex est rex regis.*

"Thirdly, because the judgment of expedient and inexpedient things is often difficult and diverse, it is meet that such laws should not proceed without due consideration of the rules of expediency set down in the word, which are these three:

"First, the rule of piety, that they may make for the glory of God. (1 Cor. 10:31)

"Secondly, the rule of charity, that no scandal come hereby to any weak brother. (1 Cor. 8:13)

"Thirdly, the rule of charity, that no man be forced to submit against his conscience (Rom. 14:14,23), nor be judged of contempt of lawful authority, because he is not suddenly persuaded of the expediency of indifferent things; for if the people be bound by God to receive such laws about such things, without any trial or satisfaction to the conscience, but must judge them expedient because the magistrate thinks them so, then the one cannot be punished in following the other, in case he shall sin in calling inexpedient expedient; but Christ says the contrary, *If the blind lead the blind, they shall both fall.*"

Truth. In this passage these worthy men lay down such a ground as the gates of hell are not able to shake, concerning the magistrates walking in indifferent things: and upon which ground that tower of Lebanon may be raised whereon there hang a thousand shields and bucklers (Cant. 4 [4]), to wit, that invincible truth, that no man is to be persecuted for cause of conscience. The ground is this, "The magistrate has not power to make what laws he please, either in restraining or constraining to the use of indifferent things." And further they confess that the reason of the law, not the will of it, must be the rule of conscience. And they add this impregnable reason, viz. "If the people be bound to receive such laws without satisfaction to conscience, then one cannot be punished for following the other, in case he shall sin contrary to Christ Jesus, who says, *If the blind lead the blind, they shall both fall.*"

Hence I argue, if the civil magistrate have no power to restrain or constrain their subjects in things in their own nature indifferent, as in eating of meats, wearing this or that garment, using this or that gesture; but that they are bound to try and examine his commands, and satisfy their own reason, conscience, and judgment before the Lord, and that they shall sin if they follow the magistrate's command, not being persuaded in their own soul and conscience that his commands are according to God: it will be much more unlawful and heinous in the magistrate to compel the subjects unto that which, according to their consciences' persuasion, is simply unlawful, as unto a falsely constituted church, ministry, worship, administration, and they shall not escape the ditch, by being led blindfold by the magistrate; but though he fall in first, yet they shall [fall] in after him and upon him, to his greater and more dreadful judgment.

In particular thus, if the magistrate may restrain me from that gesture in the supper of the Lord which I am persuaded I ought to practice, he may also restrain me by his commands from that supper of the Lord itself in such or such a church, according to my conscience.

If he cannot, as they grant, constrain me to such or such a garment in the worship of God, can he constrain me to worship God by such a ministry, and with such worship, which my soul and conscience cannot be persuaded is of God?

If he cannot command me in that circumstance of time to worship God, this or that day, can he command me to the worship itself?

Peace. Methinks I discern a threefold guilt to lie upon such civil powers as impose upon and enforce the conscience, though not unto the ministration and participation of the seals, yet either to depart from that worship which it is persuaded of, or to any exercise or worship which it has not faith in.

First, of an appearance of that Arminian, popish doctrine of freewill, as if it lay in their own power and ability to believe upon the magistrate's command, since it is confessed that what is submitted to by any without faith it is sin, be it never so true and holy. (Rom. 14 [23])

Secondly, since God only opens the heart and works the will (Phil. 2 [13]), it seems to be a high presumption to suppose that together with a command restraining from or constraining to worship, that God is also to be forced or commanded to give faith, to open the heart, to incline the will, etc.

Thirdly, a guilt of the hypocrisy of their subjects and people, in forcing them to act and practice in matters of religion and worship against the doubts and checks of their consciences, causing their bodies to worship when their souls are far off, to draw near with their lips, their hearts being far off, etc.

With less sin ten thousand-fold may a natural father force his daughter, or the father of the commonweal force all the maidens in a country to the marriage-beds of such and such men whom they cannot love, than the souls of these and other subjects to such worship or ministry, which is either a true or false,[93] because Canticles 1:16.[94]

---

[93] Underhill inserts "which is either a true or a false *bed.*"

Truth. Sweet Peace, your conclusions are undeniable, and, oh! that they might sink deep into those noble and honorable bosoms it so deeply concerns! But proceed.

CHAPTER XCV

Peace. In that fifth head they further say thus:

"Thirdly, in matters ecclesiastical we believe, first, that civil magistrates have no power to make or constitute laws about church affairs, which the Lord Jesus has not ordained in his word for the well-ordering of the church; for the apostle solemnly charges Timothy, and in him all governors of the church, before God and the Lord Jesus Christ, *who is the only Potentate, the King of kings and Lord of lords,* that the commandment given by him for the ordering of the church be kept *without spot, unrebukeable, to the appearing of the Lord Jesus Christ.* (1 Tim. 6:14,15) And this commandment given in the word, the apostle says, *is able to make the man of God perfect in all righteousness.* (2 Tim. 3:17) And, indeed, the administration of all Christ's affairs does immediately aim at spiritual and divine ends, as the worship of God, and the salvation of men's souls: and, therefore, no law nor means can be devised by the wisdom or wit of man that can be fit or able to reach such ends; but use must be made of such only as the divine wisdom and holy will of God has ordained.

"Secondly, we believe the magistrate's power in making laws about church affairs is not only thus limited and restrained by Christ to matters which concern the substance of God's worship and of church government, but also such as concern outward order: as in rites and ceremonies for uniformity's sake. For we find not in the gospel that Christ has anywhere provided for the uniformity of churches, but only for their unity.

"Paul, in matters of Christian liberty, commends the unity of their faith in the Holy Spirit, giving order that we should not judge nor condemn one another in difference of judgment and practice of such things where men live to God on both sides, even though there were

---

[94] "Persons may with less sin be forced to marry whom they cannot love than to worship where they cannot believe." (Williams's footnote)

some error on one side. (Rom. 14:1-6) How much less in things indifferent, where there may be no error on either side.

"When the apostle directs the church of Corinth that all things be done decently and in order, he meant not to give power to church officers or to civil magistrates to order whatever they should think meet for decency and order; but only to provide that all the ordinances of God be administered in the church decently, without unnatural or uncivil uncomeliness, as that of long hair, or women's prophesying, or the like; and orderly, without confusion or disturbance of edification, as the speaking of many at once in the church,

"Thirdly, we do nevertheless willingly grant that magistrates, upon due and diligent search what is the counsel and will of God in his word concerning the right ordering of' the church, may and ought to publish and declare, establish and ratify, such laws and ordinances as Christ has appointed in his word for the well ordering of church affairs: both for the gathering of the church, and the right administration of all the ordinances of' God among them, in such a manner as the Lord has appointed to edification. The law of Artaxerxes (Ezra 7:23) was not usurpation over the church's liberty; but a royal and just confirmation of them: *Whatsoever is commanded by the God of heaven...for why should there be wrath against the king and his sons?*"

Truth. Dear Peace, methinks I see before mine eyes a wall daubed up, of which Ezekiel speaks, with untempered mortar. Here they restrain the magistrate from making laws, either concerning the substance or ceremony of religion, but such only as Christ has commanded; and those, say they, they must publish and declare after the example of Artaxerxes.

I shall herein perform two things: first, examine this magistrate's duty to publish, declare, etc., such laws and ordinances as Christ has appointed.

Secondly, I shall examine that proof' from Artaxerxes. (Ezra 7:23)

In the first, methinks I hear the voice of the people of Israel (1 Sam. 8:5), *Make us a king, that may rule over us after the manner of the nations:* rejecting the Lord ruling over them by his holy word in the mouth of his prophets, and sheltering themselves under an arm of flesh; which arm of flesh God gave them in his anger, and cut off again in his wrath, after he had persecuted David, the figure of Christ Jesus, who has given his people the scepter and sword of his word and Spirit, and refused a temporal crown or weapons in the dispensation of his kingdom.

Where did the Lord Jesus or his messengers charge the civil magistrate, or direct Christians to petition him, to publish, declare, or establish by his arm of flesh and earthly weapons, the religion and worship of Christ Jesus?

I find the beast and false prophet, whose rise and doctrine is not from heaven, but from the sea and earth, dreadful and terrible, by a civil sword and dignity. (Rev. 13:2)

I find the beast has gotten the power and might of the kings of the earth. (Rev. 17:13)

But the Lamb's weapons are spiritually mighty (2 Cor. 10[4]), etc., his sword is two-edged, coming out of his mouth. (Rev. 1[16] His preparations for war are white horses and white harness, which are confessed by all to be of a spiritual nature. (Rev. 19)

When that whore Jezebel stabbed Naboth with her pen, in stirring up the people to stone him as a blasphemer of God and the king, what a glorious mask or veil of holiness she put on. Proclaim a fast, set a day apart for humiliation; and for confirmation, let all be ratified by the king's authority, name, and seal. (1 Kgs 21[8, 9])

Was not this recorded for all God's Naboths, standing for their spiritual interests in heavenly things—typed out by the typical earth and ground of Canaan's land—that they *through patience and comfort of the scriptures might have hope*? (Rom. 15:4)

Again, I demand, who shall here sit judge, whether the magistrate command any other substance or ceremony but what is Christ's?

By their former conclusions, every soul must judge what the magistrate commands, and is not bound, even in indifferent things, to the magistrates' law, further than his own soul, conscience, and judgment ascends to the reason of it. Here, the magistrate must make laws for that substance and ceremony which Christ appointed. But yet he must not do this with his eyes open, but blindfold and hoodwinked; for if he judge that to be the religion of Christ, and such to be the order therein, which their consciences judge otherwise, and assent not to, they profess they must submit only to Christ's laws, and therefore they are not bound to obey him.

Oh! what is this but to make use of the civil powers and governors of the world; as a guard about the spiritual bed of soul-whoredoms, in which the kings of the earth commit spiritual fornication with the great whore (Rev. 17:2), as a guard, while the inhabitants of the earth are drinking themselves drunk with the wine of her fornication?

But oh! what terrifyings, what allurings are in Jeremy's curse and blessing! (Jer. 17[5]) *Cursed is the man that trusteth in man, that maketh flesh his arm,*—too, too common in spiritual matters—*and whose heart departeth from Jehovah: he shall be as a heath in the wilderness*—even in the spiritual and mystical wilderness—*and shall not see when comfort comes, but shall abide in drought in the wilderness, in a barren land,* etc.

CHAPTER XCVI

Peace. Oh! what mysteries are these to flesh and blood! How hard for flesh to forsake the arm thereof! But pass on, dear Truth, to their proof propounded (Ezra 7:23), wherein Artaxerxes confirmed by law whatever was commanded by the God of heaven.

Truth. In this scripture I mind, first, the people of God captivated under the dominion and government of the kings of Babel and Persia.

Secondly, Artaxerxes's favour to these captives,

1. Of freedom to their consciences.

2. Of bounty towards them.

3. Of exempting of some of them from common charges.

Thirdly, punishments on offenders.

Fourthly, the ground that carries him on to all this.

Fifthly, Ezra praising of God for putting this into the heart of the king.

Concerning the people of God the Jews, they were as lambs and sheep in the jaws of the lion, the dearly beloved of his soul under the devouring tyrants of the world, both the Babylonian and the Persian, far from their own nation and the government of their own anointed kings, the figures of the true King of the Jews, the Lord Jesus Christ.

In this respect it is clear that the Jews were no more subject to the kings of Babylon and Persia in spiritual things than the vessels of the sanctuary were subject to the king of Babel's use. (Dan. 5)

Concerning this king, I consider, first, his person: a Gentile idolater, an oppressing tyrant, one of those devouring beasts. (Dan. 7,8) A hand of bloody conquest set the crown upon the head of these monarchs; and although in civil things they might challenge subjection, yet why should they now sit down in the throne of Israel, and govern the people and church of God in spiritual things?

Secondly, consider his acts of favor, and they will not amount to a positive command that any of the Jews should go up to build the temple, nor that any of them should practice his own worship, which he kept and judged the best for his own soul and people.

It is true, he freely permits them and exercises a bounteous assistance to them. All which argues no more, but that sometimes it pleases God to open the hearts of tyrants greatly to favor and further his people. Such favor found Nehemiah and Daniel, and others of God's people have and shall find, so often as it pleases him to honor them that honor him before the sons of men.

Peace. Who sees not how little this scripture contributes to their tenent? But why, say some, should this king confirm all with such severe punishments? And why, for all this, should Ezra give thanks to God, if it were not imitable for aftertimes?

Truth. The law of God, which he confirmed, he knew not, and therefore neither was, nor could he be a judge in the case.

And for his ground, what was it but the common terrors and convictions of an affrighted conscience?

In such fits and pangs, what have not Pharaohs, Sauls, Ahabs, Herods, Agrippas spoken? And what wonderful decrees have Nebuchadnezzar, Cyrus, Darius, Artaxerxes, put forth concerning the God of Israel (Dan. 3,6; Ezra 1,7, etc.); and yet as far from being charged with, as they were from being affected to, the spiritual crown of governing the worship of God, and the conscience of his people.

It is true, Ezra most piously and justly gave thanks to God for putting such a thing into the heart of the king; but what makes this pattern for the laws of civil governors now under the gospel? It suited well with that national state of God's church that the Gentile king should release them, permit them to return to their own land, assist them with other favors, and enable them to execute punishments upon offenders according to their national state.

But did God put such a thing as this into the heart of the king, viz., to restrain upon pain of death all the millions of men under his dominion from the idolatries of their several and respective countries? To constrain them all, upon the like penalty, to conform to the worship of the God of Israel, to build him a temple, erect an altar, ordain priests, offer sacrifice, observe the fasts and feasts of Israel? Yea, did God put it into the king's heart to send Levites into all the parts of his dominion, compelling them to hear, which is but a natural thing, as some unsoundly speak, unto which all are bound to submit?

Well, however, Ezra gives thanks to God for the king; and so should all that fear God in all countries, if he would please to put it into the hearts of the kings, states, and parliaments, to take off the yokes of violence, and permit at least the consciences of their subjects, and especially such as in truth make conscience of their worships to the God of Israel: and yet, no cause for Ezra then, or God's Ezras and Israelites now, to acknowledge the care and charge of God's worship, church, and ordinances, to lie upon the shoulders of Artaxerxes, or any other civil prince or ruler.

Lastly, for the confirmation or ratification which they suppose magistrates are bound to give to the laws of Christ, I answer, God's cause, Christ's truth, and the two-edged sword of his word, never stood in need of a temporal sword or a human witness to confirm and ratify them. If we receive the witness of an honest man, the witness of the most holy God is greater. (1 John 5 [9])

The result and sum of the whole matter is this: 1. It may please God sometimes to stir up the rulers of the earth to permit and tolerate, to favor and countenance God's people in their worships, though only out of some strong conviction of conscience or fear of wrath, etc.: and yet themselves neither understand God's worship, nor leave their own state, idolatry, or country's worship.

For this God's people ought to give thanks unto God; yea, and all men from this example may learn not to charge upon the magistrates' conscience—besides the care of the civil peace, the bodies and goods of men—the spiritual peace, in the worship of God and souls of men; but hence are magistrates instructed favorably to permit their subjects in their worships, although themselves be not persuaded to submit to them, as Nebuchadnezzar, Cyrus, Darius, and Artaxerxes did.

CHAPTER XCVII

Peace. The sixth question is this: How far the church is subject to their laws?

"All those," say they, "who are members of the commonweal are bound to be subject to all the just and righteous laws thereof, and therefore, membership in churches not cutting men off from membership in commonweals, they are bound to be subject, even every soul (Rom. 13:1), as Christ himself and the apostles were in their places wherein they lived. And therefore to exempt the clergy, as the papists do, from civil subjection, and to say that *generatio clerici* is *corruptio subditi*, is both sinful and scandalous to the gospel of God; and though all are equally subject, yet church members are more especially bound to yield subjection, and the most eminent most especially bound, not only because conscience does more strongly bind, but also because their ill examples are more infectious to others, pernicious to the state, and provoke God's wrath to bring vengeance on the state.

"Hence, if the whole church, or officers of the church, shall sin against the state, or any person, by sedition, contempt of authority, heresy, blasphemy, oppression, slander, or shall withdraw any of their members from the service of the state without the consent thereof, their persons and estates are liable to civil punishments of magistrates, according to their righteous and wholesome laws." (Exod. 22:20; Lev. 24:16; Deut. 13:6, 18:10)

Truth. What concerns this head in civil things, I gladly subscribe unto: what concerns heresy, blasphemy, etc., I have plentifully before spoken to, and shall here only say two things.

First, those scriptures produced concern only the people of God in a church estate, and must have reference only to the church of Christ Jesus, which, as Mr. Cotton confesses,[95] is not national but congregational, of so many as may meet in one place (1 Cor. 14[23]), and therefore no civil state can be the antitype and parallel: to which purpose, upon the eleventh question, I shall at large show the difference between the national church and state of Israel, and all other states and nations in the world.

---

[95] John Cotton, *The Way of the Church*, chapter 1, proposition 1.

Secondly, if the rulers of the earth are bound to put to death all that worship other gods than the true God, or that blaspheme (that is, speak evil of in a lesser or higher degree) that one true God: it must unavoidably follow, that the *beloved for the Father's sake*, [Rom. 11:28] the Jews, whose very religion blasphemes Christ in the highest degree—I say, they are actually sons of' death, and all to be immediately executed according to those quoted scriptures. And—

Secondly, the towns, cities, nations, and kingdoms of the world, must generally be put to the sword, if they speedily renounce not their gods and worships, and so cease to blaspheme the true God by their idolatries. This bloody consequence cannot be avoided by any scripture rule, for if that rule be of force (Deut. 13,18), not to spare or show mercy upon person or city falling to idolatry, that bars out all favor or partiality; and then what heaps upon heaps in the slaughter-houses and shambles of civil wars must the world come to, as I have formerly noted; and that unnecessarily, it being not required by the Lord Jesus for his sake, and the magistrate's power and weapons being essentially civil, and so not reaching to the impiety or ungodliness but the incivility and unrighteousness of tongue or hand.

CHAPTER XCVIII

Peace. Dear Truth, these are the poisoned daggers stabbing at my tender heart! Oh, when shall the Prince of peace appear, and reconcile the bloody sons of men! But let me now propose their seventh head: viz.,

"In what order may the magistrate execute punishment on a church or church member that offends his laws?

"First, gross and public, notorious sins, which are against the light of conscience, as heresy, etc., there the magistrate keeping him under safe ward should send the offender first to the church to heal his conscience, still provided that the church be both able and willing thereunto: by which means the magistrate shall convince such a one's conscience that he seeks his healing, rather than his hurt.

"The censure also against him shall proceed with more power and blessing, and none shall have cause to say that the magistrate persecutes men for their consciences, but that he justly punishes such a one for sinning rather against his conscience. (Titus 3:10)

"Secondly, in private offences how the magistrate may proceed, see Chapter XII. It is not material whether the church or magistrate take it first in hand. Only with this caution, that if the state take it first in hand, they are not to proceed to death or banishment until the church has taken their course with him, to bring him to repentance, provided that the church be willing and ready thereunto.

"Secondly, in such sins wherein men plead conscience, as heresy," etc.

Truth. Here I have many just exceptions and considerations to present.

First, they propose a distinction of some sins: some are against the light of conscience, etc., and they instance in heresy.

Answer. I have before discussed this point of a heretic sinning against light of conscience. And I shall add that however they lay this down as an infallible conclusion, that all heresy is against light of conscience, yet—to pass by the discussion of the nature of heresy, in which respect it may so be that even themselves may be found heretical, yea, and that in fundamentals—how do all idolaters after light presented, and exhortations powerfully pressed, either Turks or pagans, Jews or anti-Christians, strongly even to the death hold fast, or rather are held fast by their delusions.

Yea, God's people themselves, being deluded and captivated, are strongly confident even against some fundamentals, especially of worship: and yet not against the light, but according to the light or eye of a deceived conscience.

Now, all these consciences walk on confidently and constantly, even to the suffering of death and torments; and are more strongly confirmed in their belief and conscience, because such bloody and cruel courses of persecution are used toward them.

Secondly, speaks not the scripture expressly of the Jew (Isa. 6; Matt. 13; Acts 28) that God has given them the spirit of slumber, eyes that they should not see, etc.? All which must be spoken of the very conscience which he that has the golden key of David can only shut and open, and all the picklocks or swords in all the smiths' shops in the world can neither by force or fraud prevent his time.

Is it not said of anti-Christians (2 Thess. 2) that God has sent them strong delusions, so strong and efficacious that they believe a lie, and that so confidently, and some so conscientiously, that death itself cannot part between the delusion and their conscience?

"Again, the magistrate," say they, "keeping him in safe ward: that is, the heretic, the blasphemer, idolater," etc.

Peace. I here ask all men that love even the civil peace, where the Lord Jesus had spoken a tittle of a prison or safe ward to this purpose?

Truth. We find indeed a prison threatened by God to his irreconciled enemies, neglecting to account with him. (Matt. 5 [25])

We find a prison into which persecutors cast the saints. So John, so Paul, and the apostles (Matt. 14:10, etc.) were cast; and the great commander of, and caster into prison, is the devil. (Rev. 2 [10])

We find a spiritual prison, indeed, a prison for spirits (1 Pet. 3:19), the spirits formerly rebellious against Christ Jesus, speaking by Noah unto them, now kept in safe ward against the judgement of the great day.

In excommunication, a soul obstinate in sin is delivered to Satan his jailer, and he keeps him in safe ward until it pleases God to release him.

There is a prison for the devil himself a thousand years (Rev. 20 [2,3]), and a lake of fire and brimstone, into which the beast and false prophet, and all not written in the Lamb's book, and the devil that deceived them, shall eternally be there secured and tormented.

But neither among these, nor in any other passage of the New Testament, do we find a prison appointed by Christ Jesus for the heretic, blasphemer, idolater, etc., being not otherwise guilty against the civil state.

It is true, Antichrist, by the help of civil powers, has his prisons to keep Christ Jesus and his members fast: such prisons may well be called the bishop's prisons, the pope's, the devil's prisons. These inquisition-houses have ever been more terrible than the magistrate's.

At first, persecuting bishops borrowed prisons of the civil magistrate, as now their successors do still in the world; but afterward they wrung the keys out of the magistrates' hands, and hung them at their own girdles, and would have prisons of their own, as doubtless will that generation still do, if God prevent them not.

CHAPTER XCIX

Peace. Again, say they, the magistrate should send him first to the church to heal his conscience.

Truth. Is not this as the prophet speaks, like mother like daughter? [Ezek. 16:44] So the mother of whoredoms, the church of Rome, teaches and practices with all her heretics: first, let the holy church convince them, and then deliver them to the secular power to receive the punishment of heretics.

Peace. Methinks also they approach near that popish tenent, *ex opere operato:* for their exhortations and admonitions must necessarily be so operative and prevalent that if the heretic repent not he now sins against his conscience: not remembering that peradventure (2 Tim. 2:[25]), *If peradventure, God will give them repentance;* and how strong delusions are, and believing of lies, and how hard it is to be undeceived, especially in spirituals!

Truth. And as it may so prove, when a heretic indeed is brought to this college of physicians to have his conscience healed, and the heretic is to cure another. So also when any of Christ's witnesses, supposed heretics, are brought before them, how does the Lord Jesus suffer whippings and stabs, when his name, and truths, and witnesses, and ordinances are all profaned and blasphemed.

Besides, suppose a man to be a heretic, and yet suppose him brought as the magistrate's prisoner, though to a true church, to heal his conscience: what promise of presence and blessing has the Lord Jesus made to his church and spouse in such a way? And how common is it for heretics either to be desperately hardened by such cruel courses (yet pretending soul-healing), or else through fear and terror to practice gross hypocrisy, even against their consciences? So that these chirurgeons[96] and physicians, pretending to heal consciences by such a course, wound them deeper, and declare themselves chirurgeons and physicians of no value.

Peace. But what think you of the proviso added to their proposition, viz., "Provided the church be able and willing"?

Truth. Doubtless this proviso derogates not a little from the nature of the spouse of Christ. For she, like that gracious woman (Prov. 31:26) *opens her mouth with wisdom, and in her tongue is the law of grace:* she is

---

[96] Surgeon.

the pillar and ground of truth (1 Tim. 3:15),[97] the golden candlestick from whence true light shines: the angels or ministers thereof able to try false apostles (Rev. 2:2), and convince *the gainsayers.* (Titus 1:9)

Again, according to their principles of suppressing persons and churches, falsely worshipping, how can they permit such a blind and dead church not able and willing to heal a wounded conscience?

Peace. What should be the reason of this their expression?

Truth. Doubtless their consciences tell them how few of those churches which they yet acknowledge churches are able and willing to hold forth Christ Jesus the Sun of righteousness, healing with his wings the doubting and afflicted conscience.

Lastly, their conscience tells them that a servant of Christ Jesus may possibly be sent as a heretic to be healed by a false church, which church will never be willing to deal with him, or never be able to convince him.

Peace. Yea, but they say, "by such a course the magistrate shall convince such a one's conscience that he seeks his good," etc.

Truth. If a man thus bound be sent to a church to be healed in his conscience, either he is a heretic or he is not.

Admit he be: yet he disputes in fear, as the poor thief, the mouse disputes with a terrible persecuting cat who, while she seems to play and gently toss, yet the conclusion is a proud, insulting, and devouring cruelty.

If no heretic, but an innocent and faithful witness of any truth of Jesus, disputes he not as a lamb in the lion's paw, being sure in the end to be torn in pieces?

Peace. They add, "The censure, this way, proceeds with more power and blessing."

Truth. All power and blessing is from the blessed Son of God, unto whom all power is given from the Father, in heaven and earth. He has promised his presence with his messengers, preaching and baptizing to the world's end, ratifying in heaven what they bind or loose on earth.

But let any man show me such a commission, instruction, and promise, given by the Son of God to civil powers in these spiritual affairs of his Christian kingdom and worship.

---

[97] Williams mistakenly cites 2 Timothy 2.

Peace. Lastly, they conclude, "This course of first sending the heretic to be healed by the church takes away all excuse; for none can say that he is persecuted for his conscience, but for sinning against his conscience."

Truth. Jezebel, placing poor Naboth before the elders as a blasphemer of God and the king, and sanctifying the plotted and intended murder with a day of humiliation, may seem to take away all excuse, and to conclude the blasphemer worthy to be stoned. But Jehovah, the God of recompenses (Jer. 51[56]), when he makes inquisition for blood, will find both Jezebel and Ahab guilty, and make the dogs a feast with the flesh of' Jezebel, and leave not to Ahab a man to piss against the wall [1 Kgs 21:21]; for (as Paul in his own plea) there was nothing committed worthy of' death: and *against thee, O king,* says Daniel, *I have not sinned* (Dan. 6 [22]) in any civil fact against the state.

CHAPTER C

Peace. Their eighth question is this, viz., what power magistrates have about the gathering of churches?

"First, the magistrate has power, and it is his duty to encourage and countenance such persons as voluntarily join themselves in holy covenant, both by his presence (if it may be) and promise of protection, they accepting the right hand of fellowship from other neighbor churches.

"Secondly, he has power to forbid all idolatrous and corrupt assemblies, who offer to put themselves under their patronage, and shall attempt to join themselves into a church-estate, and if' they shall not hearken, to force them therefrom by the power of the sword. (Ps. 101:8) For our tolerating many religions in a state in several churches, besides the provoking of God, may in time not only corrupt, leaven, divide, and so destroy the peace of the churches, but also dissolve the continuity of the state, especially ours, whose walls are made of the stones of the churches, it being also contrary to the end of our planting in this part of the world, which was not only to enjoy the pure ordinances, but to enjoy them all in purity.

"Thirdly, he has power to compel all men within his grant to hear the word: for hearing the word of God is a duty which the light of nature leads even heathens to. The Ninevites heard Jonah, though a stranger,

and unknown unto them to be an extraordinary prophet. (Jonah 3) And
Eglon, the king of Moab, hearing that Ehud had a message from God, he
rose out of his seat for more reverent attention. (Jud. 3:20)

"Yet he has no power to compel all men to become members of
churches, because he has not power to make them fit members for the
church, which is not wrought by the power of the sword, but by the
power of the word; nor may he force the churches to accept of any for
members but those whom the churches themselves can freely approve
of."

Truth. To the first branch of this head I answer that the magistrate
should encourage and countenance the church, yea, and protect the
persons of the church from violence, disturbance, etc., it being truly
noble and glorious by how much the spouse and queen of' the Lord Jesus
transcends the ladies, queens, and empresses of the world in glory,
beauty, chastity, and innocency.

It is true, all magistrates in the world do this: viz., encourage and
protect the church or assembly of worshippers which they judge to be
true and approve of; but not permitting other consciences than their
own. It has come to pass in all ages, and yet doubtless will, that the Lord
Jesus and his queen are driven and persecuted out of the world.

To the second, that the magistrate ought to suppress all churches
which he judges false, he quotes Psalm 101:8, *Betimes I will cut off the
wicked of the land; that I may cut off all evil doers from the city of Jehovah:*
unto which he adds four reasons.

Peace. Dear Truth, first, a word to that scripture, so often quoted,
and so much boasted of.

Truth. Concerning that holy land of Canaan, concerning the city of
Jehovah, Jerusalem, out of which king David here resolves to cut off all
the wicked and evil doers, I shall speak more largely on the eleventh head
or question, in the differences between that and all other lands.

At present I answer, there is no holy land or city of the Lord, no
King of Zion, etc., but the church of Jesus Christ, and the King thereof,
according to 1 Peter 2:9, *Ye are a holy nation*; and Jerusalem is the holy
people of God in the true profession of Christianity (Heb. 12; Gal. 4; Rev.
21) out of which the Lord Jesus by his holy ordinances, in such a
government, and by such governors as he has appointed, he cuts off every
wicked person and evil doer.

If Christ Jesus had intended any difference of place, cities or countries, doubtless Jerusalem and Samaria had been thought of, or the cities of Asia, wherein the Christian religion was so gloriously planted.

But the Lord Jesus disclaims Jerusalem and Samaria from having any respect of holiness more than other cities. (John 4 [21])

And the Spirit of God evidently testifies that the churches were in the cities and countries, not that the whole cities or countries were God's holy land and cities, out of which all false worshippers and wicked persons were to be cut. (Rev. 2,3)

The devil's throne was in the city of Pergamos in respect of the state and persecution of it, and yet there was also the throne of the Lord Jesus set up in his church of worshippers in Pergamos, out of which the Balaamites, and Nicolaitanes, and every false worshipper were to be cast, though not out of the city of Pergamos: for then Pergamos must have been thrown out of Pergamos, and the world out of the world.

CHAPTER CI

Peace. Oh! that my head were a fountain, and mine eyes rivers of tears, to lament my children, the children of peace and light, thus darkening that and other lightsome scriptures with such dark and direful clouds of blood.

Truth. Sweet Peace, your tears are seasonable and precious, and bottled up in the heavens; but let me add a second consideration from that scripture. If that scripture may now literally be applied to nations and cities, in a parallel to Canaan and Jerusalem, since the gospel and this Psalm 101 be literally to be applied to cities, towns, and countries in Europe and America, not only such as assay to join themselves (as they here speak) in a corrupt church estate, but such as know no church estate, nor God, nor Christ, yea, every wicked person and evil doer, must be hanged or stoned, etc., as it was in Israel; and if so, how many thousands and millions of men and women in the several kingdoms and governments of the world must be cut off from their lands, and destroyed from their cities, as this scripture speaks!

Thirdly, since those persons in the New English plantations accounted unfit for church estate yet remain all members of the church of England, from which New England dares not separate, no, not in their sacraments (as some of the Independents have published),[98] what riddle or mystery, or rather fallacy of Satan is this!

Peace. It will not be offence to charity to make conjecture: first, herein New England churches secretly call their mother whore, not daring in America to join with their own mother's children, though unexcommunicate: no, nor permit them to worship God after their consciences, and as their mother has taught them this secretly and silently, they have a mind to do, which publicly they would seem to disclaim and profess against.

Secondly, if such members of Old England should be suffered to enjoy their consciences in New England—however it is pretended they would profane ordinances for which they are unfit (as true it is in that natural persons are not fit for spiritual worship), yet this appears not to be the bottom, for in Old England the New English join with Old in the ministration of the word, prayer, singing, contribution, maintenance of the ministry, etc.—if, I say, they should set up churches after their conscience, the greatness and multitudes of their own assemblies would decay, and with all the contributions and maintenance of their ministers, unto which all or most have been forced.

Truth. Dear Peace, these are more than conjectures, thousands now espy; and all that love the purity of the worship of the living God should lament such halting. I shall add this, not only do they partially neglect to cut off the wicked of the land, but such as themselves esteemed beloved and godly have they driven forth, and keep out others which would come unto them, eminently godly by their own confession; because differing in conscience and worship from them, and consequently not to be suffered in their holy land of Canaan.

But having examined that scripture alleged, let us now weigh their reasons.

First, say they, the not cutting off by the sword, but tolerating many religions in a state would provoke God, unto which I answer, first (and

---

[98] The views of the Independents: "In the late times, when we had no hopes of returning to our own country, we held communion with them, and offered to receive the Lord's Supper some that came to visit us in our exile, whom we knew to be godly, upon that relation and membership they held in their parish churches in England, they professing themselves to be members thereof, and belonging thereunto." "An Apologetical Narration, humbly submitted to the Honorable Houses of Parliament," (1643) cited in Caldwell's edition (1867).

here being no scripture produced to these reasons, shall the sooner answer), that no proof can be made from the institutions of the Lord Jesus that all religions but one are to be cut off by the civil sword; that national church in that typical land of Canaan being abolished, and the Christian commonweal or church instituted.

Secondly, I affirm that the cutting off by the sword other consciences and religions, is (contrarily) most provoking unto God, expressly against his will concerning the tares (Matt. 13), as I have before proved; as also the bloody mother of all those monstrous mischiefs, where such cutting off is used, both to the souls and bodies of men.

Thirdly, let conscience and experience speak how in the not cutting off their many religions, it has pleased God not only not to be provoked, but to prosper the state of the United Provinces,[99] our next neighbors, and that to admiration.

Peace. The second reason is, such tolerating would leaven, divide, and destroy the peace of the churches.

Truth. This must also be denied upon so many former scriptures and reasons produced, proving the power of the Lord Jesus, and the sufficiency of his spiritual power in his church, for the purging forth and conquering of the least evil: yea, and for the bringing every thought in subjection unto Christ Jesus. (II Corinthians 10)

I add, they have not produced one scripture, nor can, to prove that the permitting of leaven of false doctrine in the world or civil state will leaven the churches: only we find that the permission of leaven in persons, doctrines, or practices in the church, that indeed will corrupt and spread (1 Cor. 5; Gal. 5); but this reason should never have been alleged were not the particular churches in New England but as so many implicit parish churches in one implicit national church.

Peace. Their third reason is, it will dissolve the continuity of the state, especially theirs, where the walls are made of the stones of the churches.

Truth. I answer briefly to this bare affirmation thus, that the true church is a wall spiritual and mystical. (Cant. 8:9)

That consequently a false church or company is a false or pretended wall, and none of Christ's.

The civil state, power, and government is a civil wall, etc., and

---

[99] United Provinces of the Netherlands (1579-1795).

Lastly, the walls of earth or stone about a city, are the natural or artificial wall or defense of it.

Now, in consideration of these four walls, I desire it may be proved from the scriptures of truth how the false spiritual wall, or company of false worshippers suffered in a city, can be able to destroy the true Christian wall, or company of believers.

Again, how this false spiritual wall, or false church permitted, can destroy the civil wall, the state and government of the city and citizens, any more than it can destroy the natural or artificial wall of earth or stone.

Spiritual may destroy spiritual, if a stronger and victorious; but spiritual cannot reach to artificial or civil.

Peace. Yea, but they fear the false spiritual wall may destroy their civil, because it is made of the stones of churches.

T'ruth. If this have reference to that practice among them, viz., that none but members of churches enjoy civil freedom among them, ordinarily, in imitation of that national church and state of the Jews, then I answer, they that follow Moses' church constitution, which the New English by such a practice implicitly do, must cease to pretend to the Lord Jesus Christ and his institutions.

Secondly, we shall find lawful civil states, both before and since Christ Jesus, in which we find not any tidings of the true God or Christ.

Lastly, their civil New English state, framed out of their churches, may yet stand, subsist, and flourish, although they did—as by the word of the Lord they ought—permit either Jews, or Turks, or anti-Christians to live among them subject unto their civil government.

CHAPTER CII

Peace. One branch more, viz., the third, remains of this head, and it concerns the hearing of the word; "Unto which," say they, "all men are to be compelled; because hearing of the word is a duty which even nature leads heathens to." For this they quote the practice of the Ninevites hearing Jonah, and Eglon, king of Moab, his rising up to Ehud's pretended message from God. (Jud. 3)

Truth. I must deny that position: for light of nature leads men to hear that only which nature conceives to be good for it, and therefore not to hear a messenger, minister, or preacher, whom conscience persuades is a false messenger or deceiver, and comes to deceive my soul: as millions of men and women in their several respective religions and consciences are so persuaded, conceiving their own to be true.

Secondly, as concerning the instances, Jonah did not compel the Ninevites to hear that message which he brought unto them.

Besides, the matter of compulsion to a constant worship of the word in church estate, which is the question, comes not near Jonah's case.

Nor did Christ Jesus or any of his ambassadors so practice; but if persons refused to hear, the command of the Lord Jesus to his messengers was only to depart from them, shaking off the dust of their feet with a denunciation of God's wrath against them. (Matt. 10; Acts 14)

Concerning Eglon's rising up: first, Ehud compelled not that king either to hear or reverence, and all that can be imitable in Eglon is a voluntary and willing reverence, which persons ought to express to what they are persuaded comes from God.

But how do both these instances mightily convince and condemn themselves, who not only profess to turn away from, but also persecute or hurt all such as shall dare to profess a ministry or church estate differing from their own, though for personal godliness and excellency of gifts reverenced by themselves.

Thirdly, to the point of compulsion: it has pleased the Lord Jesus to appoint a twofold ministry of his word.

First, for unbelievers and their conversion, according to Matt. 18:19, Mark 16:15,16, and the constant practice of the apostles in the first preaching of the gospel.

Secondly, a ministry of feeding and nourishing up such as are converted and brought into church estate, according to Ephesians 4, etc. Now to neither of these do we find any compulsion appointed by the Lord Jesus, or practiced by any of his.

The compulsion preached and practiced in New England is not to the hearing of that ministry sent forth to convert unbelievers, and to constitute churches, for such a ministry they practice not; but to the hearing of the word of edification, exhortation, consolation, dispensed only in the churches of worshippers. I apply,—

When Paul came first to Corinth to preach Jesus Christ, by their rule the magistrates of Corinth ought by the sword to have compelled all the people of Corinth to hear Paul.

Secondly, after a church of Christ was gathered, by their rule the magistrates of Corinth ought to have compelled the people still, even those who had refused his doctrine (for the few only of the church embraced it) to have heard the word still, and to have kept one day in seven to the Christian's God, and to have come to the Christian's church all their days. And what is this but a settled formality of religion and worship, unto which a people are brought by the power of the sword?

And however they affirm that persons are not to be compelled to be members of churches, nor the church compelled to receive any: yet if persons be compelled to forsake their religion which their hearts cleave to, and to come to church, to the worship of the word, prayers, psalms, and contributions, and this all their days, I ask whether this be not this people's religion, unto which submitting, they shall be quiet all their days, without the enforcing them to the practice of any other religion? And if this be not so, then I ask, will it not inevitably follow that they not only permit but enforce people to be of no religion at all, all their days?

This toleration of religion, or rather irreligious compulsion, is above all tolerations monstrous, to wit, to compel men to be of no religion all their days. I desire all men, and these worthy authors of this model, to lay their hands upon their heart, and to consider whether this compulsion of men to hear the word, as they say, whether it carries men, to wit, to be of no religion all their days, worse than the very Indians, who dare not live without religion according as they are persuaded.

Lastly, I add—from the ordinance of the Lord Jesus, and practice of the apostles (Acts 2: 42), where the word and prayer is joined with the exercise of their fellowship and breaking of bread, in which exercises the church continued constantly—that it is apparent that a civil state may as lawfully compel men by the civil sword to the breaking of bread, or Lord's Supper, as to the word, or prayer, or fellowship.

For, first, they are all of the same nature, ordinance in the church (I speak of the feeding ministry in the church, unto which persons are compelled) and church worship. Secondly, every conscience in the world is fearful, at least shy of the priests and ministers of other gods and worships, and of holding spiritual fellowship in any of their services; which is the case of many a soul, viz., to question the ministers themselves, as well as the supper itself.

CHAPTER CIII

Peace. Dear Truth, this pressing of men to the spiritual battles of Christ Jesus is the cause why (as it is commonly with pressed soldiers) that so many thousands fly in the day of battle. But I present you with the ninth question, viz. what power the magistrate has in providing of church officers?

"First," say they, "the election of church officers being the proper act of the church, therefore the magistrate has no power, either as prince or patron, to assume such power unto himself. Whom Christ sends to preach by his supreme power, the magistrate may send forth by his power subordinate, to gather churches, and may force people to hear them, but not invest them with office among them.

"Secondly, the maintenance of church officers being to arise from all those who are ordinarily taught thereby (Gal. 6:6), hence it is the duty of the civil magistrate to contend with the people, as Nehemiah did (13:10,11), who do neglect and forsake the due maintenance of the church of God, and to command them to give such portions for the maintenance of church officers, as the gospel commands to be offered to them, freely and bountifully. (2 Cor. 9:5,6,7) According as Hezekiah commanded the people to give to the priests and Levites the portions appointed by the law, that *they might be encouraged in the law of the Lord.* (2 Chr. 31:4)

"Thirdly, the furnishing the church with set officers, depending much upon erecting and maintenance of schools, and good education of youth, and it lying chiefly in the hand of the magistrate to provide for the furthering thereof, they may therefore and should so far provide for the churches as to erect schools, take care for fit governors and tutors, and commend it to all the churches, if they see it meet, that in all the churches within the jurisdiction, once in a year, and if it may be, the Sabbath before the general court of election, there be a free-will offering of all people for the maintenance of such schools: and the monies of every town so given, to be brought on the day of election to the treasury of the college, and the monies to be disposed by such who are so chosen for the disposing thereof."

Truth. In the choice of officers, it is very obscure what they mean by this supreme power of Christ Jesus sending to preach.

We know the commission of the Lord Jesus to his first messengers to go into all nations to preach and gather churches, and they were immediately sent forth by him. But Mr. Cotton elsewhere holds that there is now extant no immediate ministry from Christ, but mediate, that is, from the church.

Let us, first, see how they agree with themselves, and, secondly, how they agree with the magistrate in this business.

First, if they hold a sending forth to preach by Christ's supreme power, according to Matthew 28, Mark 16, Romans 10, they must necessarily grant a time when the church is not, but is to be constituted out of the nations and peoples now converted by this preaching: whence, according to the course of scripture, the nature of the work, and their own grant in this place, it is apparent that there is a ministry before the church, gathering and espousing the church to Christ: and therefore their other tenent must needs be too light, viz., that there is no ministry but that which is mediate from the church.

Peace. Blessed Truth, this doctrine of a ministry before the church is harsh and deep, yet most true, most sweet. Yet you know their ground, that two or three godly persons may join themselves together, become a church, make officers, send them forth to preach, to convert, to baptize, and gather new churches.

Truth. I answer, first, we find not in the first institution and pattern, that ever any such two, or three, or more, did gather and constitute themselves a church of Christ, without a ministry sent from God to invite and call them by the word, and to receive them unto fellowship with God upon the receiving of that word and message. And therefore it may very well be queried, how, without such a ministry, two or three become a church? And how the power of Christ is conveyed unto them? Who espoused this people unto Jesus Christ, as the church at Corinth was espoused by Paul? (2 Cor. 11[2]) If it be said, themselves, or if it be said, the scriptures, let one instance be produced in the first patterns and practices of such a practice.

It has been generally confessed that there is no coming to the marriage-feast without a messenger inviting, sent from God to the souls of men. (Matt. 22; Luke 14; Rom. 10)

We find when the Thessalonians turned to God from their idols, to serve the living and true God (1 Thess. 1:9), it pleased God to bring a word of power unto them by the mouth of Paul in the same place.

Peace. You know, dear Truth, it is a common plea that God's people now are converted already, and therefore may congregate themselves, etc.

Truth. Two things must here be cleared.

First, does their conversion amount to external turning from idols (1 Thess. 1:9), beside their internal repentance, from sins against the faith, love? etc. Secondly, who wrought this conversion, who begot these children? For though the Corinthians might have ten thousand teachers, yet Paul had begotten them by the word.

It is true, as Mr. Cotton himself elsewhere acknowledges, God sends many preachers in the way of his providence, even in Babel mystical, though not according to his ordinance and institution. So even in the wilderness God provides for the sustentation of the woman (Rev. 12), by which provision, even in the most popish times and places, yea, and by most false and popish callings (now in this lightsome age confessed so to be), God has done great things to the personal conversion, consolation, and salvation of his people.

But as there seems yet to be desired such constitution of the Christian church, as the first institution and pattern calls for: so also such a calling and converting of God's people from anti-Christian idols to the Christian worship; and therefore such a ministry, according to the first pattern, sent from Christ Jesus to renew and restore the worship and ordinances of God in Christ.

Lastly, if it should be granted that without a ministry sent from Christ to gather churches, that God's people in this country may be called, converted from anti-Christian idols to the true worship of God in the true church estate and ordinances, will it not follow that in all other countries of the world God's elect must or may be so converted from their several respective false worships and idolatries, and brought into the true Christian church estate without such a ministry sent unto them? Or are there two ways appointed by the Lord Jesus, one for this country, and another for the rest of the world? Or lastly, if two or three more, without a ministry, shall arise up, become a church, make ministers, etc., I ask whether those two or three or more, must not be accounted immediately and extraordinarily stirred up by God? And whether this be that supreme power of Christ Jesus which they speak of, sending forth two or three private persons to make a church and ministers, without a true ministry of Christ Jesus first sent unto themselves? Is this that commission which all ministers pretend unto (Matt. 28:19, etc.), first, in the hands of two or three private persons becoming a church, without a mediate call from which church, say they, there can be no true ministry, and yet also confess that Christ sends forth to preach by his supreme power, and the magistrate by his power subordinate to gather churches?

CHAPTER CIV

Peace. You have taken great pains to show the irreconcilableness of those their two assertions, viz., first, there is now no ministry, as they say, but what is mediate from the church; and yet, secondly, Christ Jesus sends preachers forth by his supreme power to gather the church. I now wait to hear, how, as they say, "the magistrate may send forth by his power subordinate to gather churches, enforcing the people to hear," etc.

Truth. If there be a ministry sent forth by Christ's supreme power, and a ministry sent forth by the magistrate's subordinate power, to gather churches, I ask, what is the difference between these two? Is there any gathering of churches but by that commission (Matt. 28), Teach and baptize? And is the civil magistrate entrusted with a power from Christ, as his deputy, to give this commission, and so to send out ministers to preach and baptize?

As there is nothing in the testament of Christ concerning such a delegation or assignment of such power of Christ to the civil magistrate: so I also ask, since in every free state civil magistrates have no power but what the peoples of those states, lands, and countries betrust them with, whether or no, by this means, it must not follow that Christ Jesus has left with the peoples and nations of the world his spiritual kingly power to grant commissions, and send out ministers to themselves, to preach, convert, and baptize themselves? How inevitably this follows upon their conclusion of power in magistrates to send, etc., and what unchristian and unreasonable consequences must flow from hence, let all consider in the fear of God.

Jehoshaphat's sending forth the Levites to teach in Judah (2 Chr. 17), etc., as they allege it not, so elsewhere it shall more fully appear to be a type and figure of Christ Jesus, the only king of his church, providing for the feeding of his church and people by his true Christian priests and Levites, viz., the ministry which in the gospel he has appointed.

CHAPTER CV

Peace. We have examined the ministry; be pleased, dear Truth, to speak to the second branch of this head: viz., the maintenance of it. They affirm that the magistrate may force out the minister's maintenance from all that are taught by them, and that after the pattern of Israel; and the argument from 1 Corinthians 9 and Galatians 6:6.

Truth. This theme, viz., concerning the maintenance of priests and ministers of worship is indeed the apple of the eye, the Diana of the [Ephesians][100] etc.; yet all that love Christ Jesus in sincerity, and souls in and from him will readily profess to abhor filthy lucre (Titus 1 [7]), and the wages of Balaam, both more common and frequent than easily is discernible.

To that scripture (Gal. 6:6), *Let him that is taught in the word make him that teacheth partaker of all his goods*: I answer, that teaching was of persons converted, believers entered into the school and family of Christ, the church; which church being rightly gathered, is also rightly invested with the power of the Lord Jesus, to force every soul therein by spiritual weapons and penalties to do its duty.

But this forcing of the magistrate is intended and practiced to all sorts of persons, without as well as within the church, unconverted, natural and dead in sin, as well as those that live and, feeding, enjoy the benefits of spiritual food.

Now for those sorts of persons to whom Christ Jesus sends his word out of church estate, Jews or Gentiles, according to the parable of Matthew 13, highway hearers, stony ground, and thorny ground hearers, we never find tittle of any maintenance to be expected, least of all to be forced and exacted from them. By civil power they cannot be forced, for it is no civil payment or business, no matter of Caesar, but concerning God: nor by spiritual power, which has nothing to do with those which are without. (1 Cor. 5)

It is reasonable to expect and demand of such as live within the state a civil maintenance of their civil officers, and to force it where it is denied. It is reasonable for a schoolmaster to demand his recompense for his labor in his school; but it is not reasonable to expect or force it from strangers, enemies, rebels to that city, from such as come not within, or

---

[100] "Diana of the Diana" in the first edition (Acts 19:28).

else would not be received into the school. What is the church of Christ Jesus, but the city, the school, and family of Christ? The officers of this city, school, family, may reasonably expect maintenance from such they minister unto, but not from strangers, enemies, etc.

Peace. It is most true that sin goes in a link; for that tenent that all the men of the world may be compelled to hear Christ preached, and enjoy the labors of the teacher as well as the church itself, forces on another also as evil, viz., that they should also be compelled to pay, as being most equal[101] and reasonable to pay for their conversion.

Truth. Some use to urge that text of Luke 14 [23], *Compel them to come in.* Compel them to mass, say the papists; compel them to church and common prayer, say the Protestants; compel them to the meeting, say the New English. In all these compulsions they disagree among themselves; but in this, viz., Compel them to pay, in this they all agree.

There is a double violence, which both error and falsehood use to the souls of men.

First, moral and persuasive; such was the persuasion first used to Joseph by his mistress; such was the persuasions of Tamar from Amnon; such was the compelling of the young man by the harlot (Pro. 7), she caught him by her much fair speech and kisses. And thus is the whole world compelled to the worship of the golden image. (Dan. 3).

The second compulsion is civil; such as Joseph's mistress began to practice upon Joseph, to attain her desires; such as Amnon practiced on Tamar to satisfy his brutish lust ; and such was Nebuchadnezzar's second compulsion, his fiery furnace (Dan. 3); and mystical Nebuchaduezzar's killing all that receive not his mark. (Rev. 13)

The first sort of these violences, to wit, by powerful argument and persuasion, the ministers of the gospel also use. Hence all those powerful persuasions of wisdom's maidens. (Pro. 9) Hence, says Paul, *knowing the terror of the Lord, we persuade men* (2 Cor. 5); and pull some out of the fire, says Jude; such must that compulsion be (Luke 14[23]), viz., the powerful persuasions of the word, being that two-edged sword coming out of the mouth of Christ Jesus in his true ministers, sent forth to invite poor sinners to partake of the feast of the Lamb of God. The civil ministers of the commonweal cannot be sent upon this business with their civil weapons and compulsions, but the spiritual minister of the

---

[101] Fair.

gospel, with his spiritual sword of Christ's mouth, a sword with two edges.

But more particularly, the contributions of Christ's kingdom are all holy and spiritual, though consisting of material earthly substance, (as is water in baptism, bread and wine in the supper) and joined with prayer and the Lord's Supper. (Acts 2:42)

Hence, as prayer is called God's sacrifice, so are the contributions and mutual supplies of the saints, sacrifices. (Phil. 4[18])

Hence, also, as it is impossible for natural men to be capable of God's worship, and to feed, be nourished, and edified by any spiritual ordinance, no more than a dead child can suck the breast, or a dead man feast; so also is it as impossible for a dead man, yet lodged in the grave of nature, to contribute spiritually, I mean according to scripture's rule, as for a dead man to pay a reckoning.

I question not but natural men may for the outward act preach, pray, contribute, etc.; but neither are they worshippers suitable to him who is a Spirit (John 4[24]), nor can they, least of all, be forced to worship, or the maintenance of it, without a guilt of their hypocrisy.

*Peace.*They will say, what is to be done for their souls?

*Truth.*The apostles, whom we profess to imitate, preachedthe word of the Lord to unbelievers without mingling in worship with them, and such preachers and preaching such as pretend to be the true ministry of Christ ought to be and practice: not forcing them all their days to come to church and pay their duties, either so confessing that this is their religion unto which they are forced, or else that, as before, they are forced to be of no religion all their days.

The way to subdue rebels is not by correspondence and communion with them, by forcing them to keep the city watches, and pay assessments, etc., which all may be practiced, upon compulsion, treacherously; the first work with such is powerfully to subdue their judgments and wills, to lay down their weapons, and yield willing subjection, then come they orderly into the city, and so to city privileges.

CHAPTER CVI

Peace. Please you now, dear Truth, to discuss the scriptures from the Old Testament, Nehemiah 13 and 2 Chronicles 31.

Truth. God gave unto that national church of the Jews that excellent land of Canaan, and therein houses furnished, orchards, gardens, vineyards, olive-yards, fields, wells, etc.; they might well, in this settled abundance and the promised continuation and increase of it, afford a large temporal supply to their priests and Levites, even to the tenth of all they did possess.

God's people are now, in the gospel, brought into a spiritual land of Canaan, flowing with spiritual milk and honey, and they abound with spiritual and heavenly comforts, though in a poor and persecuted condition; therefore all enforced settled maintenance is not suitable to the gospel, as it was to the ministry of priests and Levites in the law.

Secondly, in the change of the church estate there was also a change of the priesthood and of the law. (Heb. 7 [12]) Nor did the Lord Jesus appoint that in his church, and for the maintenance of his ministry, the civil sword of the magistrate; but that the spiritual sword of the ministry should alone compel.

3. Therefore, the compulsion used under Hezekiah and Nehemiah was by the civil and corporal sword, a type (in that typical state) not of another material and corporal, but of a heavenly and spiritual, even the sword of the Spirit, with which Christ fights (Rev. 2 [12]),[102] which is exceeding sharp, entering in between the soul and spirit (Hebrews 4 [12]) and bringing every thought into captivity to the obedience of Christ Jesus. [II Corinthians 10:5] He that submits not at the shaking of this sword is cut off by it; and he that despises this sword, all the power in the world cannot make him a true worshipper, or by his purse a maintainer of God's worship.

Lastly, if any man professing to be a minister of Christ Jesus shall bring men before the magistrate, as the practice has been, both in Old and New England for not paying him his wages or his due: I ask, if the voluntary consent of the party has not obliged him, how can either the officers of the parish, church, or of the civil state, compel this or that man to pay so much, more or less, to maintain such a worship or ministry?[103] I ask further, if the determining what is each man's due to pay, why may they not determine the tenth and more, as some desired

---

[102] Williams mistakenly cites Revelation 3.
[103] "No man should be bound to worship, nor maintain a worship against his consent." (Williams's footnote)

(others opposing) in New England, and force men not only to maintenance, but to a Jewish maintenance?

Peace. Yea; but, say they, is not the laborer worthy of his hire?

Truth. Yea, from them that hire him, from the church, to whom he labors or ministers, not from the civil state: no more than the minister of the civil state is worthy of his hire from the church, but from the civil state; in which I grant the persons in the church ought to be assistant in their civil respects.

Peace. What maintenance, say they, shall the ministry of the gospel have?

Truth. We find two ways of maintenance for the ministry of the gospel proposed for our direction in the New Testament.

First, the free and willing contribution of the saints, according to 1 Corinthians 16, Luke 8:3, etc., upon which both the Lord Jesus, and his ministers lived.

Secondly, the diligent work and labor of their own hands, as Paul tells the Thessalonians, and that in two cases:

1. Either in the inabilities and necessities of the church.

2. Or for the greater advantage of Christ's truth. As when Paul saw it would more advantage the name of Christ, he denies himself', and falls to work among the Corinthians and Thessalonians.

Let none call these cases extraordinary: for if persecution be the portion of Christ's sheep, and the business or work of Christ must be dearer to us than our right eye or lives, such as will follow Paul, and follow the Lord Jesus must not think much at, but rejoice in, poverties, necessities, hunger, cold, nakedness, etc. The stewards of Christ Jesus must be like their Lord, and abhor to steal as the evil steward, pretending that he shamed to beg, but peremptorily dig he could not. [Luke 16:3]

CHAPTER CVII

Peace. One and the last branch, dear Truth, remains concerning schools. "The churches," say they, "much depend upon the schools, and the schools upon the magistrates."

Truth. I honor schools for tongues and arts; but the institution of Europe's universities, devoting persons (as is said) for scholars in a monastical way, forbidding marriage, and labor too, I hold as far from the mind of Jesus Christ as it is from propagating his name and worship.

We count the universities the fountains, the seminaries, or seed-plots of all piety; but have not those fountains ever sent what streams the times have liked? And ever changed their taste and color to the prince's eye and palate?

For any depending of the church of Christ upon such schools, I find not a tittle in the Testament of Christ Jesus.

I find the church of Christ frequently compared to a school. All believers are his disciples or scholars, yea, women also. (Acts 9:36) There was a certain disciple, or scholar, called Dorcas.

Have not the universities sacrilegiously stolen this blessed name of Christ's scholars from his people? Is not the very scripture language itself become absurd, to wit, to call God's people, especially women, as Dorcas, scholars ?

Peace. Some will object, how shall the scriptures be brought to light from out of popish darkness, except these schools of prophets convey them to us?

Truth. I know no schools of prophets in the New Testament, but the particular congregation of Christ Jesus. (1 Cor. 14) And I question whether anything but sin stopped and dried up the current of the Spirit in those rare gifts of tongues to God's sons and daughters, serving so admirably both for the understanding of the original scriptures, and also for the propagating of the name of Christ.

Who knows but that it may please the Lord again to clothe his people with a spirit of zeal and courage for the name of Christ; yea, and pour forth those fiery streams again of tongues and prophecy in the restoration of Zion?

If it be not his holy pleasure so to do, but that his people with daily study and labor must dig to come at the original fountains, God's people have many ways, besides the university, lazy and monkish, to attain to all excellent measure of the knowledge of those tongues.[104]

That most despised while living, and now much honored Mr. Ainsworth,[105] had scarce his peer among a thousand for the scripture originals, and yet he scarce set foot within a college-walls.

---

[104] "Tongues attainable out of Oxford and Cambridge." (Williams's footnote)

[105] Henry Ainsworth (1573-1622?), Separatist theologian, Hebrew scholar, leader of the English Separatist colony in Amsterdam, and author of commentaries on the

CHAPTER CVIII

Peace. I shall now present you with their tenth head, viz., concerning the magistrates' power in matters of doctrine. "That which is unjustly ascribed to the pope is as unjustly ascribed to the magistrates, viz., to have power of making new articles of faith, or rules of life, or of pressing upon the churches to give such public honor to the apocryphal writings, or homilies of men, as to read them to the people in the room of the oracles of God."

Truth. This position, simply considered, I acknowledge a most holy truth of God, both against the pope, and the civil magistrates' challenge, both pretending to be the vicars of Christ Jesus upon the earth. Yet two things here I shall propose to consideration:

First, since the parliament of England thrust the pope out of his chair in England, and set down King Henry VIII and his successors in the pope's room, establishing them supreme governors of the church of England: since such an absolute government is given by all men to them to be guardians of the first table and worship of God, to set up the true worship, to suppress all false, and that by the power of the sword; and therefore consequently they must judge and determine what the true is, and what the false:—

And since the magistrate is bound, by these authors' principles, to see the church, the church officers, and members do their duty, he must therefore judge what is the church's duty, and when she performs or not performs it, or when she exceeds; so likewise when the ministers perform their duty, or when they exceed it:—

And if the magistrate must judge, then certainly by his own eye, and not by the eyes of others, though assembled in a national or general council:—

Then also, upon his judgment must the people rest, as upon the mind and judgment of Christ, or else it must be confessed that he has no such power left him by Christ to compel the souls of men in matters of God's worship.

Secondly, concerning the apocrypha writings and homilies to be urged by the magistrate to be read unto the people as the oracles of God:

Pentateuch, the Psalms and Song of Solomon. He was spoken of highly by John Cotton in *The Way of Congregational Churches Cleared.*

I ask, if the homilies of England contain not in them much precious and heavenly matter? Secondly, if they were not penned, at least many of them, by excellent men for learning, holiness, and witness of Christ's truth incomparable?[106] Thirdly, were they not authorized by that most rare and pious prince, Edward VI, then head of the church of England? With what great solemnity and rejoicing were they received of thousands!

Yet now, behold their children after them sharply censure them for Apocrypha writings, and homilies thrust into the room of the word of God, and so falling into the consideration of a false and counterfeit scripture.

I demand of these worthy men whether a servant of God might then lawfully have refused to read or hear such a false scripture?

Secondly, if so, whether King Edward might have lawfully compelled such a man to yield and submit, or else have persecuted him; yea, according to the authors' principles, whether he ought to have spared him; because after the admonitions of such pious and learned men, this man shall now prove a heretic, and as an obstinate person sinning against the light of his own conscience?

In this case what shall the conscience of the subject do, awed by the dread of the Most High? What shall the magistrate do, zealous for his glorious reformation, being constantly persuaded by his clergy of his lieutenantship received from Christ ?

Again, what privilege have those worthy servants of God, either in Old or New England, to be exempted from the mistakes into which those glorious worthies in King Edward's time did fall?[107] And if so, what bloody conclusions are presented to the world, persuading men to pluck up by the roots from the land of the living all such as seem in their eyes heretical or obstinate!

---

[106] A book of homilies which were to be read in every church each week. "The composition of the first book of Homilies is generally attributed to Cranmer, Ridley, Latimer, Hopkins, and Becon. Jewel is said to have had the largest share in the second, although Archbishop Parker speaks of them as 'revised and finished, with a second part, by him and other bishops.' The first edition of the first book appeared in July, 1547." Short's *History of the Church of England,* chapter viii. Cited by Caldwell. One of the Puritans' objections to the Book of Common Prayer was its use of lessons from the Apocrypha.

[107] "Reformations are fallible." (Williams' footnote)

CHAPTER CIX

Peace. Dear Truth, what dark and dismal bloody paths do we walk in? How is your name and mine in all ages cried up, yet as an English flag in a Spanish bottom, not in truth, but dangerous treachery and abuse both of truth and peace!

We are now come to the eleventh head, which concerns the magistrates' power in worship.

"First, they have power," say they, "to reform things in the worship of God in a church corrupted, and to establish the pure worship of God, defending the same by the power of the sword against all those who shall attempt to corrupt it.

"For first, the reigning of idolatry and corruption in religion is imputed to the want of a king. (Jud. 17: 5, 6)

"Secondly, remissness in reforming religion is a fault imputed to them who suffered the high places in Israel, and in Gallio who cared not for such things. (Acts 18 [17])

"Thirdly, forwardness this way is a duty not only for kings in the Old Testament, but for princes under the New. (1 Tim. 2:2; Rom. 13:4; Isa. 49:23) Neither did the kings of Israel reform things amiss as types of Christ, but as civil magistrates, and so exemplary to all Christians. And here reformation in religion is commendable in a Persian king. (Ezra 7:23) And it is well known that remissness in princes of Christendom in matters of religion and worship, devolving the care thereof only to the clergy, and so setting the horns thereof upon the church's head, has been the cause of anti-Christian inventions, usurpations, and corruptions in the worship and temple of God.

"Secondly, they have not power to press upon the churches stinted prayers,[108] or set liturgies, whether new or old, popish or others, under color of uniformity of worship, or moral goodness of them both for matter and form, conceiving our arguments sent to our brethren in England concerning this question to evince this truth.[109]

---

[108] Fixed or limited by authority or custom; a set liturgical form, as opposed to free prayers.

[109] "A letter of many ministers in Old England requesting the judgment of their reverend brethren in New England concerning nine positions: written A.D. 1637. Together with their answer thereto returned, anno. 1639," Published 1643. The first position is "that a stinted form of prayer, or set liturgy, is unlawful."

"Thirdly, they have no power to press upon the churches, neither by law, as has been said before, nor by proclamation and command, any sacred significant ceremonies, whether more or less popish or Jewish rite, or any other device of man, be it never so little in the worship of God, under what color soever of indifferency, civility, using them without opinion of sanctity, public peace, or obedience to righteous authority, as surplice, cross, kneeling at sacrament, salt and spittle in baptism, holy days; they having been so accursed of God, so abused by man, the imposing of some ever making way for the urging of more, the receiving of some making the conscience bow to the burden of all.

"Fourthly, they have not power to govern and rule the acts of worship in the church of God.

"It is with a magistrate in a state in respect of the acts of those who worship in a church as it is with a prince in a ship, wherein, though he be governor of their persons, else he should not be their prince, yet, is not governor of the actions of the mariners, then he should be pilot: indeed if the pilot shall manifestly err in his action, he may reprove him, and so any other passenger may: or if he offend against the life and goods of any, he may in due time and place civilly punish him, which no other passenger can do; for, it is proper to Christ, the head of the church, as to prescribe so to rule the actions of his own worship in the ways of his servants. (Isa. 9:6,7) The government of the church is upon his shoulder, which no civil officer ought to attempt. And therefore magistrates have no power to limit a minister, either to what he shall preach or pray, or in what manner they shall worship God, lest hereby they shall advance themselves above Christ, and limit his Spirit."

Truth. In this general head are proposed two things. First, what the magistrate ought to do positively, concerning the worship of God.

Secondly. What he may do in the worship of God.

What he ought to do is comprised in these particulars:—

First, he ought to reform the worship of God when it is corrupted.

Secondly, he ought to establish a pure worship of God.

Thirdly, he ought to defend it by the sword: he ought to restrain idolatry by the sword, and to cut off offenders, as former passages have opened.

For the proof of this positive part of his duty, are propounded three sorts of scriptures.

First, from the practice of the kings of Israel and Judah.

Secondly, some from the New Testament.

Thirdly, from the practice of kings of other nations.

Unto which I answer,—

First, concerning this latter, the Babylonian and Persian kings—Nebuchadnezzar, Cyrus, Darius, Artaxerxes—I conceive I have sufficiently before proved that these idolatrous princes making such acts concerning the God of Israel, whom they did not worship nor know, nor meant so to do, did only permit, and tolerate, and countenance the Jewish worship; and out of strong convictions that this God of Israel was able to do them good, as well as their own gods, to bring wrath upon them and their kingdoms, as they believed their own also did, in which respect all the kings of the world may be easily brought to the like; but are no precedent or pattern for all princes and civil magistrates in the world, to challenge or assume the power of ruling or governing the church of Christ, and of wearing the spiritual crown of the Lord, which he alone wears in a spiritual way by his officers and governors after his own holy appointment.

Secondly, for those of the New Testament I have, as I believe, fully and sufficiently answered.

So also this prophecy of Isaiah 49 [23].

Lastly, however I have often touched those scriptures produced from the practice of the kings of Israel and Judah, yet, because so great a weight of this controversy lies upon this precedent of the Old Testament, from the duties of this nature enjoined to those kings and governors and their practices, obeying or disobeying, accordingly commended or reproved, I shall, with the help of Christ Jesus, the true King of Israel, declare and demonstrate how weak and brittle this supposed pillar of marble is to bear up and sustain such a mighty burden and weight of so many high concernments as are laid upon it. In which I shall evidently prove that the state of Israel as a national state, made up of spiritual and civil power, so far as it attended upon the spiritual, was merely figurative, and typing out the Christian churches consisting of both Jews and Gentiles, enjoying the true power of the Lord Jesus, establishing, reforming, correcting, defending in all cases concerning the kingdom and government.

CHAPTER CX

Peace. Blessed be the God of truth, the God of peace, who has so long preserved us in this our retired conference without interruptions. His mercy still shields us while you express and I listen to that so much imitated, yet most inimitable state of Israel.

Yet, before you descend to particulars, dear Truth, let me cast one mite into your great treasury, concerning that instance, just now mentioned, of the Persian kings.

Methinks those precedents of Cyrus, Darius, and Artaxerxes, are strong against New England's tenent and practice. Those princes professedly gave free permission and bountiful encouragement to the consciences of the Jews to use and practice their religion, which religion was most eminently contrary to their own religion and their country's worship.

Truth. I shall, sweet Peace, with more delight pass on these rough ways, from your kind acceptance and unwearied patience in attention.

In this discovery of that vast and mighty difference between that state of Israel and all other states, only to be matched and paralleled by the Christian church or Israel, I shall select some main and principal considerations concerning that state, wherein the irreconcilable differences and disproportion may appear.

First, I shall consider the very land and country of Canaan itself, and present some considerations proving it to be a nonesuch.[110]

First, this land was espied out, and chosen by the Lord, out of all the countries of the world, to be the seat of his church and people. (Ezek. 20:6)

But now there is no respect of earth, of places, or countries with the Lord. So testified the Lord Jesus Christ himself to the woman of Samaria (John 4 [21]), professing that neither at that mountain, nor at Jerusalem, should men worship the Father.

While that national state of the church of the Jews remained, the tribes were bound to go up to Jerusalem to worship. (Psalms 122) But now, *in every nation,* not the whole land or country as it was with Canaan, *he that fears God and works righteousness is accepted with him.* (Acts 10:35) This then appeared in that large commission of the Lord

---

[110] A person or thing without equal.

Jesus to his first ministers: *Go into all nations* [Matthew 28:19], and not only into Canaan, to carry tidings of mercy, etc.

Secondly, the former inhabitants thereof, seven great and mighty nations (Deut. 7[1]), were all devoted to destruction by the Lord's own mouth, which was to be performed by the impartial hand of the children of Israel, without any sparing or showing mercy.

But so now it has not pleased the Lord to devote any people to present destruction, commanding his people to kill and slay without covenant or compassion. (Deut. 7:2)

Where have emperors, kings, or generals an immediate call from God to destroy whole cities, city after city, men, women, children, old and young, as Joshua practiced? (Josh. 6, 10, etc.)

This did Israel to these seven nations that they themselves might succeed them in their cities, habitations, and possessions.

This only is true in a spiritual antitype, when God's people by the sword, the two-edged sword of God's Spirit, slay the ungodly and become heirs, yea, fellow heirs with Christ Jesus. (Rom. 8[17]) God's meek people inherit the earth. (Matthew 5[5]) They mystically, like Noah (Heb. 11[7]), condemn the whole unbelieving world, both by present and future sentence. (1 Cor. 6:2)

CHAPTER CXI

Thirdly, the very materials, the gold and silver of the idols of this land, were odious and abominable, and dangerous to the people of Israel, that they might not desire it nor take it to themselves (Deut. 7:25,26), lest themselves also become a curse, and like unto those cursed, abominable things. Whereas we find not any such accursed nature in the materials of idols or images now; but that the idolatrous forms being changed, the silver and gold may be cast and coined, and other materials lawfully employed and used.

Yet this we find in the antitype, that gold, silver: yea, house, land: yea, wives, children: yea, life itself, as they allure and draw us from God in Christ, are to be abominated and hated by us, without which hatred and indignation, against the most plausible and pleasing enticings, from Christ Jesus, it is impossible for any man to be a true Christian. (Luke 14:26)

Fourthly, this land, this earth, was a holy land. (Zechariah 2:12) Ceremonially and typically holy, fields, gardens, orchards, houses, etc., which holiness the world knows not now in one land or country, house, field, garden, etc., one above another.

Yet in the spiritual land of Canaan, the Christian church, all things are made holy and pure, in all lands, to the pure (Titus 1[16]); meats and drinks are sanctified, that is, dedicated to the holy use of the thankful believers (I Timothy 4 [5]); yea, and the unbelieving husband, wife, and their children, are sanctified and made holy to believers, insomuch that that golden inscription, peculiar to the forehead of the high priest, "Holiness to Jehovah,"[111] shall be written upon the very bridles of the horses, as all are dedicated to the service of Christ Jesus in the gospel's peace and holiness.

Fifthly, the Lord expressly calls it his own land (Lev. 25:3; Hos. 9:3), Jehovah's land, a term proper unto spiritual Canaan, the church of God, which must needs be in respect of his choice of that land to be the seat and residence of his church and ordinances.

But now the partition-wall is broken down, and in respect of the Lord's special propriety to one country more than another, what difference between Asia and Africa, between Europe and America, between England and Turkey, London and Constantinople?

This land, among many other glorious titles given to it, was called Emanuel's land, that is, God with us, Christ his land, or Christian land. (Isa. 8:8)

But now, Jerusalem from above is not material and earthly, but spiritual. (Gal. 4[25]; Heb. 12[22]) Material Jerusalem is no more the Lord's city than Jericho, Nineveh, or Babel, in respect of place or country: for even at Babel literal was a church of Jesus Christ. (1 Pet. 5 [13])

It is true that Antichrist has christened all those countries whereon the whore sits (Rev. 17), with the title of Christ's land, or Christian land.

And Hondius,[112] in his map of the Christian world, makes this land to extend to all Asia, a great part of Africa, all Europe, and a vast part of America, even so far as his unchristian christenings has gone. But as every false Christ has false teachers, false Christians, false faith, hope, love, etc.,

---

[111] Exodus 28:36, 39:30.
[112] Joffe Hondius (1546-1611), Dutch engraver and geographer, who enlarged and improved the Grand Atlas of Mercator.

and in the end false salvation, so does he also counterfeit the false name of Christ, Christians, Christian land or country.

Sixthly, this land was to keep her Sabbaths unto God. Six years they were to sow their fields, and prune their vines, but in the seventh year they were not to sow their fields, nor prune their vineyards, but to eat that which grew of itself or own accord.

But such observations does not God now lay upon any fields, vineyards, etc., under the gospel.

Yet, in the spiritual land of Canaan, the true church, there is a spiritual soul-rest or Sabbath, a quiet depending upon God, a living by faith in him, a making him our portion, and casting all care upon him who cares for us [1 Pet. 5:7]: yea, sometimes he feeds his by immediate, gracious works of providence, when comforts arise out of the earth, without secondary means or causes, as here, or as elsewhere, manna descended from heaven.

Seventhly, such portions and possessions of lands, fields, houses, vineyards, were sold with caution or proviso of returning again in the year of jubilee to the right owners. (Lev. 25:23)

Such cautions, such provisos, are not now enjoined by God in the sale of lands, fields, inheritances, nor no such jubilee or redemption to be expected.

Yea, this also finds a fulfilling in the spiritual Canaan, or church of God, unto which the silver trumpet of jubilee, the gospel, has sounded a spiritual restitution of all their spiritual rights and inheritances, which either they have lost in the fall of the first man Adam, or in their particular falls, when they are captive, and sold unto sin (Rom. 7 [14]), or, lastly, in the spiritual captivity of Babel's bondage. How sweet then is the name of a Savior, in whom is the joyful sound of a deliverance and redemption!

Eighthly, this land or country was a figure or type of the kingdom of heaven above, begun here below in the church and kingdom of God. (Heb. 4:8; 11:9,10) Hence was a birthright so precious in Canaan's land: hence Naboth so inexorable and resolute in refusing to part with his inheritance to King Ahab, counting all Ahab's seeming reasonable offers most unreasonable, as soliciting him to part with a garden plot of Canaan's land, though his refusal cost him his very life.

What land, what country now is Israel's parallel and antitype, but that holy mystical nation, the church of God, peculiar and called out to him out of every nation and country, (I Peter 2:9) in which every true spiritual Naboth has his spiritual inheritance, which he dares not part with, though it be to his king or sovereign, and though such his refusal cost him this present life?

CHAPTER CXII

Peace. Doubtless that Canaan land was not a pattern for all lands: it was a nonesuch, unparalleled, and unmatchable.

Truth. Many other considerations of the same nature I might annex, but I pick here and there a flower, and pass on to a second head concerning the people themselves, wherein the state of the people shall appear unmatchable: but only by the true church and Israel of God.

First, the people of Israel were all the seed or offspring of one man, Abraham (Psa. 105:6), and so downward the seed of Isaac and Jacob, hence called the Israel of God, that is, wrestlers and prevailers with God, distinguished into twelve tribes, all sprung out of Israel's loins.

But now, few nations of the world but are a mixed seed; the people of England especially: the Britons, Picts, Romans, Saxons, Danes, and Normans, by a wonderful providence of God, being become one English people.

Only the spiritual Israel and seed of God, the new born, are but one. Christ is the seed (Gal. 3[16]), and they only that are Christ's are only Abraham's seed, and heirs according to the promise.

This spiritual seed is the only antitype of the former figurative and typical, a seed which all Christians ought to propagate, yea, even the unmarried men and women who are not capable of natural offspring, for thus is this called the seed of Christ, who lived and died unmarried. (Isa. 49:21)

Secondly, this people was selected and separated to the Lord, his covenant and worship, from all the people and nations of the world beside, to be his peculiar and only people. (Lev. 20:26, etc.)

Therefore, such as returned from Babylon to Jerusalem, they separated themselves to eat the Passover. (Ezra 6 [21]) And in that solemn humiliation and confession before the Lord (Neh. 9[2]) the children of Israel separated themselves from all strangers.

This separation of theirs was so famous that it extended not only to circumcision, the Passover, and matters of God's worship, but even to temporal and civil things: thus (Ezra 9), they separated or put away their very wives, which they had taken of the strange nations, contrary to the commandment of the Lord.

But where has the God of heaven, in the gospel, separated whole nations or kingdoms, English, Scotch, Iris, French, Dutch, etc., as a peculiar people and antitype of the people of Israel? Yea, where the least footing in all the scripture for a national church after Christ's coming?

Can any people in the world pattern this sampler but the new-born Israel, such as fear God in every nation (Acts 10:35), commanded to come forth, and separate from all unclean things or persons (2 Cor. 6 [17]), and though not bound to put away strange wives as Israel did, because of that peculiar respect upon them in civil things, yet to be holy or set apart to the Lord in all manner of' civil conversation (1 Pet. 1[1]): only to marry in the Lord, yea, and to marry as if they married not (1 Corinthians 7[29]): yea, to hate wife and children, father, mother, house, and land, yea, and life itself for the Lord Jesus.(Luke 14[26])

Thirdly, this seed of Abraham thus separate from all people unto the Lord was wonderfully redeemed and brought from Egypt bondage, through the Red Sea, and the wilderness, unto the land of Canaan, by many strange signs and wonderful miracles, wrought by the outstretched hand of the Lord, famous and dreadful, and to be admired by all succeeding peoples and generations. *Ask now from one side of the heaven unto the other, whether there has been such a thing as this?* etc. (Deut. 4:32-34)

And we may ask again from one side of the heaven unto the other, whether the Lord has now so miraculously redeemed and brought unto himself any nation or people, as he did this people of' Israel.

Peace. The English, Scotch, Dutch, etc., are apt to make themselves the parallels, as wonderfully come forth of popery, etc.

Truth. 1. But first, whole nations are no churches under the gospel.

2. Secondly, bring the nations of Europe professing Protestantism to the balance of the sanctuary, and ponder well whether the body, bulk, the general, or one hundredth part of such peoples, be truly turned to God from popery:—

Who knows not how easy it is to turn, and turn, and turn again, whole nations from one religion to another?

Who knows not that within the compass of one poor span of twelve years' revolution, all England has become from half-papist, half-Protestant, to be absolute Protestants; from absolute Protestants, to absolute papists; from absolute papists, changing as fashions, to absolute Protestants?

I will not say, as some worthy witnesses of Christ have uttered, that all England and Europe must again submit their fair necks to the pope's yoke; but this I say, many scriptures concerning the destruction of the beast and the whore look that way. And I add, they that feel the pulse of the people seriously must confess that a victorious sword and a Spanish Inquisition will soon make millions face about as they were in the forefathers' time.

CHAPTER CXIII

Peace. Oh! that the steersmen of the nations might remember this, be wise and kiss the Son, lest he go on in this his dreadful anger, and dash them in pieces here and eternally.

Truth. I therefore, thirdly, add, that only such as are Abraham's seed, circumcised in heart, new-born, Israel (or wrestlers with God), are the antitype of the former Israel; these are only the holy nation (1 Pet. 2[9]), wonderfully redeemed from the Egypt of this world (Titus 2:14), brought through the Red Sea of baptism (1 Cor. 10 [2]), through the wilderness of afflictions, and of the peoples (Deut. 8; Ezek. 20), into the kingdom of heaven begun below, even that Christian land of promise where flow the everlasting streams and rivers of spiritual milk and honey.

Fourthly, all this people universally, in typical and ceremonial respect, were holy and clean in this their separation and sequestration unto God (Exod. 19:5). Hence, even in respect of their natural birth in that land, they were an holy seed, and Ezra makes it the matter of his great complaint (Ezra 9:1, 2), *The holy seed have mingled themselves.*

But where is now that nation, or country, upon the face of the earth, thus clean and holy unto God, and bound to so many ceremonial cleansings and purgings?

Are not all the nations of the earth alike clean unto God? Or rather, alike unclean, until it pleases the Father of mercies to call some out to the knowledge and grace of his Son, making them to see their filthiness, and strangeness from the commonweal of Israel, and to wash in the blood of the Lamb of God?

This taking away the difference between nation and nation, country and country, is most fully and admirably declared in that great vision of all sorts of living creatures presented unto Peter (Acts 10), whereby it pleased the Lord to inform Peter of the abolishing of the difference between Jew and Gentile in any holy or unholy, clean or unclean respect.

Fifthly—not only to speak of all, but to select one or two more—this people of Israel in that national state were a type of all the children of God in all ages under the profession of the gospel, who are therefore called the children of Abraham, and the Israel of God (Gal. 3; 6[16]), a kingly priesthood and holy nation (1 Pet. 2:9), in a clear and manifest antitype to the former Israel (Exod. 19:6).

Hence, Christians now are figuratively, in this respect, called Jews (Rev. 3[9]), where lies a clear distinction of the true and false Christian under the consideration of the true and false Jew: *Behold I will make them of the synagogue of Satan that say they are Jews and are not, but do lie* (Rev. 3[9]). But such a typical respect we find not now upon any people, nation, or country of the whole world; but out of all nations, tongues, and languages is God pleased to call some, and redeem them to himself (Rev. 5:9), and has made no difference between the Jews and Gentiles, Greeks and Scythians (Gal. 3[28]), who by regeneration, or second birth, become the Israel of God (Gal. 6[16]), the temple of God (1 Cor. 3[17]), and the true Jerusalem. (Heb. 12[22])

Lastly, all this whole nation or people, as they were of one typical seed of Abraham, and sealed with a shameful and painful ordinance of cutting off the foreskin, which differenced them from all the world beside: so also were they bound to such and such solemnities of figurative worships. Among many others I shall end this passage concerning the people with a famous observation out of Numbers 9:13, viz., all that whole nation was bound to celebrate and keep the feast of the Passover in his season, or else they were to be put to death. But does God require a whole nation, country, or kingdom now thus to celebrate the spiritual passover, the supper and feast of the Lamb Christ Jesus, at such a time once a year, and that whosoever shall not so do shall be put to death? What horrible profanations, what gross hypocrisies, yea, what wonderful desolations, sooner or later, must needs follow upon such a course!

It is true, the people of Israel, brought into covenant with God in Abraham, and so successively born in covenant with God, might, in that state of a national church, solemnly covenant and swear that whosoever would not seek Jehovah, the God of Israel, should be put to death (2 Chr. 15[12,13], whether small or great, whether man or woman.

But may whole nations or kingdoms now, according to any one tittle expressed by Christ Jesus to that purpose, follow that pattern of Israel, and put to death all, both men and women, great and small, that according to the rules of the gospel are not born again, penitent, humble, heavenly, patient? etc. What a world of hypocrisy from hence is practiced by thousands, that for fear will stoop to give that God their bodies in a form, whom yet in truth their hearts affect not!

Yea, also what a world of profanation of the holy name and holy ordinances of the Lord, in prostituting the holy things of God, like the vessels of the sanctuary (Dan. 5), to profane, impenitent, and unregenerate persons!

Lastly, what slaughters, both of men and women, must this necessarily bring into the world, by the insurrections and civil wars about religion and conscience! Yea, what slaughters of the innocent and faithful witnesses of Christ Jesus, who choose to be slain all the day long for Christ's sake [Rom. 8:36; Psa. 44:22], and to fight for their Lord and Master Christ, only with spiritual and Christian weapons!

CHAPTER CXIV

Peace. It seems, dear Truth, a mighty gulf between that people and nation, and the nations of the world then extant and ever since.

Truth. As sure as the blessed substance to all those shadows, Christ Jesus, is come, so unmatchable and never to be paralleled by any national state was that Israel in the figure, or shadow.

And yet the Israel of God now, the regenerate or new born, the circumcised in heart by repentance and mortification, who willingly submit unto the Lord Jesus as their only King and Head, may fitly parallel and answer that Israel in the type, without such danger of hypocrisy, of such horrible profanations, and of firing the civil state in such bloody combustions as all ages have brought forth upon this compelling a whole nation or kingdom to be the antitype of Israel.

Peace. Were this light entertained, some hopes would shine forth for my return and restoration.

Truth. I have yet to add a third consideration, concerning the kings and governors of that land and people.

They were to be, unless in their captivities, of their brethren, members of the true church of God: as appears in the history of Moses, the elders of Israel, and the judges and kings of Israel.But first, who can deny but that there may be now many lawful governors, magistrates, and kings in the nations of the world, where is no true church of Jesus Christ?

Secondly, we know the many excellent gifts wherewith it has pleased God to furnish many, enabling them for public service to their countries both in peace and war, as all ages and experience testify, on whose souls he has not yet pleased to shine in the face of Jesus Christ: which gifts and talents must all lie buried in the earth, unless such persons may lawfully be called and chosen to, and improved in public service, notwithstanding their different or contrary conscience or worship.

Thirdly, if none but true Christians, members of Christ Jesus, might be civil magistrates, and publicly entrusted with civil affairs, then none but members of churches, Christians, should be husbands of wives, fathers of children, masters of servants. But against this doctrine the whole creation, the whole world, may justly rise up in arms, as not only contrary to true piety, but common humanity itself. For if a commonweal be lawful among men that have not heard of God nor Christ, certainly their officers, ministers, and governors must be lawful also.

Fourthly, it is notoriously known to be the dangerous doctrine professed by some papists that princes degenerating from their religion and turning heretics are to be deposed, and their subjects actually discharged from their obedience. Which doctrine all such must necessarily hold, however most loath to own it, that hold the magistrate guardian of both tables; and consequently such an one as is enabled to judge, yea, and to demonstrate to all men the worship of God: yea, and being thus governor and head of the church, he must necessarily be a part of it himself; which when by heresy he falls from—though it may be by truth, miscalled heresy—he falls from his calling of magistracy, and is utterly disabled from his (pretended) guardianship and government of the church.

Lastly, we may remember the practice of the Lord Jesus and his followers, commanding and practicing Christ's obedience to the higher powers, though we find not one civil magistrate a Christian in all the first churches. But contrarily, the civil magistrate at that time was the bloody beast, made up—as Daniel seems to imply concerning the Roman state (Dan. 7:7)—of the lion, the bear, and the leopard. (Rev. 13:2)

CHAPTER CXV

Peace. By these weights we may try the weight of that commonly received and not questioned opinion, viz., that the civil state and the spiritual, the church and the commonweal, they are like Hippocrates' twins, they are born together, grow up together, laugh together, weep together, sicken and die together.

Truth. A witty, yet a most dangerous fiction of the father of lies, who, hardened in rebellion against God, persuades God's people to drink down such deadly poison, though he knows the truth of these five particulars, which I shall remind you of:

First, many flourishing states in the world have been and are at this day, which hear not of Jesus Christ, and, therefore have not the presence and concurrence of a church of Christ with them.

Secondly, there have been many thousands of God's people, who in their personal estate and life of grace were awake to God; but in respect of church estate, they knew no other than a church of dead stones, the parish church; or though some light be of late come in through some cranny, yet they seek not after, or least of all are joined to any true church of God, consisting of living and believing stones.

So that by these New English ministers' principles, not only is the door of calling to magistracy shut against natural and unregenerate men, though excellently fitted for civil offices, but also against the best and ablest servants of God, except they be entered into church estate: so that thousands of God's own people, excellently qualified, not knowing or not entering into such a church estate, shall not be accounted fit for civil services.

Thirdly, admit that a civil magistrate be neither a member of a true church of Christ, if any be in his dominions, nor in his person fear God, yet may he (possibly) give free permission without molestation, yea, and sometimes encouragement and assistance, to the service and church of God. Thus, we find Abraham permitted to build and set up an altar to his God wheresoever he came among the idolatrous nations in the land of Canaan. Thus Cyrus proclaims liberty to all the people of God in his dominions, freely to go up and build the temple of God at Jerusalem, and Artaxerxes after him confirmed it.

Thus, the Roman emperors, and governors under them, permitted the church of God, the Jews, in the Lord Christ's time, their temple and worship, although in civil things they were subject to the Romans.

Fourthly, the scriptures of truth and the records of time concur in this, that the first churches of Christ Jesus, the lights, patterns, and precedents to all succeeding ages, were gathered and governed without the aid, assistance, or countenance of any civil authority, from which they suffered great persecutions for the name of the Lord Jesus professed among them.

The nations, rulers, and kings of the earth tumultuously rage against the Lord and his anointed. (Psa. 2:1,2) Yet, verse 6, it has pleased the Father to set the Lord Jesus King upon his holy hill of Zion.

Christ Jesus would not be pleased to make use of the civil magistrate to assist him in his spiritual kingdom, nor would he yet be daunted or discouraged in his servants by all their threats and terrors: for *love is strong as death*, and the coals thereof give a most vehement flame, and are not quenched by all the waters and floods of mightiest opposition. (Cant. 8[6,7])

Christ's church is like a chaste and loving wife, in whose heart is fixed her husband's love, who has found the tenderness of his love towards her, and has been made fruitful by him, and therefore seeks she not the smiles, nor fears the frowns of all the emperors in the world to bring her Christ unto her, or keep him from her.

Lastly, we find in the tyrannical usurpations of the Romish Antichrist, the ten horns—which some of good note conceive to be the ten kingdoms into which the Roman empire was quartered and divided—are expressly said (Rev. 17:13) to have one mind to give their power and strength unto the beast; yea, verse 17, their kingdom unto the beast, until the words of God shall be fulfilled. Whence it follows that all those nations that are gilded over with the name of Christ have under that mask or vizard (as some executioners and tormenters in the Inquisition use to torment) persecuted the Lord Jesus Christ, either with a more open, gross, and bloody, or with a more subtle, secret, and gentle violence.

Let us cast our eyes about, turn over the records, and examine the experience of past and present generations, and see if all particular observations amount not to this sum, viz., that the great whore has committed fornication with the kings of the earth, and made drunk thereof nations with the cup of the wine of her fornications: in which drunkenness and whoredom (as whores use to practice) she has robbed the kings and nations of their power and strength, and Jezebel-like, having procured the kings' names and seals, she drinks drunk (Rev. 17[6]) with the blood of Naboth, who, because he dares not part with his rightful inheritance in the land of Canaan, the blessed land of promise and salvation in Christ, as a traitor to the civil state and blasphemer against God, she, under the color of a day of humiliation in prayer and fasting, stones to death.

CHAPTER CXVI

Peace. Dear Truth, how are you hidden from the eyes of men in these mysteries? How should men weep abundantly with John, that the Lamb may please to open these blessed seals unto them! [Revelation 5:4]

Truth. Oh, that men more prized their Maker's fear! Then should they be more acquainted with their Maker's counsels, for his secret is with them that fear him. (Psa. 25[14])

I pass on to a second difference.

The kings of Israel and Judah were all solemnly anointed with oil (Psa. 89:20),[113] *I have found David my servant, with my oil have I anointed him.* Whence the kings of Israel and Judah were honored with that mystical and glorious title of the anointed, or Christ of the Lord, Lamentations 4:20, *the breath of our nostrils, the anointed of Jehovah, was taken in their pits,* &c.

Which anointing and title however, the man of sin, together with the crown and diadem of spiritual Israel, the church of God, he has given to some of the kings of the earth, that so he may in lieu thereof dispose of

---

[113] Williams mistakenly cites Psalm 39:20.

their civil crowns the easier: yet shall we find it an incommunicable privilege and prerogative of the saints and people of God.

For as the Lord Jesus himself in the antitype was not anointed with material but spiritual oil (Psa. 45 [7]), with *the oil of gladness*; and (Luke 4:18 from Isaiah 61:1)[114] with the Spirit of God, *The Spirit of the Lord is upon me, the Lord hath anointed me to preach good tidings,* etc.; so also all his members are anointed with the Holy Spirit of God. (2 Cor. 1:21; 1 John 2:20)

Hence is it that Christians rejoice in that name, as carrying the very express title of the anointed of the Lord; which most superstitiously and sacrilegiously has been applied only unto kings.

Peace. Oh! dear Truth, how does the great searcher of all hearts find out the thefts of the anti-Christian world! How are men carried in the dark they know not whither! How is that heavenly charge, *Touch not mine anointed,* etc. (Psa. 105[15]), common to all Christians, or anointed with Christ their head, by way of monopoly or privilege appropriated to kings and princes!

Truth. It will not be here unseasonable to call to mind that admirable prophecy (Ezek. 21:26,27), *Thus saith Jehovah God, remove the diadem, take away the crown; this shall not be the same; exalt him that is low, and abase him that is high; I will overturn, overturn, overturn, until he come whose right it is ; and I will give it him.* The matter is a crown and diadem to be taken from a usurper's head, and set upon the head of the right owner.

Peace. Doubtless this mystically intends the spiritual crown of' the Lord Jesus, for these many hundred years set upon the heads of the competitors and co-rivals of the Lord Jesus, upon whose glorious head, in his messengers and churches, the crown shall be established. The anointing, the title, and the crown and power, must return to the Lord Jesus in his saints, unto whom alone belongs his power and authority in ecclesiastical or spiritual cases.

---

[114] Williams mistakenly cites Luke 4:14.

CHAPTER CXVII

Truth. I therefore proceed to a third difference between those kings and governors of Israel and Judah, and all kings and rulers of the earth. Look upon the administrations of the kings of Israel and Judah, and well weigh the power and authority which those kings of Israel and Judah exercised in ecclesiastical and spiritual causes; and upon a due search we shall not find the same scepter of spiritual power in the hand of civil authority, which was settled in the hands of the kings of Israel and Judah.

David appointed the orders of the priests and singers, he brought the ark to Jerusalem, he prepared for the building of the temple, the pattern whereof he delivered to Solomon: yet David herein could not be a type of the kings and rulers of the earth, but of the king of heaven, Christ Jesus: for,

First, David, as he was a king, so was he also a prophet (Acts 2:30); and therefore a type, as Moses also was, of that great prophet, the Son of God. And they that plead for David's kingly power, must also by the same rule plead for his prophetical, by which he swayed the scepter of Israel in church affairs.

Secondly, it is expressly said (2 Chr. 28:11-13) that the pattern which David gave to Solomon, concerning the matter of the temple and worship of God, he had it by the Spirit, which was no other but a figure of the immediate inspiration of the Spirit of God unto the Lord Jesus, the true spiritual king of Israel (John 1:49), *Rabbi, thou art the Son of God; Rabbi, thou art the King of Israel.*

Again, what civil magistrate may now act as Solomon, a type of Christ, does act? (1 Kgs 2:26, 27) Solomon thrust out Abiathar from being priest unto Jehovah.

Peace. Some object that Abiathar was a man of death, ver. 26, worthy to die, as having followed Adonijah; and therefore Solomon executed no more than civil justice upon him.

Truth. Solomon remits the civil punishment, and inflicts upon him a spiritual; but by what right, but as he was king of the church, a figure of Christ?

Abiathar's life is spared with respect to his former good service in following after David; but yet he is turned out from the priesthood.

But now put the case: suppose that any of the officers of the New England churches should prove false to the state, and be discovered joining with a French Monsieur, or Spanish Don, thirsting after conquest and dominion, to further their invasions of that country; yet for some former faithful service to the state, he should not be adjudged to civil punishment:—I ask now, might their governors, or their general court (their parliament), depose such a man, a pastor, teacher, or elder, from his holy calling or office in God's house?

Or suppose, in a partial and corrupt state, a member or officer of a church should escape with his life upon the commission of murder, ought not a church of Christ upon repentance to receive him? I suppose it will not be said that he ought to execute himself; or that the church may use it civil sword against him. In these cases may such persons, spared in civil punishments for some reason of or by partiality of state, be punished spiritually by the civil magistrate, as Abiathar was? Let the very enemies of Zion be judges.

Secondly, if Solomon in thrusting out of Abiathar was a pattern and precedent unto all civil magistrates, why not also in putting Zadok in his room ([1 Kgs 2]35)? But against this the pope, the bishops, the Presbyterians, and the Independents, will all cry out against such a practice, in their several respective claims and challenges for their ministries.

We find the liberty of the subjects of Christ in the choice of an apostle (Acts 1), of a deacon (Acts 6), of elders (Acts 14), and guided by the assistance either of the apostles or evangelists (1 Tim. 1; Titus 1) without the least influence of any civil magistrate, which shows the beauty of their liberty.

The parliaments of England have by right free choice of their speaker: yet some princes have thus far been gratified as to nominate, yea, and implicitly to commend a speaker to them. Wise men have seen the evil consequences of those influences, though but in civil things; how much far greater and stronger are those snares when the golden keys of the Son of God are delivered into the hands of civil authority!

Peace. You know the noise raised concerning those famous acts of Asa, Hezekiah, Jehoshaphat, Josiah. What think you of the fast proclaimed by Jehoshaphat? (2 Chr. 20:3)

Truth. I find it to be the duty of kings and all in authority to encourage Christ's messengers of truth proclaiming repentance, etc.

But under the gospel, to enforce all natural and unregenerate people to acts of worship, what precedent has Christ Jesus given us?

First, it is true Jehoshaphat proclaimed a fast, etc.; but was he not in matters spiritual a type of Christ, the true king of Israel?

Secondly, Jehoshaphat calls the members of the true church to church service and worship of God.

But consider, if civil powers now may judge of and determine the actions of worship proper to the saints: if they may appoint the time of the church's worship, fasting, and prayer, etc., why may they not as well forbid those times which a church of Christ shall make choice of, seeing it is a branch of the same root to forbid what likes not, as well as to enjoin what pleases?

And if in those most solemn duties and exercises, why not also in other ordinary meetings and worships? And if so, where is the power of the Lord Jesus bequeathed to his ministers and churches, of which the power of those things was but a shadow?

CHAPTER CXVIII

Peace. The liberty of the subject sounds most sweet; London and Oxford both profess to fight for. How much infinitely more sweet is that true soul liberty according to Christ Jesus!

I know you would not take from Caesar aught, although it were to give to God; and what is God's and his people's I wish that Caesar may not take. Yet, for the satisfaction of some, be pleased to glance upon Josiah, his famous acts in the church of God, concerning the worship of God, the priests, Levites, and their services, compelling the people to keep the Passover, making himself a covenant before the Lord, and compelling all that were found in Jerusalem and Benjamin to stand to it.

Truth. To these famous practices of Josiah I shall parallel the practices of England's kings; and first, *de jure*, a word or two of their right: then, *de facto*, discuss what has been done.

First, *de jure.* Josiah was a precious branch of that royal root King David, who was immediately designed by God: and when the golden links of the royal chain broke in the usurpations of the Roman conqueror, it pleased the most wise God to send a Son of David, a Son of God, to begin again that royal line, to sit upon the throne of his father David. (Luke 1:32; Acts 2:30)

It is not so with the Gentile princes, rulers, and magistrates, whether monarchical, aristocratical, or democratical, who, though government in general be from God, yet, receive their callings, power, and authority, both kings and parliaments, mediately from the people.

Secondly, Josiah and those kings were kings and governors over the then true and only church of God national, brought into the covenant of God in Abraham, and so downward: and they might well be forced to stand to that covenant into which, with such immediate signs and miracles, they had been brought.

But what commission from Christ Jesus had Henry VIII, Edward VI, or any, Josiah-like, to force the many hundred thousands of English men and women, without such immediate signs and miracles that Israel had, to enter into a holy and spiritual covenant with the invisible God, the Father of spirits, or upon pain of death, as in Josiah's time, to stand to that which they never made, nor before evangelical repentance are possibly capable of?

Now secondly, *de facto,* let it be well remembered concerning the kings of England professing reformation. The foundation of all was laid in Henry VIII. The pope challenges to be the vicar of Christ Jesus here upon earth, to have power of reforming the church, redressing abuses, etc. Henry VIII falls out with the pope, and challenges that very power to himself of which he had despoiled the pope, as appears by that act of parliament establishing Henry VIII the supreme head and governor in all cases ecclesiastical, etc. It pleased the most high God to plague the pope by Henry VIII his means. But neither pope nor king can ever prove such power from Christ derived to either of them.

Secondly, as before intimated, let us view the works and acts of England's imitation of Josiah's practice. Henry VII leaves England under the slavish bondage of the pope's yoke. Henry VIII reforms all England to a new fashion, half papist, half Protestant. King Edward VI turns about the wheels of the state, and works the whole land to absolute Protestantism. Queen Mary, succeeding to the helm, steers a direct contrary course, breaks in pieces all that Edward wrought, and brings forth an old edition of England's reformation all popish. Mary not living out half her days, as the prophet speaks of bloody persons, Elizabeth, like Joseph, advances from the prison to the palace, and from the irons to the crown, she plucks up all her sister Mary's plants, and sounds a trumpet all Protestant.

What sober man stands not amazed at these revolutions? And yet, like mother like daughter: and how zealous are we, their offspring, for another impression, and better edition of a national Canaan, in imitation of Judah and Josiah, which, if attained, who knows how soon succeeding kings or parliaments will quite pull down and abrogate?

Thirdly, in all these formings and reformings, a national church of natural, unregenerate men was (like wax) the subject matter of all these forms and changes, whether popish or Protestant: concerning which national state, the time is yet to come whenever the Lord Jesus has given a word of institution and appointment.

CHAPTER CXIX

Peace. You bring to mind, dear Truth, a plea of some wiser papists for the pope's supremacy, viz., that it was no such exorbitant or unheard of power and jurisdiction, which the pope challenged, but the very same which a woman, Queen Elizabeth herself challenged, styling herself a papissa or she-pope: withal pleading, that in point of reason it was far more suitable that the Lord Jesus would delegate his power rather to a clergyman than a layman, as Henry VIII; or a woman, as his daughter Elizabeth.

Truth. I believe that neither one or the other hit the white,[115] yet I believe the papists' arrows fall the nearest to it in this particular, viz., that the government of the church of Christ should rather belong to such as profess a ministry or office spiritual, than to such as are merely temporal and civil.

So that in conclusion, the whole controversy concerning the government of Christ's kingdom or church, will be found to lie between the true and false ministry, both challenging the true commission, power, and keys from Christ.

Peace. This all glorious diadem of the kingly power of the Lord Jesus has been the eye-sore of the world, and that which the kings and rulers of the world have always lift up their hands unto.

The first report of a new king of the Jews puts Herod and all Jerusalem into frights; and the power of this most glorious King of kings

---

[115] "The central part of a target, which anciently was painted white." (Underhill) "Twas I won the wager, though you hit the white." Shakespeare, *Taming of the Shrew, V,ii.*

over the souls and consciences of men, or over their lives and worships, is still the white that all the princes of this world shoot at, and are enraged at the tidings of the true heir, the Lord Jesus, in his servants.

Truth. You well mind, dear Peace, a twofold exaltation of the Lord Jesus; one in the souls and spirits of men, and so he is exalted by all that truly love him, though yet remaining in Babel's captivity, and before they hearken to the voice of the Lord, "Come forth of Babel, my people."

A second exaltation of Christ Jesus, upon the throne of David his father, in his church and congregation, which is his spiritual kingdom here below.

I confess there is a tumultuous rage at his entrance into his throne in the soul and consciences of any of his chosen; but against his second exaltation in his true kingly power and government, either monarchical in himself, or ministerial in the hands of his ministers and churches, are mustered up, and shall be in the battles of Christ yet to be fought, all the powers of the gates of earth and hell.

But I shall mention one difference more between the kings of Israel and Judah, and all other kings and rulers of the Gentiles.

Those kings as kings of Israel were invested with a typical and figurative respect, with which now no civil power in the world can be invested.

They wore a double crown: first, civil; secondly, spiritual: in which respect they typed out the spiritual king crown of Israel, Christ Jesus.

When I say they were types, I make them not in all respects so to be; but as kings and governors over the church and kingdom of God, therein types.

Hence all those saviors and deliverers, which it pleased God to stir up extraordinarily to his people, Gideon, Baruch, Sampson, etc.; in that respect of their being saviors, judges, and deliverers of God's people, so were they types of Jesus Christ, either monarchically ruling by himself immediately, or ministerially by such whom he pleases to send to vindicate the liberties and inheritances of his people.

CHAPTER CXXA[116]

Peace. It must needs be confessed that since the kings of Israel were ceremonially anointed with oil: and, secondly, in that they sat upon the throne of David, which is expressly applied to Christ Jesus (Luke 1:32; Acts 2:30; John 1:49), their crowns were figurative and ceremonial; but some here question whether or no they were not types of civil powers and rulers now, when kings and queens shall be nursing fathers and nursing mothers, etc.

Truth. For answer unto such, let them first remember that the dispute lies not concerning the monarchical power of the Lord Jesus, the power of making laws, and making ordinances to his saints and subjects; but concerning a deputed and ministerial power, and this distinction the very pope himself acknowledges.

There are three great competitors for this deputed or ministerial power of the Lord Jesus.

First, the arch-vicar or Satan, the pretended vicar of Christ on earth, who sits as God over the temple of God, exalting himself not only above all that is called God, but over the souls and consciences of all his vassals, yea, over the Spirit of Christ, over the holy scriptures, yea, and God himself (Dan. 8,11; Rev. 15; together with 2 Thess. 2)

This pretender, although he professes to claim but the ministerial power of Christ, to declare his ordinances, to preach, baptize, ordain ministers, and yet does he upon the point challenge the monarchical or absolute power also, being full of self-exalting and blaspheming (Dan. 7:25; 11:36; Rev. 13:6), speaking blasphemies against the God of' heaven, thinking to change times and laws; but he is the son of perdition arising out of the bottomless pit, and comes to destruction (Rev. 17), for so has the Lord Jesus decreed to consume him by the breath of his mouth. (2 Thess. 2)

The second great competitor to this crown of the Lord Jesus is the civil magistrate, whether emperors, kings, or other inferior officers of state, who are made to believe, by the false prophets of the world, that they are the antitypes of' the kings of Israel and Judah, and wear the crown of Christ.

---

[116] There are two chapters numbered CXX in the first edition. That error has been repeated here, and designated A and B, in order to maintain a correlation with the first edition.

Under the wing of the civil magistrate do three great factions shelter themselves, and mutually oppose each other, striving as for life who shall sit down under the shadow of that arm of flesh.

First, the prelacy, who, though some extravagants of late have inclined to waive the king, and to creep under the wings of the pope, yet so far depends upon the king, that it is justly said they are the king's bishops.

Secondly, the presbytery, who, though in truth they ascribe not so much to the civil magistrate as some too grossly do, yet they give so much to the civil magistrate as to make him absolutely the head of the church: for, if they make him the reformer of the church, the suppressor of schismatics and heretics, the protector and defender of the church, etc., what is this, in true, plain English, but to make him the judge of the true and false church, judge of what is truth and what error, who is schismatical, who heretical, unless they make him only an executioner, as the pope does in his punishing of heretics?

I doubt not but the aristocratical government of Presbyterians may well subsist in a monarchy, not only regulated but also tyrannical; yet does it more naturally delight in the element of an aristocratical government of state, and so may properly be said to be—as the prelates the king's, so these—the state-bishop's.

The third, though not so great, yet growing faction is that (so called) Independent. I prejudice not the personal worth of any of the three sorts: this latter, as I believe this discourse has manifested, jumps with the prelates, and, though not more fully, yet more explicitly than the Presbyterians, casts down the crown of the Lord Jesus at the feet of the civil magistrate. And although they pretend to receive their ministry from the choice of two or three private persons in church covenant, yet would they fain persuade the mother of Old England to imitate her daughter New England's practice, viz., to keep out the Presbyterians, and only to embrace themselves, both as the state's and the people's bishops.

The third competition for this crown and power of the Lord Jesus is of those that separate both from one and the other, yet divided also among themselves into many several professions.

Of these, they that go furthest profess they must yet come nearer to the ways of the Son of God: and doubtless, so far as they have gone, they bid the most, and make the fairest plea for the purity and power of Christ Jesus. Let the rest of the inhabitants of the world be judges.

Let all the former well be viewed in their external state, pomp, riches, conformity to the world, etc. And on the other side, let the latter be considered, in their more thorough departure from sin and sinful worship, their condescending (generally) to the lowest and meanest contentments of this life, their exposing of themselves for Christ to greater sufferings, and their desiring no civil sword nor arm of flesh, but the two-edged sword of God's Spirit to try out the matter by: and then let the inhabitants of the world judge which come nearest to the doctrine, holiness, poverty, patience, and practice of the Lord Jesus Christ; and whether or no these latter deserve not so much of humanity and subjects' liberty, as (not offending the civil state) in the freedom of their souls, to enjoy the common air to breathe in.

CHAPTER CXXB

Peace. Dear Truth, you have shown me a little draught of Zion's sorrows, her children tearing out their mother's bowels. Oh! when will he that stablishes, comforts, and builds up Zion, look down from heaven, and have mercy on her? etc.

Truth. The vision yet does tarry, says Habakkuk [2:3], but will most surely come; and therefore the patient and believing must wait for it.

But to your last proposition, whether the kings of Israel and Judah were not types of civil magistrates. Now, I suppose, by what has been already spoken, these things will be evident:—

First, that those former types of the land, of the people, of their worships, were types and figures of a spiritual land, spiritual people, and spiritual worship under Christ. Therefore, consequently, their saviors, redeemers, deliverers, judges, kings, must also have their spiritual antitypes, and so consequently not civil but spiritual governors and rulers, lest the very essential nature of types, figures, and shadows be overthrown.

Secondly, although the magistrate by a civil sword might well compel that national church to the external exercise of their national worship: yet it is not possible, according to the rule of the New Testament, to compel whole nations to true repentance and regeneration, without which (so far as may be discerned true) the worship national and holy name of God is profaned and blasphemed.

An arm of flesh and sword of steel cannot reach to cut the darkness of the mind, the hardness and unbelief of the heart, and kindly operate upon the soul's affections to forsake a long-continued father's worship, and to embrace a new, though the best and truest. This work performs alone that sword out of the mouth of Christ, with two edges. (Rev. 1,3)

Thirdly, we have not one tittle in the New Testament of Christ Jesus concerning such a parallel, neither from himself nor from his ministers, with whom he conversed forty days after his resurrection, instructing them in the matters of his kingdom. (Acts 1[3])

Neither find we any such commission or direction given to the civil magistrate to this purpose, nor to the saints for their submission in matters spiritual, but the contrary. (Acts 4,5; 1 Cor. 7:23; Col. 2:18)

Fourthly, we have formerly viewed the very matter and essence of a civil magistrate, and find it the same in all parts of the world, wherever people live upon the face of the earth, agreeing together in towns, cities, provinces, kingdoms:—I say the same essentially civil, both from, [1.] the rise and fountain whence it springs, to wit, the people's choice and free consent; [2.] the object of it, viz., the commonweal, or safety of such a people in their bodies and goods, as the authors of this model have themselves confessed.

This civil nature of the magistrate we have proved to receive no addition of power from the magistrate being a Christian, no more than it receives diminution from his not being a Christian, even as the commonweal is a true commonweal, although it have not heard of Christianity; and Christianity professed in it, as in Pergamos, Ephesus, etc., makes it never no more a commonweal; and Christianity taken away, and the candlestick removed, makes it nevertheless a commonweal.

Fifthly, the Spirit of God expressly relates the work of the civil magistrate under the gospel (Rom. 13), expressly mentioning, as the magistrates' object, the duties of the civil of the second table, concerning the bodies and goods of the subject.

The reward or wages which people owe for such a work, to wit, not the contribution of the church for any spiritual work, but tribute, toll, custom, which are wages payable by all sorts of men, natives and foreigners, who enjoy the same benefit of public peace and commerce in the nation.

Sixthly, since civil magistrates, whether kings or parliaments, states, and governors, can receive no more in justice than what the people give:

and are, therefore, but the eyes, and hands, and instruments of the people, simply considered, without respect to this or that religion; it must inevitably follow, as formerly I have touched, that if magistrates have received their power from the people, then the greatest number of the people of every land have received from Christ Jesus a power to establish, correct, reform his saints and servants, his wife and spouse, the church: and she that by the express word of the Lord (Psa. 149[8]), binds kings in chains, and nobles in links of iron, must herself be subject to the changeable pleasures of the people of the world, which lies in wickedness (1 John 5[19]) even in matters of heavenly and spiritual nature.

Hence, therefore, in all controversies concerning the church, ministry and worship, the last appeal must come to the bar of the people or commonweal, where all may personally meet, as in some commonweals of small number, or in greater by their representatives.

Hence, then, no person esteemed a believer, and added to the church:

No officer chosen and ordained:—

No person cast forth and excommunicated, but as the commonweal and people please; and in conclusion, no church of Christ in this land or world, and consequently no visible Christ the head of it. Yea, yet higher, consequently no God in the world worshipped according to the institutions of Christ Jesus, except the several peoples of the nations of the world shall give allowance.

Peace. Dear Truth, oh! whither have our forefathers and teachers led us? Higher than to God himself, by these doctrines driven out of the world, you cannot rise: and yet so high must the inevitable and undeniable consequences of these their doctrines reach, if men walk by their own common principles.

Truth. I may therefore here seasonably add a seventh, which is a necessary consequence of all the former arguments, and an argument itself: viz., we find expressly a spiritual power of Christ Jesus in the hands of his saints, ministers, and churches, to be the true antitype of those former figures in all the prophecies concerning Christ's spiritual power. (Isa. 9; Dan. 7; Mic. 4, etc., compared with Luke 1:32; Acts 2:30; 1 Cor. 5; Matt. 18; Mark 13:34, etc.)

CHAPTER CXXI

Peace. Glorious and conquering Truth, methinks I see most evidently your glorious conquests: how mighty are your spiritual weapons (2 Corinthians 10[4]) to break down those mighty and strongholds and castles, which men have fortified themselves withal against you? Oh! that even the thoughts of men may submit and bow down to the captivity of Jesus Christ! [2 Cor. 10:5]

Truth. Your kind encouragement makes me proceed more cheerfully to a fourth difference from the laws and statutes of this land, different from all the laws and statutes of the world, and paralleled only by the laws and ordinances of spiritual Israel.

First, then, consider we the law-maker, or rather the law-publisher, or prophet, as Moses calls himself. (Deut. 18[16] and Acts 3[22]) He is expressly called that prophet who figured out Christ Jesus who was to come, like unto Moses, greater than Moses, as the son is greater than the servant.

Such lawgivers, or law-publishers, never had any state or people as Moses the type, or Christ Jesus, miraculously stirred up and sent as the mouth of God between God and his people.

Secondly, concerning the laws themselves: it is true, the second table contains the law of nature, the law moral and civil, yet such a law was also given to this people as never to any people in the world: such was the law of worship (Psalm 147) peculiarly given to Jacob, and God did not deal so with other nations: which laws for the matter of the worship in all those wonderful significant sacrifices, and for the manner by such a priesthood, such a place of tabernacle, and afterward of temple, such times and solemnities of festivals, were never to be paralleled by any other nation, but only by the true Christian Israel established by Jesus Christ among Jews and Gentiles throughout the world.

Thirdly, the law of the ten words (Deut. 10), the epitome of all the rest, it pleased the most high God to frame and pen twice with his own most holy and dreadful finger upon Mount Sinai, which he never did to any other nation before or since, but only to that spiritual Israel, the people and the church of God, in whose hearts of flesh he writes his laws, according to Jeremiah 31, Hebrews 8 and 10.

Peace. Such promulgation of such laws, by such a prophet, must needs be matchless and unparalleled.

Truth. In the fifth place, consider we the punishments and rewards annexed to the breach or observation of these laws.

First, those which were of a temporal and present consideration of this life: blessings and curses of all sorts opened at large (Lev. 26; Deut. 28), which cannot possibly be made good in any state, country, or kingdom, but in a spiritual sense in the church and kingdom of Christ.

The reason is this: such a temporal prosperity of outward peace and plenty of all things, of increase of children, of cattle, of honor, of health, of success, of victory, suits not temporally with the afflicted and persecuted estate of God's people now: and therefore spiritual and soul-blessedness must be the antitype, viz., in the midst of revilings, and all manner of evil speeches for Christ's sake, soul-blessedness. In the midst of afflictions and persecutions, soul-blessedness. (Matt. 5; Luke 6) And yet herein the Israel of God should enjoy their spiritual peace. (Gal. 6:16)

Out of that blessed temporal estate to be cast, or carried captive was their excommunication or casting out of God's sight. (2 Kgs 17:23) Therefore was the blasphemer, the false prophet, the idolater, to be cast out or cut off from this holy land: which punishment cannot be paralleled by the punishment of any state or kingdom in the world, but only by the excommunicating or outcasting of person or church from the fellowship of the saints and churches of Christ Jesus in the gospel.

And therefore, as before I have noted, the putting away of the false prophet by stoning him to death (Deut. 13), is fitly answered, and that in the very same words, in the antitype, when, by the general consent or stoning of the whole assembly, any wicked person is put away from among them, that is, spiritually cut off out of the land of the spiritually living, the people or church of God. (1 Cor. 5; Gal. 5)

Lastly, the great and high reward or punishment of the keeping or breach of these laws to Israel, was such as cannot suit with any state or kingdom in the world beside. The reward of the observation was life, eternal life. The breach of any one of these laws was death, eternal death, or damnation from the presence of the Lord (so Rom. 10, James 2), such a covenant God made not before nor since with any state or people in the world. For, *Christ is the end of the law for righteousness to every one that believeth.* (Rom. 10:4) And, *he that believeth in that Son of God, hath eternal life; he that believeth not hath not life, but is condemned already.* (John 3 [36]; 1 John 5)

CHAPTER CXXII

Peace. Dear Truth, you have most lively set forth the unparalleled state of that typical land and people of the Jews in their peace and quiet government: let me now request you, in the last place, to glance at the difference of the wars of this people from the wars of other nations and of their having no antitype but the churches of Christ Jesus.

[Truth] First, all nations about Israel, more or less, some time or other, had indignation against this people—Egyptians, Edomites, Moabites, Ammonites, Midianites, Philistines, Assyrians, and Babylonians, etc., as appears in the history of Moses, Samuel, Judges, and Kings, and in all the prophets: you have an express catalogue of them (Psalm 83), sometimes many hundred thousand enemies in pitched field against them: of Ethiopians ten hundred thousand at once in the days of Asa (II Chronicles 14 [9]), and at other times as the sand upon the sea shore.

Such enemies the Lord Jesus foretold his Israel, *The world shall hate you.* (John 15 [18, 19] *You shall be hated of all men for my name's sake.* (Matt. 24 [9]) *All that will live godly in Christ Jesus must be persecuted,* or hunted. (2 Tim. 3 [12]) And not only by flesh and blood, but also by *principalities, powers, spiritual wickedness in high places* (Eph. 6 [12]), by the whole pagan world under the Roman emperors, and the whole anti-Christian world under the Roman popes (Rev. 12, 13), by the kings of the earth (Rev. 17), and Gog and Magog, like the sand upon the shore. (Rev. 20)

Peace. Such enemies, such armies, no history, no experience proves ever to have come against one poor nation as against Israel in the type; and never was nor shall be known to come against any state or country now, but the Israel of God, the spiritual Jews, Christ's true followers in all parts and quarters of the world.

Beside all these without, Israel is betrayed within her own bowels: bloody Sauls, Absaloms, Shebas, Adonijahs, Jeroboams, Athaliahs, raising insurrections, conspiracies, tumults in the antitype and parallel, the spiritual state of the Christian church.

Secondly, consider we the famous and wonderful battles, victories, captivities, deliverances, which it pleased the God of Israel to dispense to that people and nation, and let us search if they can be paralleled by any state or people, but mystically and spiritually the true Christian Israel of God. (Gal. 6 [16])

How famous was the bondage and slavery of that people and nation four hundred and thirty years in the land of Egypt, and as famous, glorious, and miraculous was their return through the Red Sea, a figure of baptism (1 Cor. 10 [2], and Egypt a figure of all Egypt now? (Rev. 11:8)

How famous was the seventy years' captivity of the Jews in Babel, transported from the land of Canaan, and at the full period returned again to Jerusalem, a type of the captivity of God's people now, spiritually captivated in spiritual Babel. (Rev. 18:4)

Time would fail me to speak of Joshua's conquest of literal Canaan; the slaughter of thirty-one kings, of the miraculous taking of Jericho and other cities; Gideon's miraculous battle against the Midianites; Jonathan and his armor-bearer against the Philistines; David, by his five smooth stones against Goliath; Asa, Jehoshaphat, Hezekiah, their mighty and miraculous victories against so many hundred thousand enemies, and that sometimes without a blow given.

What state, what kingdom, what wars and combats, victories and deliverances, can parallel this people, but the spiritual and mystical Israel of God in every nation and country of the world, typed out by that small typical handful in that little spot of ground, the land of Canaan?

The Israel of God now, men and women, fight under the great Lord General, the Lord Jesus Christ: their weapons, armor, and artillery, is like themselves, spiritual, set forth from top to toe (Eph. 6); so mighty and so potent that they break down the strongest holds and castles, yea, in the very souls of men, and carry into captivity the very thoughts of men, subjecting them to Christ Jesus. They are spiritual conquerors, as in all the seven churches of Asia, *He that overcometh: He that overcometh*. (Rev. 2,3)

Their victories and conquests in this country are contrary to those of this world, for when they are slain and slaughtered, yet then they conquer. So overcame they the devil in the Roman emperors (Rev. 12[11]), *by the blood of the Lamb*: 2. *by the word of their testimony*: 3. the cheerful spilling of their own blood for Christ; for *they loved not their lives unto the death*: and in all this *they are more than conquerors through him that loved them*. (Romans 8[37])

This glorious army of white troopers, horses and harness—Christ Jesus and his true Israel (Rev.19)—gloriously conquer and overcome the beast, the false prophet, and the kings of the earth, up in arms against them (Rev.19); and, lastly, reigning with Christ a thousand years, they conquer the devil himself, and the numberless armies, like the sand on the sea shore, of Gog and Magog: and yet not a tittle of mention of any sword, helmet, breastplate, shield, or horse, but what is spiritual and of a heavenly nature. All which wars of Israel have been, may be, and shall be fulfilled mystically and spiritually.

I could further insist on other particulars of Israel's unparalleled state, and might display those excellent passages which it pleases God to mention. (Neh 9)

CHAPTER CXXIII

Peace. You have, dear Truth, as in a glass, presented the face of old and new Israel, and as in water face answers to face, so does the face of typical Israel to the face of the antitype, between whom, and not between Canaan and the civil nations and countries of the world now, there is an admirable consent and harmony. But I have heard some say, was not the civil state and judicials of that people precedential?

Truth. I have in part, and might further discover, that from the king upon his throne to the very beasts, yea, the excrements of their bodies (as we see in their going to war [Deut. 23:12]), their civils, morals, and naturals were carried on in types; and however I acknowledge that what was simply moral, civil, and natural in Israel's state, in their constitutions, laws, punishments, may be imitated and followed by the states, countries, cities, and kingdoms of the world: yet who can question the lawfulness of other forms of government, laws, and punishments which differ, since civil constitutions are men's ordinances or creation (2 Pet. 2:13), unto which God's people are commanded even for the Lord's sake to submit themselves, which if they were unlawful they ought not to do?

Peace. Having thus far proceeded in examining whether God has charged the civil state with the establishing of the spiritual and religious, what conceive you of that next assertion, viz., "It is well known that the remissness of princes in Christendom in matters of religion and worship, devolving the care thereof only to the clergy, and so setting their horns upon the church's head, has been the cause of anti-Christian invention, usurpation, and corruption in the worship and temple of God."

Truth. It is lamentably come to pass by God's just permission, Satan's policy, the people's sin, the malice of the wicked against Christ, and the corruption of princes and magistrates, that so many inventions, usurpations, and corruptions are risen in the worship and temple of God throughout that part of the world which is called Christian, and may most properly be called the pope's Christendom in opposition to Christ Jesus his true Christian commonweal, or church, the true Christendom; but that this has arisen from princes' remissness in not keeping their watch to establish the purity of religion, doctrine, and worship, and to punish, according to Israel's pattern, all false ministers, by rooting them and their worships out of the world, that, I say, can never be evinced; and the many thousands of glorious souls under the altar whose blood has been spilt by this position, and the many hundred thousand souls, driven out of their bodies by civil wars, and the many millions of souls forced to hypocrisy and ruin eternal, by enforced uniformities in worship, will to all eternity proclaim the contrary.

Indeed, it shows a most injurious idleness and unfaithfulness in such as profess to be messengers of Christ Jesus to cast the heaviest weight of their care upon the kings and rulers of the earth, yea, upon the very commonweals, bodies of people, that is, the world itself, who have fundamentally in themselves the root of power to set up what government and governors they shall agree upon.

Secondly, it shows abundance of carnal diffidence and distrust of the glorious power and gracious presence of the Lord Jesus, who has given his promise and word to be with such his messengers to the end of the world. (Matt. 28 [20])

That dog that fears to meet a man in the path, runs on with boldness at his master's coming and presence at his back.

Thirdly, what imprudence and indiscretion is it in the most common affairs of life, to conceive that emperors, kings, and rulers of the earth, must not only be qualified with political and state abilities to make and execute such civil laws which may concern the common rights, peace, and safety, which is work and business, load and burden enough for the ablest shoulders in the commonweal; but also furnished with such spiritual and heavenly abilities to govern the spiritual and Christian commonweal, the flock and church of Christ, to pull down, and set up religion, to judge, determine, and punish in spiritual controversies, even to death or banishment. And beside that not only the several sorts of civil officers, which the people shall choose and set up, must be so authorized, but that all respective commonweals or bodies of people are charged (much more) by God with this work and business, radically and fundamentally, because all true civil magistrates, have not the least inch of civil power, but what is measured out to them from the free consent of the whole: even as a committee of parliament cannot further act than the power of the house shall arm and enable them.

Concerning that objection which may arise from the kings of Israel and Judah, who were born members of God's church, and trained up therein all their days, which thousands of lawful magistrates in the world, possibly born and bred in false worships, pagan or anti-Christian, never heard of, and were therein types of the great anointed, the King of Israel, I have spoken sufficiently to such as have an ear to hear: and therefore,

Lastly, so unsuitable is the commixing and entangling of the civil with the spiritual charge and government, that (except it was for subsistence, as we see in Paul and Barnabas working with their own hands) the Lord Jesus, and his apostles, kept themselves to one. If ever any in this world was able to manage both the spiritual and civil, church and commonweal, it was the Lord Jesus, wisdom itself: yea, he was the true heir to the crown of Israel, being the son of David: yet being sought for by the people to be made a king (John 6 [15])[117] he refused, and would not give a precedent to any king, prince, or ruler, to manage both swords, and to assume the charge of both tables.

Now concerning princes, I desire it may be remembered who were most injurious and dangerous to Christianity, whether Nero, Domitian, Julian, etc., persecutors: or Constantine,[118] Theodosius, etc., who assumed this power and authority in and over the church in spiritual things. It is confessed by the answerer and others of note that under these latter, the church, the Christian state, religion, and worship, were most corrupted: under Constantine Christians fell asleep on the beds of carnal ease and liberty; insomuch that some apply to his times that sleep of the church (Canticles 5:2), *I sleep, though mine heart waketh.*[119]

---

[117] Williams mistakenly cited John 5.

[118] "Nero and the persecuting emperors were not so injurious to Christianity as Constantine and others who assumed a power in spiritual things. Under Constantine Christianity fell into corruption, and Christians fell asleep." (Williams's footnote)

[119] John Cotton wrote, "Constantine came into the Church, enjoyed the fellowship of it, did partake in all the parts of it, yea and richly endowed; so that the Church and all her friends did eat and drink, yea and did drink abundantly of wealth, preferments, etc., whence it was that she fell into a deep sleep. Canticles 5:2-6:4." "A Brief Exposition of the Whole Book of Canticles, or Song of Solomon; Lively Describing the Estate of the Church

CHAPTER CXXIV

Peace. Yea, but some will say, this was not through their assuming of this power, but the ill-managing of it.

Truth. Yet are they commonly brought as the great precedents for all succeeding princes and rulers in after ages: and in this very controversy, their practices are brought as precedential to establish persecution for conscience.

Secondly, those emperors and other princes and magistrates acted in religion according to their consciences' persuasion, and beyond the light and persuasion of conscience can no man living walk in any fear of God. Hence have they forced their subjects to uniformity and conformity unto their own consciences, whatever they were, though not willing to have been forced themselves in the matters of God and conscience.

Thirdly, had not the light of their eye of conscience, and the consciences also of their teachers, been darkened, they could not have been condemned for want of heavenly affection, rare devotion, wonderful care and diligence, propounding to themselves the best patterns of the kings of Judah, David, Solomon, Asa, Jehoshaphat, Josiah, Hezekiah. But here they lost the path, and themselves, in persuading themselves to be the parallels and antitypes to those figurative and typical princes: whence they conceived themselves bound to make their cities, kingdoms, empires, new holy lands of Canaan, and themselves governors and judges in spiritual causes, compelling all consciences to Christ, and persecuting the contrary with fire and sword.

Upon these roots, how was, how is it possible, but that such bitter fruits should grow of corruption of Christianity, persecution of such godly who happily see more of Christ than such rulers themselves: their dominions and jurisdictions being overwhelmed with enforced dissimulation and hypocrisy, and (where power of resistance) with flames of civil combustion: as at this very day, he that runs may read and tremble at?

Peace. They add further that the princes of Christendom, setting their horns upon the church's head, have been the cause of anti-Christian inventions, etc.

---

in All the Ages Thereof, Written by the Learned and Godly Divine John Cotton," London, 1642.

Truth. If they mean that the princes of Europe, giving their power
and authority to the seven-headed and ten-horned beast of Rome, have
been the cause, etc., I confess it to be one concurring cause: yet withal it
must be remembered that even before such princes set their horns, or
authority, upon the beast's head, even when they did, as I may say, but
lend their horns to the bishops, even then rose up many anti-Christian
abominations. And though I confess there is but small difference, in some
respect, between the setting their horns upon the priests' heads, whereby
they are enabled immediately to push and gore whoever cross their
doctrine and practice, and the lending of their horns, that is, pushing
and goring such themselves, as are declared by their bishops and priests
to be heretical, as was and is practiced in some countries before and since
the pope rose: yet I confidently affirm that neither the Lord Jesus nor his
first ordained ministers and churches (gathered by such ministers) did
ever wear, or crave the help of such horns in spiritual and Christian
affairs. The spiritual power of the Lord Jesus in the hands of his true
ministers and churches, according to Balaam's prophecy (Numbers 23),
is the horn of that unicorn, or rhinoceros (Psalm 92 [10]), which is the
strongest horn in the world: in comparison of which the strongest horns
of the bulls of Bashan break as sticks and reeds. History tells us how that
unicorn, or one-horned beast, the rhinoceros, took up a bull like a tennis
ball in the theatre at Rome, before the emperor, according to that record
of the poet: *Quantus erat cornu cui pila tauru erat!*[120]

Unto this spiritual power of the Lord Jesus, the souls and thoughts
of the highest kings and emperors must subject. (Matthew 16,18; I
Corinthians 5, 10)

CHAPTER CXXV

Peace. Dear Truth, you know the noise is made from those
prophecies (Isa. 49 [23]),[121] kings and queens shall be nursing fathers,

---

[120] Marcus Valerius Martialis (b. 38/41–d. 103), *On the Spectacles.*
He, who with armed nostril wildly glar'd,
Has fought the battles, he had not declared,
How did his headlong rage the pit apall!
How slashed the horn, that made the bull a ball!
[121] Williams mistakenly cites Isaiah 46.

etc., and (Rev. 21 [24]) the kings of the earth shall bring their glory and honor to the new Jerusalem, etc.

Truth. I answer with that mournful prophet (Psa. 74), I see not that man, that prophet, that can tell us how long. How many excellent penmen fight each against other with their pens (like swords) in the application of those prophecies of David, Isaiah, Jeremiah, Ezekiel, Daniel, Zechariah, John, when and how those prophecies shall be fulfilled!

Secondly, whenever those prophecies are fulfilled, yet shall those kings not be heads, governors, and judges in ecclesiastical or spiritual causes; but be themselves judged and ruled, if within the church, by the power of the Lord Jesus therein. Hence, says Isaiah, those kings and queens shall lick the dust of your feet, etc.

Peace. Some will here ask, What may the magistrate then lawfully do with his civil horn, or power, in matters of religion?

Truth. His horn not being the horn of that unicorn, or rhinoceros, the power of the Lord Jesus in spiritual cases: his sword not the two-edged sword of the Spirit, the word of God, hanging not about the loins or side, but at the lips, and proceeding out of the mouth of his ministers, but of a human and civil nature and constitution; it must consequently be of a human and civil operation for who knows not that operation follows constitution? And therefore I shall end this passage with this consideration:

The civil magistrate either respects that religion and worship which his conscience is persuaded is true, and upon which he ventures his soul: or else that which he is persuaded are false.

Concerning the first; if that which the magistrate believes to be true, be true, I say he owes a three-fold duty unto it:

First, approbation and countenance, a reverent esteem and honorable testimony, according to Isaiah 49 and Revelation 21, with a tender respect of truth, and the professors of it.

Secondly, personal submission of his own soul to the power of the Lord Jesus in that spiritual government and kingdom, according to Matthew 18 and 1 Corinthians 5.

Thirdly, protection of such true professors of Christ, whether apart, or met together, as also of their estates from violence and injury, according to Romans 13.

Now secondly, if it be a false religion, unto which the magistrate dare not adjoin, yet, he owes,

First, permission, for approbation he owes not to what is evil, and this according to Matthew 13:30, for public peace and quiet sake.

Secondly, he owes protection to the persons of his subjects, though of a false worship, that no injury be offered either to the persons or goods of any. (Rom. 13)

Peace. Dear Truth, in this eleventh head concerning the magistrates' power in worship, you have examined what is affirmed that the magistrate may do in point of worship; there remains a second, to wit, that which they say the magistrate may not do in worship.

They say, "The magistrate may not bring in set forms of prayer: nor secondly, bring in significant ceremonies: nor thirdly, not govern and rule the acts of worship in the church of God;" for which they bring an excellent similitude of a prince or magistrate in a ship, where he has no governing power over the actions of the mariners: and secondly, that excellent prophecy concerning Christ Jesus, that his government should be upon his shoulders. (Isa. 9:6,7)

Truth. Unto all this I willingly subscribe: yet can I not pass by a most injurious and unequal practice toward the civil magistrate: ceremonies, holy days, common prayer, and whatever else dislikes their consciences, that the magistrate must not bring in. Others again, as learned, as godly, as wise, have conceived the magistrate may approve or permit these in the church, and all men are bound in obedience to obey him. How shall the magistrate's conscience be herein (between both) torn and distracted, if indeed the power either of establishing or abolishing in church matters be committed to him!

Secondly, methinks in this case they deal with the civil magistrate as the soldiers dealt with the Lord Jesus: first, they take off his own clothes, and put upon him a purple robe, plait a crown of thorns on his had, bow the knee, and salute him by the name of King of the Jews.

They tell him that he is the keeper of both tables, he must see the church do her duty, he must establish the true church, true ministry, true ordinances, he must keep her in this purity. Again, he must abolish superstition, and punish false churches, false ministers, even to banishment and death.

Thus indeed do they make the blood run down the head of the civil magistrate, from the thorny vexation of that power which sometimes they crown him with; whence in great states, kingdoms, or monarchies, necessarily arise delegations of that spiritual power, high commissions, etc.[122]

Anon again they take off this purple robe, put him into his own clothes, and tell him that he has no power to command what is against their conscience. They cannot conform to a set form of prayer, nor to ceremonies, nor holy days, etc., although the civil magistrate (that most pious prince, Edward VI and his famous bishops, afterwards burnt for Christ) were of another conscience. Which of these two consciences shall stand? If either magistrate must put forth his civil power in these cases: the strongest arm of flesh, and most conquering, bloody sword of steel can alone decide the question.

I confess it is most true, that no magistrate, as no other superior, is to be obeyed in any matter displeasing to God: yet, when in matters of worship we ascribe the absolute headship and government to the magistrate, as to keep the church pure, and force her to her duty, ministers and people, and yet take unto ourselves power to judge what is right in our own eyes, and to judge the magistrate in and for those very things wherein we confess he has power to see us do our duty, and therefore consequently must judge what our duty is, what is this but to play with magistrates, with the souls of men, with heaven, with God, with Christ Jesus? etc.

CHAPTER CXXVI

Peace. Pass on, holy Truth, to that similitude whereby they illustrate that negative assertion: "The prince in the ship, " say they, "is governor over the bodies of all in the ship; but he has no power to govern the ship or the mariners in the actions of' it. If the pilot manifestly err in his action, the prince may reprove him," and so, say they, may any passenger; "if he offend against the life or goods of' any, the prince may in due time and place punish him, which no private person may."

---

[122] An ecclesiastical court established by the crown. In its time it became a controversial instrument of repression, used against those who refused to acknowledge the authority of the Church of England. The first commission was held under Edward VI in 1549, though the term high commission did not appear until 1570. The High Commission was abolished in 1641.

Truth. Although, dear Peace, we both agree that civil powers may not enjoin such devices, no nor enforce on any God's institutions, since Christ Jesus his coming: yet, for further illustration, I shall propose some queries concerning the civil magistrate's passing in the ship of the church, wherein Christ Jesus has appointed his ministers and officers as governors and pilots, etc.

If in a ship at sea, wherein the governor or pilot of a ship undertakes to carry the ship to such a port, the civil magistrate (suppose a king or emperor) shall command the master such and such a course, to steer upon such or such a point, which the master knows is not their course, and which if they steer he shall never bring the ship to that port or harbor, what shall the master do? Surely all men will say, the master of the ship is to present reasons and arguments from his mariner's art, if the prince be capable of them, or else in humble and submissive manner to persuade the prince not to interrupt them in their course and duty properly belonging to them, to wit, governing of the ship, steering of the course, etc.

If the master of the ship command the mariners thus and thus, in cunning[123] the ship, managing the helm, trimming the sail, and the prince command the mariners a different or contrary course, who is to be obeyed?

It is confessed that the mariners may lawfully disobey the prince, and obey the governor of the ship in the actions of the ship.

Thirdly, what if the prince have as much skill, which is rare, as the pilot himself? I conceive it will be answered, that the master of the ship and pilot, in what concerns the ship, are chief and above, in respect of their office, the prince himself, and their commands ought to be attended by all the mariners, unless it be in manifest error, wherein it is granted any passenger may reprove the pilot.

Fourthly, I ask, if the prince and his attendants be unskillful in the ship's affairs, whether every sailor and mariner, the youngest and lowest, be not, so far as concerns the ship, to be preferred before the prince's followers, and the prince himself? And their counsel and advice more to be attended to, and their service more to be desired and respected, and the prince to be requested to stand by and let the business alone in their hands?

---

[123] Caldwell cites *Dictionarium Brittanicum* (1736): "The cunning of a ship is the directing the person at helm how to steer her."

Fifthly, in case a willful king and his attendants, out of opinion of
their skill, or willfulness or passion, would so steer the course, trim sail,
etc., as that in the judgment of the master and seamen the ship and lives
shall be endangered: whether, in case humble persuasions prevail not,
ought not the ship's company to refuse to act in such a course, yea, and,
in case power be in their hands, resist and suppress these dangerous
practices of the prince and his followers, and so save the ship?

Lastly, suppose the master, out of base fear and cowardice, or
covetous desire of reward, shall yield to gratify the mind of the prince,
contrary to the rules of art and experience, etc., and the ship come in
danger, and perish, and the prince with it: if the master get to shore,
whether may he not be justly questioned, yea, and suffer as guilty of the
prince's death, and those that perished with him? These cases are clear,
wherein, according to this similitude, the prince ought not to govern and
rule the actions of the ship, but such whose office, and charge, and skill it
is.

The result of all is this: the church of Christ is the ship, wherein the
prince—if a member, for otherwise the case is altered—is a passenger. In
this ship the officers and governors, such as are appointed by the Lord
Jesus, they are the chief, and, in those respects, above the prince himself,
and are to be obeyed and submitted to in their works and
administrations, even before the prince himself.

In this respect every Christian in the church, man or woman, if of
more knowledge and grace of Christ, ought to be of higher esteem,
concerning religion and Christianity, than all the princes in the world
who have either none or less grace or knowledge of Christ: although in
civil things all civil reverence, honor, and obedience ought to be yielded
by all men.

Therefore, if in matters of religion the king command what is
contrary to Christ's rule, though according to his persuasion and
conscience, who sees not that, according to the similitude, he ought not
to be obeyed? Yea, and (in case) boldly, with spiritual force and power, he
ought to be resisted. And if any officer of the church of Christ shall out
of baseness yield to the command of the prince, to the danger of the
church and souls committed to his charge, the souls that perish,
notwithstanding the prince's command shall be laid to his charge.

If so, then I rejoin thus: how agree these truths of this similitude
with those former positions, viz., that the civil magistrate is keeper of

both tables, that he is to see the church do her duty, that he ought to establish the true religion, suppress and punish the false, and so consequently must discern, judge, and determine what the true gathering and governing of the church is, what the duty of every minister of Christ is, what the true ordinances are, and what the true administrations of them; and where men fail, correct, punish, and reform by the civil sword? I desire it may be answered, in the fear and presence of Him whose eyes are as a flame of fire, if this be not --according to the similitude, though contrary to their scope in proposing of it—to be governor of the ship of the church, to see the master, pilot, and mariners do their duty, in setting the course, steering the ship, trimming the sails, keeping the watch, etc., and where they fail, to punish them; and therefore, by undeniable consequence, to judge and determine what their duties are, when they do right, and when they do wrong: and this not only to manifest error, (for then they say every passenger may reprove) but in their ordinary course and practice.

The similitude of a physician obeying the prince in the body politic, but prescribing to the prince concerning the prince's body, wherein the prince, unless the physician manifestly err, is to be obedient to the physician, and not to be judge of the physician in his art, but to be ruled and judged as touching the state of his body by the physician—I say this similitude and many others suiting with the former of a ship, might be alleged to prove the distinction of the civil and spiritual estate, and that according to the rule of the Lord Jesus in the gospel, the civil magistrate is only to attend the calling of the civil magistracy concerning the bodies and goods of the subjects, and is himself, if a member of the church and within, subject to the power of the Lord Jesus therein, as any member of the church is. (1 Cor. 5)

CHAPTER CXXVII

Peace. Dear Truth, you have uprightly and aptly untied the knots of that eleventh head; let me present you with the twelfth head, which is, concerning the magistrates' power in the censures of the church.

"First," say they, "he has no power to execute, or to substitute any civil officer to execute any church censure, under the notion of civil or eccleciastical men.

"Secondly, though a magistrate may immediately civilly censure such an offender whose secret sins are made manifest by their casting out to be injurious to the good of the state, yet such offences of excommunicate persons, which manifestly hurt not the good of the state, he ought not to proceed against them, sooner or later, until the church has made her complaint to him, and given in their just reasons for help from them. For to give liberty to magistrates, without exception, to punish all excommunicate persons within so many months, may prove injurious to the person who needs, to the church who may desire, and to God who calls for longer indulgence from the hands of them.

"Thirdly, for persons not excommunicate, the magistrate has no power immediately to censure such offences of the church members by the power of' the sword, but only for such as immediately hurt the peace of the state: because the proper end of civil government being the preservation of the peace and welfare of the state, they ought not to break down those bounds, and so to censure immediately for such sins which hurt not their peace.

"Hence, first, magistrates have no power to censure for secret sins, as deadness, unbelief, because they are secret, and not yet come forth immediately to hurt the peace of the state; we say immediately, for every sin, even original sin remotely hurts the civil state.

"Secondly, hence they have no power to censure for such private sins in church members, which being not heinous may be best healed in a private way by the churches themselves. For that which may be best healed by the church, and yet is prosecuted by the state, may make a deeper wound and greater rent in the peace both of' church and state. The magistrates also being members of' the church, are bound to the rule of' Christ, viz., not to produce any thing in public against a brother, which may be best healed in a private way.

"Now we call that private,

"First, which is only remaining in families, not known of others: and therefore a magistrate to hear and prosecute the complaint of children against their parents, servants against masters, wives against their husbands, without acquainting the church first, transgresses the rule of Christ.

"Secondly, that which is between members of the same church, or of' divers churches: for it was a double fault of the Corinthians (1 Cor. 6), first to go to law, secondly, to go it before an infidel, seeing the church was able to judge of such kind of differences by some arbitrators among themselves. So that the magistrates should refer the differences of church members to private healing, and try that way first, by means whereof the churches should be free from much scandal, and the state from much trouble, and the hearts of the godly from much grief in beholding such breaches.

"Thirdly, such offences which the conscience of a brother dealing with another privately, dares not as yet publish openly, coming to the notice of the magistrate accidentally, he ought not to make public as yet, nor to require the grand jury to present the same, no more than the other private brother who is dealing with him, until he see some issue of the private way.

"Thirdly, hence they have no power to put any to an oath, *ex officio*, to accuse themselves, or the brethren, in case either *criminis suspecti*, or *praetensi*, because this preserves not, but hurts many ways the peace of the state, and abuses the ordinance of an oath, which is ordained to end controversies, not to begin them. (Heb. 6:16)

"Fourthly, hence they have no power to censure any for such offences as break either no civil law of God, or law of the state published according to it: for the peace of the state being preserved by wholesome laws, when they are not hurt, the peace is not hurt."

Truth. In this passage, as I said before, I observe how weakly and partially they deal with the souls of magistrates, in telling them they are the guardians of both tables, must see the church do her duty, punish, etc., and yet in this passage the elders or ministers of the churches not only sit judges over the magistrates' actions in church affairs, but in civil also, straightening and enlarging his commission according to the particular interests of their own ends, or, at the best, their consciences.

I grant the word of the Lord is the only rule, light, and lantern in all cases concerning God or man, and that the ministers of the gospel are to teach this way, hold out this lantern unto the feet of all men; but to give such an absolute power in spiritual things to the civil magistrate, and yet after their own ends or consciences to abridge it, is but the former sporting with holy things, and to walk in contradictions, as before I noted.

Many of the particulars I acknowledge true, where the magistrate is a member of the church; yet some passages call for explication, and some for observation.

First, in that they say the civil magistrate ought not to proceed against the offences of an excommunicate person, which manifestly hurt not the good of the state, until the church has made her complaint for help from them, I observe two things:

First, a clear grant that when the church complains for help, then the magistrate may punish such offences as hurt not the good of the state: and yet in a few lines after they say, the magistrates have no power to censure such offences of church members by the power of the civil sword, but only such as do immediately hurt the peace of the civil state; and they add the reason, because the proper end of the civil government being the preservation of the peace and welfare of the state, they ought not break down those bounds, and so to censure immediately for such sins which hurt not their peace. And in the last place, they acknowledge the magistrate has no power to punish any for any such offences as break no civil law of God, or law of the state published according to it: "for the peace of the state," say they, "being preserved by wholesome laws, when they are not hurt, the peace is not hurt."

CHAPTER CXXVIII

Peace. Dear Truth, here are excellent confessions, unto which both truth and grace may gladly assent; but what is your second observation from hence?

Truth. I observe secondly, what a deep charge of weakness is laid upon the church of Christ, the laws, government, and officers thereof, and consequently upon the Lord Jesus himself: to wit, that the church is not enabled with all the power of Christ to censure sufficiently an offender—on whom yet they have executed the deepest censure in the world, to wit, cutting off from Christ, shutting out of heaven, casting to the devil—which offender's crime reaches not to hurt the good of the civil state; but that she is forced to make complaint to the civil state, and the officers thereof, for their help.

Oh! let not this be told in Gath, nor heard in Askelon! And oh! how dim must needs that eye be which is bloodshot with that bloody and cruel tenent of persecution for cause of conscience!

Peace. But what should be meant by this passage, viz., "that they cannot give liberty to the magistrate to punish without exception all excommunicate persons, within so many months"?

Truth. It may be this has reference to a law made formerly in New England, that if an excommunicate person repented not within, as I have heard, three months after sentence of excommunication, then the civil magistrate might proceed against him.[124]

These worthy men see cause to question this law upon good reasons rendered, though it appears not by their words that they wholly condemn it, only they desire a longer time, implying that after some longer time the magistrate may proceed: and indeed I see not, but according to such principles, if the magistrate himself should be cast out, he ought to be proceeded against by the civil state, and consequently deposed and punished, as the pope teaches: yea, though happily he had not offended against either bodies or goods of any subject.

Thirdly, from this confession, that the magistrate ought not to punish for many sins above mentioned, I observe how they cross the plea which commonly they bring for the magistrates punishing of false doctrines, heretics, etc., viz., Romans 13, The magistrate is to punish them that do evil; and when it is answered, True, evil against the second table, which is there only spoken of, and against the bodies and goods of the subject, which are the proper object of the civil magistrate, as they confess: it is replied, Why? Is not idolatry sin? Heresy, sin? Schism and false worship, sin? Yet here in this passage many evils, many sins, even of parents against their children, masters against their servants, husbands against their wives, the magistrate ought not to meddle with.

Fourthly, I dare not assent to that assertion, "That even original sin remotely hurts the civil state." It is true some do, as inclinations to murder, theft, whoredom, slander, disobedience to parents, and magistrates; but blindness of mind, hardness of heart, inclination to choose or worship this or that God, this or that Christ, beside the true, these hurt not remotely the civil state, as not concerning it, but the spiritual.

---

[124] In Massachusetts a law was passed on September 6, 1638, stating that "whosoever shall stand excommunicate for the space of six months, without laboring what in him or her lies to be restored, such person shall be presented to the Court of Assistants, and there proceeded with by fine, imprisonment, or further." The law was repealed a year later.

Peace. Let me, in the last place, remind you of their charge against the magistrate, and which will necessarily turn to my wrong and prejudice: they say, the magistrate, in hearing and prosecuting the complaints of children against their parents, of servants against their masters, of wives against their husbands, without acquainting the church first, transgresses the rule of Christ.

Truth. Sweet Peace, they that pretend to be your dearest friends, will prove your bitter enemies.

First, I ask for one rule out of the testament of the Lord Jesus to prove this deep charge and accusation against the civil magistrate.

Secondly, this is built upon a supposition of what rarely falls out in the world, to wit, that there must necessarily be a true church of Christ in every lawful state, unto whom these complaints must go: whereas, how many thousand commonweals have been and are, where the name of Christ has not (or not truly) been founded.

Thirdly, the magistrates' office, according to their own grant, properly respecting the bodies and goods of their own subjects, and the whole body of the commonweal being made up of families, as the members constituting that body, I see not how, according to the rule of Christ (Rom. 13), the magistrate may refuse to hear and help the just complaints of any such petitioners—children, wives, and servants—against oppression, etc.

Peace. I have long observed that such as have been ready to ascribe to the civil magistrate and his sword more than God has ascribed, have also been most ready to cut off the skirts, and, in case of his inclining to another conscience than their own to spoil him of the robe of that due authority with which it has pleased God and the people to invest and clothe him.

But I shall now present you with the thirteenth head, whose title is,

CHAPTER CXXIX

What power magistrates have in public assemblies of churches.

"First," say they, "the churches have power to assemble and continue such assemblies for the performance of all God's ordinances, without or against the consent of the magistrate, *renuente magistratu,* because

"Christians are commanded so to do. (Matt. 28:18-20)

"Also, because an angel from God commanded the apostles so to do. (Acts 5:20)

"Likewise, from the practice of the apostles, who were not rebellious or seditious, yet they did so. (Acts 4:18-20; 5: 27, 28)

"Further, from the practice of the primitive church at Jerusalem, who did meet, preach, pray, minister sacraments, censures (Acts 4:23), *renuente magistratu.*

"Moreover, from the exhortation to the Hebrews (10:25) not to forsake their assemblies, though it were in dangerous times; and if they might do this under professed enemies, then we may much more under Christian magistrates, else we were worse under Christian magistrates than heathen: therefore magistrates may not hinder them herein, as Pharaoh did the people from sacrificing, for wrath will be upon the realm, and the king and his sons. (Ezra 7:23)

"Secondly, it has been a usurpation of foreign countries and magistrates to take upon them to determine times and places of worship; rather let the churches be left herein to their inoffensive liberty.

"Thirdly, concerning the power of synod assemblies:—

"First, in corrupt times, the magistrate, desirous to make reformation of religion, may and should call those who are most fit in several churches to assemble together in a synod, to discuss and declare from the Word of God matters of doctrine and worship, and to help forward the reformation of the churches of God: this did Josiah.

"Secondly, in the reformed times, he ought to give liberty to the elders of several churches to assemble themselves by their own mutual and voluntary agreement, at convenient times, as the means appointed by God whereby he may mediately reform matters amiss in churches, which immediately he cannot nor might not to do.

"Thirdly, those meetings for this end we conceive may be of two sorts.

"1. Monthly, of some of the elders and messengers of the churches.

"2. Annual, of all the messengers and elders of the churches.

"First, monthly, of some: first, those members of churches which are nearest together, and so may most conveniently assemble together, may, by mutual agreement, once in a month, consult of such things as make for the good of the churches.

"Secondly, the time of this meeting may be sometimes at one place, sometimes at another, upon the lecture day of every church where lectures are: and let the lecture that day be ended by eleven of the clock.

"Thirdly, let the end of this assembly be to do nothing by way of authority, but by way of counsel, as the need of churches shall require.

"Secondly, annual, of all the elders within our jurisdiction or others, whereto the churches may send once in the year to consult together for the public welfare of all the churches.

"First, let the place be sometimes at one church, sometimes at another, as reasons for the present may require.

"Secondly, let all the churches send their weighty questions and cases, six weeks or a month before the set time, to the church where the assembly is to be held, and the officers thereof disperse them speedily to all the churches, that so they may have time to come prepared to the discussing of them.

"Thirdly, let this assembly do nothing by authority, but only by counsel, in all cases which fall out, leaving the determination of all things to particular churches within themselves, who are to judge and so to receive all doctrines and directions agreeing only with the word of God."

The grounds of these assemblies.

"First, need of each other's help, in regard of daily emergent troubles, doubts, and controversies.

"Secondly, love of each other's fellowship.

"Thirdly, of God's glory, out of a public spirit to seek the welfare of the churches, as well as their own. (1 Cor. 10:33; 2 Cor. 11:28)[125]

"Fourthly, the great blessing and special presence of God upon such assemblies hitherto.

"Fifthly, the good report the elders and brethren of churches shall have hereby, by whose communion of love others shall know they are the disciples of Christ."

---

[125] Williams mistakenly cites 2 Cor. 11:23.

CHAPTER CXXX

Truth. I may well compare this passage to a double picture; on the first part or side of it a most fair and beautiful countenance of the pure and holy Word of God: on the latter side or part, a most sour and uncomely, deformed look of a mere human invention.

Concerning the former, they prove the true and unquestionable power and privilege of the churches of Christ to assemble and practice all the holy ordinances of God, without or against the consent of the magistrate.

Their arguments from Christ's and the angels' voice, from the apostles' and churches' practice, I desire may take deep impression, written by the point of a diamond, the finger of God's Spirit, in all hearts whom it may concern.

This liberty of the churches of Christ, he enlarges and amplifies so far that he calls it a usurpation of some magistrates to determine the time and place of worship: and says, that rather the churches should be left to their inoffensive liberty.

Upon which grant I must renew my former query, whether this be not to walk in contradictions, to hold with light yet walk in darkness? For,—

How can they say the magistrate is appointed by God and Christ the guardian of the Christian church and worship, bound to set up the true church, ministry, and ordinances, to see the church do her duty, that is, to force her to it by the civil sword: bound to suppress the false church, ministry, and ordinances, and therefore, consequently, to judge and determine which is the true church, which is the false, and what is the duty of the church officers and members of it, and what not: and yet, say they, the churches must assemble and practice all ordinances, without his consent, yea, against it. Yea, and he has not so much power as to judge what is a convenient time and place for the churches to assemble in; which if he should do, he should be a usurper, and should abridge the church of her inoffensive liberty.

As if the master or governor of a ship had power to judge who were true and fit officers, mariners, etc., for the managing of the ship, and were bound to see them each perform his duty, and to force them thereunto, and yet he should be an usurper if he should abridge them of meeting and managing the vessel at their pleasure, when they please, and how they please, without and against his consent. Certainly, if a physician have power to judge the disease of his patient, and what course of physic he must use, can he be counted an usurper unless the patient might take what physic himself pleased, day or night, summer or winter, at home in his chamber or abroad in the air?

Secondly, by their grant in this passage, that God's people may thus assemble and practice ordinances without and against the consent of the magistrate, I infer, then also may they become a church, constitute and gather without or against the consent of' the magistrate. Therefore may the messengers of Christ preach and baptize, that is, make disciples and wash them into the true profession of Christianity, according to the commission, though the magistrate determine and publicly declare such ministers, such baptisms, such churches to be heretical.

Thirdly, it may here be questioned, what power is now given to the civil magistrate in church matters and spiritual affairs?

If it be answered that although God's people may do this against the magistrates' consent, yet others may not.

I answer, as before, who sees not herein partiality to themselves? God's people must enjoy their liberty of conscience, and not be forced; but all subjects in a kingdom or monarchy, or the whole world beside, must be compelled by the power of the civil sword to assemble thus and thus.

Secondly, I demand who shall judge whether they are God's people or no? For they say, whether the magistrate consent or consent not, that is, judge so or not, they ought to go on in the ordinances, *renuente magistratu.*

How agrees this with their former and general assertion, that the civil magistrate must set up the Christian church and worship? Therefore, by their own grant, he must judge the godly themselves, he must discern who are fit matter for the house of God, living stones, and what unfit matter, trash, and rubbish.

Those worthy men, the authors of these positions, and others of their judgment, have cause to examine their souls with fear and trembling in the presence of God upon this interrogatory, viz., whether or no this be not the bottom and root of the matter: if they could have the same supply of maintenance without the help of the civil sword, or were persuaded to live upon the voluntary contribution of poor saints, or their own labor, as the Lord Jesus and his first messengers did:—I say, if this lay not in the bottom, whether or no they could not be willingly shut of the civil power, and left only to their inoffensive liberties?

I could also put a sad query to the consciences of some, viz., what should be the reason why in their native country, where the magistrate consented not, they forebore to practice such ordinances as now they do, and intended to do so soon as they got into another place where they might set up magistrates of their own, and a civil sword? etc. How much is it to be feared that in case their magistrate should alter, or their persons be cast under a magistracy prohibiting their practice, whether they would then maintain their separate meetings without and against the consent of the magistrate, *renuente magistratu*?

Lastly, it may be questioned how it comes to pass that in pleading for the church's liberty more now under the Christian magistrate, since the Christians took that liberty in dangerous times under the heathen, why he quotes to prove such liberty Pharaoh's hindering the Israelites from worship, and (Ezra 7:23), Artaxerxes his fear of wrath upon the realm?

Are not all their hopes and arguments built upon the Christian magistrate, whom, say they, the first Christians wanted? And yet do they scare the Christian magistrate, whom they account the governor of the church, with Pharaoh and Artaxerxes, that knew not God, expecting that the Christian magistrate should act and command no more in God's worship than they.

But what can those instances of Pharaoh's evil in hindering the Israelites worshipping of God, and Artaxerxes giving liberty to Israel to worship God and build the temple, what can they prove but a duty in all princes and civil magistrates to take off the yoke of bondage, which commonly they lay on the necks of the souls of their subjects in matters of conscience and religion?

CHAPTER CXXXI

Peace. It is plausible, but not reasonable, that God's people should (considering the drift of these positions) expect more liberty under a Christian than under a heathen magistrate. Have God's people more liberty to break the command of a Christian than a heathen governor, and so to set up Christ's church and ordinances after their own conscience against his consent, more than against the consent of a heathen or unbelieving magistrate? What is become of all the great expectation what a Christian magistrate may and ought to do in establishing the church, in reforming the church, and in punishing the contrary? It is true, say men, in Christ's time, and in the time of the first ministers and churches, there were no Christian magistrates, and therefore in that case it was in vain for Christians to seek unto the heathen magistrates to govern the church,suppress heretics, etc.; but now we enjoy Christian magistrates, etc.

Truth. All reason and religion would now expect more submission thereof, in matters concerning Christ, to a Christian magistrate, than to a pagan or anti-Christian ruler! But, dear Peace, the day will discover, the fire will try (1 Cor. 3 [13]) what is but wood, hay, and stubble, though built, in men's upright intention, on that foundation, Jesus Christ.

But, to wind up all, as it is most true that magistracy in general is of God (Rom. 13), for the preservation of civil order and peace—the world otherwise would be like the sea, wherein men, like fishes, would hunt and devour each other, and the greater devour the less—so also it is true, that magistracy in special for the several kinds of it is of man. (1 Pet. 2:13) Now what kind of magistrate soever the people shall agree to set up, whether he receive Christianity before he be set in office, or whether he receive Christianity after, he receives no more power of magistracy than a magistrate that has received no Christianity. For neither of them both can receive more than the commonweal, the body of people and civil state, as men, communicate unto them, and betrust them with.

All lawful magistrates in the world, both before the coming of Christ Jesus and since, (excepting those unparalleled typical magistrates of the church of Israel) are but derivatives and agents immediately derived and employed as eyes and hands, serving for the good of the whole: hence they have and can have no more power than fundamentally lies in the bodies or fountains themselves, which power, might, or authority is not religious, Christian, etc., but natural, human, and civil.

And hence it is true that a Christian captain, Christian merchant, physician, lawyer, pilot, father, master, and so consequently magistrate, etc., is no more a captain, merchant, physician, lawyer, pilot, father, master, magistrate, etc., than a captain, merchant, etc., of any other conscience or religion.

It is true, Christianity teaches all these to act in their several callings to a higher ultimate end, from higher principles, in a more heavenly and spiritual manner, etc.

CHAPTER CXXXII

Peace. Oh! that thy light and brightness, dear Truth, might shine to the dark world in this particular: let it not therefore be grievous, if I request a little further illustration of it.

Truth. In his season, God will glorify himself in all his truths. But to gratify your desire, thus: A pagan or anti-Christian pilot may be as skilful to carry the ship to its desired port, as any Christian mariner or pilot in the world, and may perform that work with as much safety and speed: yet have they not command over the souls and consciences of their passengers, or mariners under them, although they may justly see to the labor of the one, and the civil behavior of all in the ship. A Christian pilot, he performs the same work, as likewise does the metaphorical pilot in the ship of the commonweal, from a principle of knowledge and experience; but more than this, he acts from a root of the fear of God and love to mankind in his whole course. Secondly, his aim is more to glorify God than to gain his pay, or make his voyage. Thirdly, he walks heavenly with men and God, in a constant observation of God's hand in storms, calms, etc. So that the thread of navigation being equally spun by a believing or unbelieving pilot, yet is it drawn over with the gold of godliness and Christianity by a Christian pilot, while he is holy in all manner of Christianity. (1 Pet. 1:15) But lastly, the Christian pilot's power over the souls and consciences of his sailors and passengers is not greater than that of the anti-Christian, otherwise than he can subdue the souls of any by the two-edged sword of the Spirit, the Word of God, and by his holy demeanor in his place, etc.

Peace. I shall present you with no other consideration in this first part of the picture, but this only.

Although the term heathen is most commonly appropriated to the wild naked Americans, etc., yet these worthy men justly apply it even to the civilized Romans, etc.; and consequently must it be applied to the most civilized anti-Christians, who are not the church and people of God in Christ.

Truth. The word בְּרִים in the Hebrew, and εθνη in the Greek, signifies no more than the Gentiles, or nations of the earth, which were without and not within the true typical national church of the Jews before Christ; and since his coming, the Gentiles, or nations of the world, who are without that one holy nation of the Christian Israel, the church gathered unto Christ Jesus in particular and distinct congregations all the world over.

Translators promiscuously render the words, Gentiles, heathens, nations: whence it is evident that even such as profess the name of Christ in an unregenerate and impenitent estate, whether papist, or Protestant, are yet without, that is, heathen, Gentile, or of the nations.

CHAPTER CXXXIII

Peace. Dear Truth, it is now time to cast your eye on the second part of this head or picture, uncomely and deformed.

Truth. It contains two sorts of religious meetings or assemblies.

First, more extraordinary and occasional, for which he quotes the practice of Josiah.

Answer. Josiah was in the type: so are not now the several governors of commonweals, kings or governors of the church or Israel; whose state I have proved to be a nonesuch, and not to be paralleled but in the antitype, the particular church of Christ, where Christ Jesus alone sits King in his most holy government.

Secondly, they propound meetings or assemblings ordinary, stated, and constant, yearly and monthly, unto which the civil magistrate should give liberty. For these meetings they propound plausible arguments from the necessity of them, from Christian fellowship, from God's glory, from the experience of the benefit of them, and from the good report of them, as also those two scriptures, 1 Corinthians 10:33 and 2 Corinthians 11: 28.

To these I answer, if they intend that the civil magistrate should permit liberty to the free and voluntary spiritual meetings of their subjects, I shall subscribe unto them; but if they intend that the magistrate should give liberty only unto themselves, and not to the rest of their subjects, that is to desire their own souls only to be free, and all other souls of their subjects to be kept in bondage.

Secondly, if they intend that the magistrate should enforce all the elders of such churches under their jurisdiction to keep correspondency with them in such meetings, then I say, as before, it is to cause him to give liberty with a partial hand, and unequal balance; for thus I argue: if the civil state and civil officers be of their religion and conscience, it is not proper for them to give liberty or freedom, but to give honorable testimony and approbation, and their own personal submission to the churches. But if the civil state and officers be of another conscience and worship, and shall be bound to grant permission and liberty to them, their consciences, and meetings, and not to those of his own religion and conscience also, how will this appear to be equal in the very eye of common peace and righteousness?

For those yearly and monthly meetings, as we find not any such in the first churches, so neither will those general arguments from the plausible pretense of Christian fellowship, God's glory, etc., prove such particular ways of glorifying God, without some precept or precedent of such a kind.

For those scriptures, 1 Corinthians 10:33, and 2 Corinthians 11:28, expressing the apostle Paul his zeal for glorifying God, and his care for all the churches, it is clear they concern such as are indeed Paul's successors, sent forth by Christ Jesus to preach and gather churches; but those scriptures concern not the churches themselves, nor the pastors of the churches properly, least of all the civil state and commonwealth, neither of which the churches, the pastors, or commonwealth do go forth personally with that commission (Matt. 28[19]) to preach and baptize, that is, to gather churches unto Christ.

For as for the first, the churches are not ministers of the gospel; the angels or messengers of the churches, and the churches themselves, were distinct. (Rev. 2,3)

As for the second, the pastors and elders of the church, their work is not to gather churches, but to govern and feed them. (Acts 20; 1 Pet. 5)

As for the civil magistrate, it is a ministry indeed—magistrates are God's ministers (Rom. 13:4)—but it is of another nature. And therefore none of these—the churches of Christ, the shepherds of those churches, nor the civil magistrate, succeeding the apostles or first messengers—these scriptures alleged concern not any of these to have care of all the churches.

Peace. Dear Truth, who can hear this word, but will presently cry out, Who then may rightly challenge that commission, and that promise? (Matt. 28, etc.)

Truth. Sweet Peace, in due place and season that question may be resolved; but doubtless the true successors must precede or go before the church, making disciples, and baptizing as the apostles did, who were neither the churches, nor the pastors and fixed teachers of them, but as they gathered, so had the care of the churches.

CHAPTER CXXXIV

Peace. I cease to urge this further; and, in the last place, marvel what should be the reason of that conclusion, viz., "There is no power of determination in any of these meetings, but that all must be left to the particular determination of the churches."

Truth. At the meeting at Jerusalem, when Paul and Barnabas and others were sent thither from the church of Christ at Antioch, the apostles and elders did not only consult and advise, but particularly determined the question which the church of Antioch sent to them about (Acts 15), and send their particular determinations or decrees to the churches afterward.

So that if these assemblies were of the nature of that pattern or precedent, as is generally pretended, and had such a promise of the assistance and concurrence of the Spirit as that assembly had, they might then say as that assembly did (Acts 15), *It seemeth good to the Holy Spirit and to us;* and should not leave particular determinations to the particular churches, in which sometimes are very few able guides and leaders.

Peace. But what should be the reason to persuade these worthy men to conceive the particular congregations, or churches, to be more fit and competent judges in such high points, than an assembly of so excellent and choice persons, who must only consult and advise? etc.

Truth. Doubtless there is a strong conviction in their souls of a professed promised presence of the Lord Jesus in the midst of his church, gathered after his mind and will, more than unto such kind of assemblies, though consisting of far more able persons, even the flower and cream of all the churches.

Peace. It is generally conceived that the promise of Christ's presence to the end of the world (Matt. 28[20]) is made to the church.

Truth. There is doubtless a promise of Christ's presence in the midst of his church and congregation (Matthew 18[20]), but the promise of Christ's presence (Matt. 28[20]) cannot properly and immediately belong to the church constituted and gathered, but to such ministers or messengers of Christ Jesus, whom he is pleased to employ to gather and constitute the church by converting and baptizing: unto which messengers, if Christ Jesus will be pleased to send such forth, that passage (Acts 15) will be precedential.

Peace. The fourteenth general head is this, viz., What power particular churches have particularly over magistrates.

"First," say they, "they may censure any member, though a magistrate, if by sin he deserve it.

"First, because magistrates must be subject to Christ; but Christ censures all offenders. (1 Cor. 5:4,5)

"Secondly, every brother must be subject to Christ's censure. (Matthew 18:15,16,17) But magistrates are brethren. (Deut. 17:15)

"Thirdly, they may censure all within the church. (1 Cor. 5:12) But the magistrates are within the church, for they are either without, or within, or above the church: not the first, nor the last, for so Christ is only above it.

"Fourthly, the church has a charge of all the souls of the members, and must give account thereof. (Heb. 13:17)

"Fifthly, Christ's censures are for the good of souls (1 Cor. 5:6); but magistrates must not be denied any privilege for their souls, for then they must lose a privilege of Christ by being magistrates.

"Sixthly, in church privileges Christians are all one. (Gal. 3:28; Col. 3:11)

"2. Magistrates may be censured for apparent and manifest sin against any moral law of God in their judicial proceedings, or in the execution of their office. Courts are not sanctuaries for sin; and if for no sin, then not for such especially.

"First, because sins of magistrates in court are as hateful to God. 2. And as much spoken against. (Isa. 10:1; Mic. 3:1) Thirdly, God has nowhere granted such immunity to them. Fourthly, what a brother may do privately in case of private offence, that the church may do publicly in case of public scandal. But a private brother may admonish and reprove privately in case of any private offence. (Matt. 18:16; Luke 17:3; Psa. 141:5)[126]

"Lastly, civil magistracy does not exempt any church from faithful watchfulness over any member, nor deprive a church of her due power, nor a church member of his due privilege, which is to partake of every ordinance of God, needful and requisite to their winning and salvation. *Ergo,*—

CHAPTER CXXXV

Truth. These arguments to prove the magistrate subject, even for sin committed in judicial proceeding, I judge, like Mount Zion, immovable, and every true Christian that is a magistrate will judge so with me. Yet a query or two will not be unseasonable.

First, where they name the church in this whole passage, whether they mean the church without the ministry or governors of it, or with the elders and governors jointly? And if the latter, why name they not the governors at all, since that in all administrations of the church the duty lies not upon the body of the church, but firstly and properly upon the elders?

It is true in case of the elder's obstinacy in apparent sin, the church has power over him, having as much power to take down as to set up (Col. 4[17]), *Say to Archippus,* etc.; yet in the ordinary dispensations and administrations of the ordinances, the ministers or elders thereof are first charged with duty, etc.

Hence, first for the apostles, who converted, gathered, and espoused the churches to Christ, I question whether their power to edification was not a power over the churches as many scriptures seem to imply.

Secondly, for the ordinary officers ordained for the ordinary and constant guiding, feeding, and governing the church, they were rulers, shepherds, bishops, or overseers, and to them was every letter and charge, commendation or reproof, directed. (Rev. 2:3; Acts 20) And that place by them quoted for the submission of the magistrates to the church, it mentions only submission to the rulers thereof. (Heb. 13:17) Those excellent men concealed not this out of ignorance, and therefore most

---

[126] Williams mistakenly cites Luke 19:17.

certainly in a silent way confess that their doctrine concerning the magistrates' power in church causes would seem too gross, if they should not have named the whole church, and but silently implied the governors of it. And is it not wonderful in any sober eye, how the same persons, magistrates, can be exalted over the ministers and members, as being bound to establish, reform, suppress by the civil sword in punishing the body or goods, and yet for the same actions, if the church and governors thereof so conceive, be liable to a punishment ten thousand times more transcendent, to wit, excommunication, a punishment reaching to their souls, and consciences, and eternal estate; and this not only for common sins, but for those actions which immediately concern the execution of their civil office, in judicial proceeding?

Peace. The prelates in Queen Elizabeth's days, kept with more plainness to their principles: for, acknowledging the queen to be supreme in all church causes, according to the title and power of Henry VIII, her father, taken from the pope, and given to him by the parliament, they professed that the queen was not a sheep, but under Christ the chief shepherd, and that the church had not power to excommunicate the queen.

Truth. Therefore, sweet Peace, it was esteemed capital, in that faithful witness of so much truth as he saw, even unto death, Mr. Barrowe,[127] to maintain before the lords of the council that the queen herself was subject to the power of Christ Jesus in the church: which truth overthrew that other tenent, that the queen should be head and supreme in all church causes.

Peace. Those bishops according to their principles, though bad and false, dealt plainly, though cruelly, with Mr. Barrowe: but these authors, whose principles are the same with the bishops concerning the power of the magistrate in church affairs, though they waive the title, will not call them heads or governors, which now in lighter times seems too gross, yet

---

[127] Henry Barrowe (ca.1550-1593), separatist leader, whose book *Four Causes for Separation* (1587) identified false worship, false ministry, false discipline, and a false basis for membership as grounds for separation from the Church of England. He was imprisoned in 1586 and executed seven years later. In his examination before the High Commission Barrow said, "I think the Queen Majesty supreme governor of the whole land, and over the church also, bodies and goods: but I think that no prince, neither the whole world, neither the church itself, may make any laws for the church, other than Christ has already left in his word." Caldwell, 410, citing Brook, *Lives of the Puritans,* and Neal, *History of Puritans.*

give they as much spiritual power and authority to the civil magistrates to
the full as ever the bishops gave unto them; although they yet also with
the same breath lay all their honor in the dust, and make them to lick the
dust of the feet of the churches, as it is prophesied the kings and the
queens of the earth shall do, when Christ makes them nursing fathers and
nursing mothers. (Isaiah 49)[128] The truth is, Christ Jesus is honored when
the civil magistrate, a member of the church, punishes any member of the
church with the civil sword, even to the death, for any crime against the
civil state, so deserving it; for he bears not the sword in vain.

And Christ Jesus is again most honored when for apparent sin in the
magistrate, being a member of the church, for otherwise they have not to
meddle with him, the elders with the church admonish him, and recover
his soul: or if obstinate in sin, cast him forth of their spiritual and
Christian fellowship; which doubtless they could not do were the
magistrate supreme governor under Christ in ecclesiastical or church
causes, and so consequently the true heir and successor of the apostles.

CHAPTER CXXXVI

Peace. The fifteenth head runs thus, viz., In what cases must
churches proceed with magistrates in case of offence.

"We like it well that churches be slower in proceeding to
excommunication, as of all other, so of civil magistrates, especially in
point of their judicial proceedings, unless it be in scandalous breach of a
manifest law of God, and that after notorious evidence of the fact, and
that after due seeking and waiting for satisfaction in a previous
advertisement. And though each particular church in respect of the
government of Christ be independent and absolute within itself, yet
where the commonweal consists of church members, it may be a point of
Christian wisdom to consider and consult with the court also, so far as
any thing may seem doubtful to them in the magistrate's case, which may
be further cleared by intelligence given from them; but otherwise we dare
not leave it in the power of any church to forbear to proceed and agree
upon that on earth which they plainly see Christ has resolved in his word,
and will ratify in heaven."

---

[128] "Is not this too like the pope's profession of *servus servorum Dei,* yet holding out
his slipper to the lips of princes, kings, and emperors!" (Williams's footnote)

Truth. If the scope of this head be to qualify and adorn Christian impartiality and faithfulness with Christian wisdom and tenderness, I honor and applaud such a Christian motion; but whereas that case is put which is nowhere found in the pattern of the first churches, nor suiting with the rule of Christianity, to wit, that "the commonweal should consist of church members," which must be taken privately, to wit, that none should be admitted members of the commonweal but such as are first members of the church—which must necessarily run the church upon that temptation to feel the pulse of the court concerning a delinquent magistrate before they dare proceed—I say, let such practices be brought to the touchstone of the true frame of a civil commonweal, and the true frame of the spiritual or Christian commonweal, the church of Christ, and it will be seen what wood, hay, and stubble of carnal policy and human inventions in Christ's matters are put in place of the precious stones, gold, and silver of the most high and only wise God.

CHAPTER CXXXVII

Peace. Dear Truth, we are now arrived at their last head: the title is this, viz., Their power in the liberties and privileges of these churches.

"First, all magistrates ought to be chosen out of church members. (Exod. 18:21; Deut. 17:15) *When the righteous rule, the people rejoice.* (Prov. 29:2)

"Secondly, that all free men elected, be only church members;—

"1. Because if none but church members should rule, then others should not choose, because they may elect others beside church members.

"2. From the pattern of Israel, where none had power to choose but only Israel, or such as were joined to the people of God.

"3. If it shall fall out that in the court consisting of magistrates and deputies, there be a dissent between them which may hinder the common good, that they now return for ending the same to their first principles, which are the free men, and let them be consulted with."

Truth. In this head are two branches: first, concerning the choice of magistrates, that such ought to be chosen as are church members: for which is quoted Exod. 18; Deut. 17:15; Prov. 29:2.[129]

Unto which I answer: it were to be wished that since the point is so weighty, as concerning the pilots and steersmen of kingdoms and nations, etc., on whose abilities, care, and faithfulness depends most commonly the peace and safety of the commonweals they sail in: I say, it were to be wished that they had more fully explained what they intend by this affirmative, viz., "Magistrates ought to be chosen out of church members."

For if they intend by this "ought to be chosen," a necessity of convenience, viz., that for the greater advancement of common utility and rejoicing of the people, according to the place quoted (Proverbs 29:2), it were to be desired, prayed for, and peaceably endeavored, then I readily assent unto them.

But if by this "ought" they intend such a necessity as those scriptures quoted imply, viz., that people shall sin by choosing such for magistrates as are not members of churches, as the Israelites should have sinned, if they had not, according to Jethro's counsel (Exodus 18), and according to the command of God (Deut. 17), chosen their judges and kings within themselves in Israel, then I propose these necessary queries:

First, whether those are not lawful civil combinations, societies, and communions of men, in towns, cities, states, or kingdoms, where no church of Christ is resident, yea, where his name was never yet heard of? I add to this that men of no small note, skillful in the state of the world, acknowledge that the world divided into thirty parts, twenty-five of that thirty have never yet heard of the name of Christ:[130] if their civil politics and combinations be not lawful, because they are not churches and their magistrates church members, then disorder, confusion, and all unrighteousness is lawful, and pleasing to God.

Secondly, whether in such states or commonweals where a church or churches of Christ are resident, such persons may not lawfully succeed to the crown or government in whom the fear of God, according to Jethro's

---

[129] Williams mistakenly cites Prov. 19:29.
[130] Caldwell (p. 321) implies that this is a reference to a map by Hundius, citing Williams in *Hireling Ministry*, "The world divided (say our blessed cosmographers) into thirty parts, as yet but five of thirty have heard of the sweet name of Jesus a Savior." *The Complete Writings of Roger Williams, Vol. VII* (New York: Russell and Russell, Inc., 1963).

counsel, cannot be discerned, nor are brethren of the church, according to Deuteronomy 17[15], but only are fitted with civil and moral abilities to manage the civil affairs of the civil estate.

Thirdly, since not many wise and noble are called, but the poor receive the gospel, as God has chosen the poor of the world to be rich in faith (1 Cor. 1[26]; James 2[5]), whether it may not ordinarily come to pass that there may not be found in a true church of Christ, which sometimes consists but of few persons, persons fit to be either kings or governors, etc., whose civil office is no less difficult than the office of a doctor of physic, a master or pilot of a ship, or a captain or commander of a band or army of men: for which services the children of God may be no ways qualified, though otherwise excellent for the fear of God, and the knowledge and grace of the Lord Jesus.

4. If magistrates ought, that is, ought only, to be chosen out of the church, I demand, if they ought not also to be dethroned and deposed when they cease to be of the church, either by voluntary departure from it, or by excommunication out of 'it, according to the bloody tenents and practice of some papists, with whom the Protestants, according to their principles, although they seem to abhor it, do absolutely agree?

5. Therefore, lastly, I ask, if this be not to turn the world upside down, to turn the world out of the world, to pluck up the roots and foundations of all common society in the world, to turn the garden and paradise of the church and saints into the field of the civil state of the world, and to reduce the world to the first chaos or confusion?

CHAPTER CXXXVIII

Peace. Dear Truth, you conquer and shall triumph in season, but some will say, how answer you those scriptures alleged?

Truth. I have fully and at large declared the vast differences between that holy nation of typical Israel and all other lands and countries, how unmatchable then and now, and never to be paralleled but by the true Israel and particular churches of Christ residing in all parts, and under the several civil governments of the world. In which churches, the Israel of God and kingdom of Christ Jesus, such only are to be chosen spiritual officers and governors, to manage his kingly power and authority in the church as are, according to the scriptures quoted, not pope, bishops, or civil powers, but from among themselves, brethren, fearing God, hating covetousness or filthy lucre, according to those golden rules given by the Lord Jesus. (1 Tim. 3; Titus 1)

The want of discerning this true parallel between Israel in the type then, and Israel the antitype now, is that rock whereon, through the Lord's righteous jealousy, punishing the world and chastising his people, thousands dash, and make woeful shipwreck.

The second branch, viz., that all freemen elected be only church members, I have before shown to be built on that sandy and dangerous ground of Israel's pattern. Oh! that it may please the Father of lights to discover this to all that fear his name! Then would they not sin to save a kingdom, nor run into the lamentable breach of civil peace and order in the world, nor be guilty of forcing thousands to hypocrisy in a state-worship, nor of profaning the holy name of God and Christ by putting their names and ordinances upon unclean and unholy persons, nor of shedding the blood of such heretics, etc., whom Christ would have enjoy longer patience and permission until the harvest, nor of the blood of the Lord Jesus himself in his faithful witnesses of truth, nor lastly, of the blood of so many hundred thousands slaughtered men, women, and children, by such uncivil and unchristian wars and combustions about the Christian faith and religion.

Peace. Dear Truth, before we part, I ask your faithful help once more, to two or three scriptures which many allege, and yet we have not spoken of.

Truth. Speak on. Here is some sand left in this our hour-glass of merciful opportunity. One grain of time's inestimable sand is worth a golden mountain; let us not lose it.

Peace. The first is that of the Ninevites' fast, commanded by the king of Nineveh and his nobles upon the preaching of Jonah: succeeded by God's merciful answer in sparing of the city; and quoted with honorable approbation by the Lord Jesus Christ. (Jon. 3; Matthew 12[41])

Truth. I have before proved that even Jehosaphat's fast, he being king of the national church and people of Israel, could not possibly be a type or warrant for every king or magistrate in the world, whose nations, countries, or cities cannot be churches of God now in the gospel, according to Christ Jesus.

Much less can this pattern of the king of Nineveh and his nobles be a ground for kings and magistrates now to force all their subjects under them in the matters of worship.

Peace. It will be said, why did God thus answer them?

Truth. God's mercy in hearing does not prove an action right and according to rule.

It pleases God to hear the Israelites' cry for flesh, and afterward for a king, giving both in anger to them.

It pleased God to hear Ahab's prayer, yea, and the prayer of the devils (Luke 8 [32]), although their persons and prayers in themselves abominable.

If it be said, why did Christ approve this example? I answer, the Lord Jesus Christ did not approve the king of Nineveh's compelling all to worship, but the men of Nineveh's repentance at the preaching of Jonah.

Peace. It will be said, what shall kings and magistrates now do in the plagues of sword, famine, pestilence?

Truth. Kings and magistrates must be considered, as formerly, invested with no more power than the people betrust them with.

But no people can betrust them with any spiritual power in matters of worship; but with a civil power belonging to their goods and bodies.

Kings and magistrates must be considered as either godly or ungodly.

If ungodly, his own and people's duty is repentance, and reconciling of their persons unto God, before their sacrifice can be accepted. Without repentance what have any to do with the covenant or promise of God? (Psa. 50 [16])

Again, if godly, they are to humble themselves and beg mercies for themselves and people.

Secondly, upon this advantage and occasion, they are to stir up their people, as possibly they may, to repentance; but not to force the conscience of people to worship.

If it be said, what must be attended to in this example?

Two things are most eminent in this example.

First, the great work of repentance, which God calls all men unto, upon the true preaching of his word.

Secondly, the nature of that true repentance, whether legal or evangelical. The people of Nineveh turned from the violence that was in their hands: and confident I am, if this nation shall turn, though but with a legal repentance, from that violent persecuting or hunting each of the other for religion's sake, the greatest violence and hunting in the wilderness of the whole world—even as Sodom and Gomorrah upon a legal repentance had continued until Christ's day: so consequently might England, London, etc., continue free from a general destruction, upon such a turning from their violence, until the heavens and the whole world be with fire consumed.

Peace. The second scripture is that speech of the Lord Christ (Luke 22:36), *He that hath not a sword, let him sell his coat and buy one.*

Truth. For the clearing of this scripture, I must propose and reconcile that seeming contrary command of the Lord Jesus to Peter (Matt. 26 [52]), *Put up thy sword into its place, for all that take the sword shall perish by it.*

In the former scripture (Luke 22:36), it pleased the Lord Jesus, speaking of his present trouble, to compare his former sending forth of his disciples without scrip, etc., with that present condition and trial coming upon them, wherein they should provide both scrip and sword, etc.

Yet now, first, when they tell him of two swords, he answers, It is enough: which shows his former meaning was not literal, but figurative, foreshowing his present danger above his former.

Secondly, in the same sense at the same time (Matt. 26 [52]), commanding Peter to put up his sword, he gives a threefold reason thereof.

1. (verse 52) From the event of it: *for all that take the sword shall perish by it.*

2. The needlessness of it: for with a word to his Father, he could have twelve legions of angels.

3. The counsel of God to be fulfilled in the scripture: thus it ought to be.

Peace. It is much questioned by some what should be the meaning of Christ Jesus in that speech, *All that take the sword shall perish by the sword.*

Truth. There is a three-fold taking of the sword: first, by murderous cruelty, either of private persons; or secondly, public states or societies, in wrath or revenge each against other.

Secondly, a just and righteous taking of the sword in punishing offenders against the civil peace, either more personal, private, and ordinary; or more public, oppressors, tyrants, ships, navies, etc. Neither of these can it be imagined that Christ Jesus intended to Peter.

Thirdly, there is therefore a third taking of the sword, forbidden to Peter, that is, for Christ and the gospel's cause when Christ is in danger: which made Peter strike, etc.

Peace. It seems to some most contrary to all true reason that Christ Jesus, innocency itself, should not be defended.

Truth. The foolishness of God is wiser than the wisdom of man.

It is not the purpose of God that the spiritual battles of his Son shall be fought by carnal weapons and persons.

It is not his pleasure that the world shall flame on fire with civil combustions for his Son's sake. It is directly contrary to the nature of Christ Jesus, his saints and truths, that throats of' men, which is the highest contrariety to civil converse, should be torn out for his sake who most delighted to converse with the greatest sinners.

It is the counsel of God that his servants shall overcome by three weapons of a spiritual nature (Rev. 12:11); and that all that take the sword of steel shall perish.

Lastly, it is the counsel of God that Christ Jesus shall shortly appear a most glorious judge and revenger against all his enemies, when the heavens and the earth shall flee before his most glorious presence.

Peace. I shall propose the last scripture much insisted on by many for carnal weapons in spiritual cases, Revelation 17:16, *The ten horns which thou sawest upon the beast, these shall hate the whore, and shall make her desolate and naked, and shall eat her flesh, and shall burn her with fire.*

Truth. Not to controvert with some, whether or no the beast be yet risen and extant:—

Nor secondly, whether either the beast, or the horns, or the whore, may be taken literally for any corporal beast or whore:—

Or thirdly, whether these ten horns be punctually and exactly ten kings:—

Or fourthly, whether those ten horns signify those many kings, kingdoms, and governments, who have bowed down to the pope's yoke, and have committed fornication with that great whore, the church of Rome:

Let this last be admitted, (which yet will cost some work to clear against all opposites): yet,

First, can the time be now clearly demonstrated to be come? etc.

Secondly, how will it be proved, that this hatred of this whore shall be a true, chaste, Christian hatred against anti-Christian, whorish practices? etc.

Thirdly, or rather that this hating, and desolating, and, making naked, and burning shall arise, not by way of an ordinance warranted by the institution of Christ Jesus, but by way of providence, when, as it used to be with all whores and their lovers, the church of Rome and her great lovers shall fall out, and by the righteous vengeance of God upon her, drunk with the blood of saints or holy ones, these mighty fornicators shall turn their love into hatred, which hatred shall make her a poor, desolate, naked whore, torn and consumed, etc.

Peace. You know it is a great controversy how the kings of the earth shall thus deal with the whore in the seventeenth chapter, and yet so bewail her in the eighteenth chapter.

Truth. If we take it that these kings of the earth shall first hate, and plunder, and tear, and burn this whore, and yet afterward shall relent and bewail their cruel dealing toward her: or else, that as some kings deal so terribly with her, yet others of those kings shall bewail her: if either of these two answers stand, or a better be given, yet none of them can prove it lawful for people to give power to their kings and magistrates thus to deal with them, their subjects, for their conscience; nor for magistrates to assume a title more than the people betrust them with; nor for one people out of conscience to God, and for Christ's sake, thus to kill and slaughter and burn each other. However, it may please the righteous judge, according to the famous types of Gideon's and Jehosaphat's battles, to permit in justice, and to order in wisdom, these mighty and mutual slaughters each of other.

Peace. We have now, dear Truth, through the gracious hand of God, clambered up to the top of this our tedious discourse.

Truth. Oh! it is mercy inexpressible that either you or I have had so long a breathing time, and that together!

Peace. If English ground must be drunk with English blood, oh! where shall Peace repose her wearied head and heavy heart?

Truth. Dear Peace, if you find welcome, and the God of peace miraculously please to squelch these all-devouring flames, yet where shall Truth find rest from cruel persecutions?

Peace. Oh! will not the authority of holy scriptures, the commands and declarations of the Son of God, therein produced by you, together with all the lamentable experiences of former and present slaughters, prevail with the sons of men, especially with the sons of peace, to depart from the dens of lions, and mountains of leopards,[131] and to put on the bowels, if not of Christianity, yet of humanity each to other?

Truth. Dear Peace, Habakkuk's fishes[132] keep their constant bloody game of persecutions in the world's mighty ocean; the greater taking, plundering, swallowing up the lesser. Oh! happy he whose portion is the God of Jacob, who has nothing to lose under the sun; but has a state, a house, an inheritance, a name, a crown, a life, past all the plunderers', ravishers', murderers' reach and fury!

Peace. But lo! Who's there?

Truth. Our sister Patience, whose desired company is as needful as delightful. 'Tis like the wolf will send the scattered sheep in one: the common pirate gather up the loose and scattered navy: the slaughter of the witnesses by that bloody beast unite the Independents and Presbyterians.

The God of peace, the God of truth, will shortly seal this truth, and confirm this witness, and make it evident to the whole world, that the doctrine of persecution for cause of conscience, is most evidently and lamentably contrary to the doctrine of Jesus Christ, the Prince of Peace. Amen.

FINIS.

[131] Canticles 4:8.
[132] Habakkuk 1:13-14.

Appendix

A Table

of the Principal

Contents of the Book

A Reply to the Aforesaid Answers of Mr. Cotton

Truth and Peace, their rare and seldom meeting
Two great complaints of Peace
Persecutors seldom plead Christ but Moses for their author
Strife, Christian and unchristian
A three-fold doleful cry
The wonderful providence of God in the writing of the arguments against
    persecution
A definition of persecution discussed
Conscience will not be restrained from its own worship, nor constrained to
    another
A chaste soul in God's worship compared to a chaste wife
God's people have erred from the very fundamentals of visible worship
Four sorts of spiritual foundations in the New Testament
The six fundamentals of the Christian religion
The coming out of Babel not local, but mystical
The great ignorance of God's people concerning the nature of a true church
Common prayer written against by the New English ministers
God's people have worshiped God in false worships
God is pleased sometimes to convey good unto his people beyond a promise
A notable speech of King James to a great nonconformist turned persecutor
Civil peace discussed
The difference between spiritual and civil state
Six cases wherein God's people have been usually accounted arrogant, and peace
    breakers, but most unjustly
The true causes of breach and disturbance of civil peace
A preposterous way of suppressing errors
Persecutors must needs oppress both erroneous and true consciences

All persecutors of Christ profess not to persecute him
What is meant by the heretic (Titus 3)
The word *heretic* generally mistaken
Corporal killing in the law, typing out spiritual killing in the gospel
The carriage of a soul sensible of mercy towards others in their blindness, etc.
The difference between the church and the world, wherein it is, in all places
The church and civil state confusedly made all one
The most peaceable accused for peace breaking
A large examination of what is meant by the tares, and letting of them alone
Satan's subtlety about the opening of scriptures
Two sorts of hypocrites
The Lord Jesus the great teacher of parables, and the only expounder of them
Preaching for conversion is properly out of the church
The tares proved properly to signify anti-Christians
God's kingdom on earth the visible church
The difference between the wheat and the tares, as also between these tares and
      all others
A civil magistry from the beginning of the world
The tares are to be tolerated the longest of all sinners
The danger of infection by permitting of the tares, assailed
The civil magistrate not so particularly spoken to in the New Testament as
      fathers, mothers, etc., and why
A two-fold state of Christianity: persecuted under the Roman emperors, and
      apostated under the Roman popes
Three particulars contained in that prohibition of Christ Jesus concerning the
      tares, *Let them*
alone, Matthew 13
Accompanying with idolaters, I Corinthians 5 discussed
Civil magistrates never invested by Christ Jesus with the power and title of
      defenders of the faith
God's people (Israel) ever earnest with God for an arm of flesh
The dreadful punishment of the blind Pharisees in four respects
The point of seducing, infecting, or soul-killing, examined
Strange confusions in punishments
The blood of souls (Acts 20) lies upon such as profess the ministry: the blood of
      bodies only upon the state
Usurpers and true heirs of Christ Jesus
The civil magistrate bound to preserve the bodies of their subjects, and not to
      destroy them for conscience's sake
The fire from heaven (Revelation 13:13, II Timothy 2:25-26), examined
The original of the Christian name, Acts 11
A civil sword in religion makes a nation of hypocrites, Isaiah 10

A difference of the true and false Christ and Christians
The nature of the worship of unbelieving and natural persons
Antoninus Pius' famous act concerning religion
Isaiah 2:4, Micah 4:3, concerning Christ's visible kingdom, discussed
Acts 20:29, the suppressing of spiritual wolves, discussed
It is in vain to decline the name of the head of the church, and yet to practice the
     headship
Titus 1:9-10 discussed
Unmerciful and bloody doctrine
The spiritual weapons (II Corinthians 10:4), discussed
Civil weapons most improper in spiritual causes
The spiritual artillery (Ephesians 6), applied
Romans 13, concerning civil rulers' power in spiritual causes, largely examined
Paul's appeal to Caesar examined
And cleared by five arguments
Four sorts of swords
What it to be understood by *evil*, Romans 13:4
Though evil be always evil, yet the permission of it may sometimes be good
Two sorts of commands, both from Moses and Christ
The permission of divorce in Israel (Matthew 19:17-18)
Usury in the civil state lawfully permitted
Seducing teachers, either pagans, Jewish, Turkish, or anti-Christian, may yet be
     obedient
subjects to the civil laws
Scandalous livers against the civil state
Toleration of Jezebel and Balaam (Revelation 2:14,20), examined
The Christian world has swallowed up Christianity
Christ Jesus, the deepest politician that ever was, yet commands he a toleration
     of anti-Christians
The princes of the world seldom take part with Christ Jesus
Buchanan's item to King James
King James' sayings against persecution
Forcing of conscience a soul-rape
Persecution for conscience has been the lancet which has let blood the nations.
     All spiritual whores are bloody.
Polygamy, or the many wives of the fathers
David advancing of God's worship against order
Constantine and the good emperors confessed to have done more hurt to the
     name and crown of
Christ than the bloody Neros did
The language of persecution

Christ's lilies may flourish in the church, notwithstanding the weeds in the world
    permitted
Queen Elizabeth and King James, their persecuting for cause of religion
    examined
Queen Elizabeth confessed by John Cotton to have almost fired the world in civil
    combustions
The wars between the papists and the Protestants
The wars and success of the Waldensians against three popes
God's people victorious overcomers, and with what weapons
The Christian church does not persecute, but is persecuted
The nature of excommunication
The opinion of ancient writers examined concerning the doctrine of persecution
Constraint upon conscience in Old and New England
The Indians of New England permitted in their worship of devils
In two cases a false religion will not hurt
The absolute sufficiency of the sword of the Spirit
A national church not instituted by Christ
Man has no power to make laws to bind conscience
Hearing of the word in a church estate a part of God's worship
Papists' plea for toleration of conscience
Protestant partiality in the cause of conscience
Pills to purge out the bitter humor of persecution
Superstition and persecution have had many votes and suffrages from God's own
    people
Soul-killing discussed
Phineas' act discussed
Elijah's slaughters discussed
Dangerous consequences flowing from the civil magistrate's power in spiritual
    cases
The world turned upside down
The wonderful answer of the ministers of New England to the ministers of Old
Lamentable differences even among them that fear God
The doctrine of persecution ever drives the most godly out of the world
A MODEL OF CHURCH AND CIVIL POWER, composed by Mr. Cotton and
    the ministers of New England, and sent to Salem, (as a further
    confirmation of the bloody doctrine of persecution for cause of conscience)
    examined and answered
Christ's power in the church confessed to be above all magistrates in spiritual
    things
Isaiah 49:23 lamentably twisted
The civil commonweal and the spiritual commonweal, the church, not
    inconsistent, though independent the one on the other

Christ's ordinances put upon a whole city or nation may civilize them, and
moralize, but not Christianize, before repentance first wrought
Mr. Cotton and the New English ministers' confession that the magistrate has
neither civil nor spiritual power in soul matters
The magistrate and the church (by Mr. Cotton's grounds) in one and the same
cause, made the judges on the bench and delinquents at the bar
A demonstrative illustration that the magistrate cannot have power over the
church in spiritual or
church causes
The true way of the God of peace, in differences between the church and the
magistrate
The terms *godliness* and *honesty* explained (I Timothy 2:1), and *honesty* proved
not to signify in that place the righteousness of the second table
The forcing of men to God's worship, the greatest breach of civil peace
The Roman Caesars of Christ's time described
It pleased not the Lord Jesus, in the institution of the Christian church, to
appoint and raise up any civil government to take care of his worship
The true *custodes utriusque tabulae*, and keepers of the ordinances and worship
of Jesus Christ
The kings of Egypt, Moab, Philistia, Assyria, Nineveh, were not charged with the
worship of God, as the kings of Judah were
Masters of families not charged under the gospel to force all the consciences of
their families to worship
God's people have then shined brightest in godliness when they have enjoyed
least quietness
Few magistrates, few men, spiritually good; yet divers sorts of commendable
goodness beside spiritual
Civil power originally and fundamentally in the people. Mr. Cotton and the New
English give
the power of Christ into the hands of the commonweal
Laws concerning religion of two sorts
The very Indians abhor to disturb any conscience at worship
Canons and constitutions pretended civil, but indeed ecclesiastical
A three-fold guilt lying upon civil powers, commanding the subject's soul in
worship
Persons may with less sin be forced to marry whom they cannot love, than to
worship where they cannot believe
As the cause, so the weapons of the beast and the lamb are infinitely different
Artaxerxes his decree examined
The sum of the examples of the Gentile king's decrees concerning God's worship
in scripture

The doctrine of putting to death blasphemers of Christ cuts off the hopes of the Jews partaking in
his blood

The direful effects of fighting for conscience

Error is confident as well as truth

Spiritual prisons

Some consciences not so easily healed and cured as men imagine

Persecutors dispute with heretics as a tyrannical cat with a poor mouse, and with a true witness as a
roaring lion with an innocent lamb in his paw

Persecutors endure not the name of persecutors

Psalm 101, concerning cutting of the wicked, examined

No difference of lands and countries, since Christ Jesus his coming

The New English separate in America, but not in Europe

Christ Jesus forbidding his followers to permit leaven in the church, does not forbid to permit leaven in the world

The wall (Canticles 8:9) discussed

Every religion commands its professors to hear only its own priests and ministers

Jonah his preaching to the Ninevites discussed

Hearing of the word discussed

Eglon his rising up to Ehud's message, discussed

A two-fold ministry of Christ: first, apostolic, properly converting; secondly, feeding or pastoral

The New English forcing people to church, and yet not to religion (as they say), forcing them to be
of no religion all their days

The civil state can no more lawfully compel the conscience of men to church to hear the word, than to receive the sacraments

No precedent in the word of any people converting and baptizing themselves

True conversion to visible Christianity is not only from sins against the second table, but from
false worships also

The commission (Matthew 28), discussed

The civil magistrate not betrusted with that commission

Jehosphat (II Chronicles 17), a figure of Christ Jesus in his church, not of the civil magistrate in the state

The maintenance of the ministry (Galatians 6:6), examined

Christ Jesus never appointed a maintenance of the ministry from impenitent and unbelieving

They that compel men to hear, compel them also to pay for their hearing and conversion

Luke 14, *Compel them to come in,* examined

Natural men can neither truly worship, nor maintain it

The national church of the Jews might well be forced to a settled maintenance, but not so the Christian church

The maintenance which Christ has appointed his ministry in the church

The universities of Europe causes of universal sins and plagues; yet school are honorable for tongues and arts

The true church is Christ's school, and believers his scholars

Mr. Ainsworth excellent in the tongues, yet no university man

King Henry VIII set down in the pope's chair in England

Apocrypha, homilies, and common prayer, precious to our forefathers

Reformation proved fallible

The precedent of the kings of Israel and Judah largely examined

The Persian kings' example make strongly against the doctrine of persecution

1. The difference of the land of Canaan from all lands and countries in seven particulars

2. The difference of the people of Israel from all other peoples in seven particulars

Wonderful turnings of religion in England in twelve years revolution

The pope not unlike to recover his monarchy over Europe before his downfall

Israel, God's only church, might well renew that national covenant and ceremonial worship, which other nations cannot do

The difference of the kings and governors of Israel from all kings and governors of the world, in four particulars

Five demonstrative arguments proving the unsoundness of the maxim, viz., the church and commonweal are like Hippocrates' twins

A sacrilegious prostitution of the name Christian

David immediately inspired by God in his ordering of church affairs

Solomon's deposing Abiathar (I Kings 2:26-27), discussed

The liberties of Christ's churches in the choice of her officers

A civil influence dangerous to the saints' liberties

Jehoshaphat's fast examined

Magistracy in general from God, the particular forms from the people

Israel confirmed in a national covenant by revelations, signs, and miracles; but not so any other land

Kings and nations often plant and often pluck up religions

A national church ever subject to turn and return

A woman, Papissa, or head of the church

The papists nearer to the truth, concerning the governor of the church, than most Protestants

The kingly power of the Lord Jesus troubles all the kings and rulers of the world

A two-fold exaltation of Christ

A monarchical and ministerial power of Christ

Three great competitors for the ministerial power of Christ

The pope pretends to the ministerial power of Christ, yet upon the point challenges the
monarchical also

Three great factions in England, striving for the arm of flesh

The churches of the separation ought in humanity and subjects' liberty not to be
oppressed, but at least permitted

Seven reasons proving that the kings of Israel and Judah can have no other but a spiritual
antitype

Christianity adds not to the nature of a civil commonweal, nor does want of Christianity diminish it

Most strange, yet most true consequences from the civil magistrates being the antitype of the kings of Israel and Judah

If no religion but what the commonweal approve, then no Christ, no God, but at the pleasure of the world

The true antitype of the kings of Israel and Judah

4. The difference of Israel's statutes and laws from all others in three particulars

5. The difference of Israel's punishments and rewards from all others

Temporal prosperity most proper to the national state of the Jew

The excommunication in Israel

The corporal stoning in the law, typed out spiritual stoning in the gospel

The rewards of Israel typical and unparalleled but by the spiritual wars of spiritual Israel

The famous typical captivity of the Jews

Their wonderful victories

The mystical army of white troopers

Whether the civil state of Israel was precedential

Great unfaithfulness in magistrates to cast out the burden of judging and establishing Christianity upon the commonweal

Thousands of lawful civil magistrates, who never hear of Jesus Christ

Nero and persecuting emperors not so injurious to Christianity as Constantine and others, who assumed a power in spiritual things

They who force the conscience of others, cry out of persecution when their own are forced

Constantine and others wanted not so much affection as information of judgment

Civil authority giving and lending their horns to bishops, dangerous to Christ's truth

The spiritual power of Christ Jesus compared in scripture to the incomparable horn of the rhinoceros

The nursing fathers and mothers (Isaiah 49)
The civil magistrate owes three things to the true church of Christ
The civil magistrate owes two things to false worshipers
The rise of high commissions
Pious magistrates' and ministers' consciences are persuaded for that which other
    as pious magistrates' and ministers' consciences condemn
An apt similitude discussed concerning the civil magistrate
A grievous charge against the Christian church and the king of it
A strange law in New England formerly against excommunicate persons
A dangerous doctrine against all civil magistrates
Original sin charged to hurt the civil state
They who give the magistrate more than his due are apt to disrobe him of what is
    his
A strange double picture
The great privileges of the true church of Christ
Two similitudes illustrating the true power of the magistrate
A marvelous challenge of more power under the Christian than under the
    heathen magistrate
Civil magistrates, derivatives from the fountains or bodies of people
A believing magistrate no more a magistrate than an unbelieving
The excellency of Christianity in all callings
The magistrate like a pilot in the ship of the commonweal
The terms *heathen* and *Christian* magistrate
The unjust and partial liberty to some consciences, and bondage unto all others
The commission (Matthew 28:19-20), not proper to pastors and teachers, least of
    all to the civil magistrates
Unto whom now belongs the care of all the churches, etc
Acts 15 commonly misapplied
The promise of Christ's presence (Matthew 18), distinct from that Matthew 28
Church administration firstly charged upon the minsters thereof
Queen Elizabeth's bishops truer to their principles than many of a better spirit
    and profession
Mr. Barrowe's profession concerning Queen Elizabeth
The inventions of men swerving from the true essentials of civil and spiritual
    commonweals
A great question, viz., whether only church members, that is, godly persons, in a
    particular church state be only eligible into the magistracy
The world being divided into thirty parts, twenty-five never heard of Christ
Lawful civil states where churches of Christ are not
Few Christians wise and noble, and qualified for affairs of state

Index of Names

Index of Scriptures

4:25 198
5 126, 127, 151, 177, 223
5:9 121
6:6 181, 185
6:16 203, 222, 224

Ephesians
2 153
2:20 34, 94
4 97, 179
4:5 81
5 66
6 66, 96, 224
6:6 158
6:12 223

Philippians
1:29 81
2:13 160
3:17 20, 52
4:18 187

Colossians
2:18 219
2:21-22 158
3 66
3:11 252
4 66
4:17 253

I Thessalonians
1:9 182, 183
2
5:21 9

II Thessalonians
2 64
2:18

I Timothy
1 211
1:4 48
2 138, 149

2:1-2 64, 138, 143, 145, 193
3 258
3:12
3:15 172
4:5 198
4:16 127
5:20 74
6:14 148, 161
6:19 34

II Timothy
2 66, 105, 126
2:24-26 52, 76, 78, 171
3:17 161
4:17 41

Titus
1 211, 258
1:7 185
1:9-11 85, 172
1:16 198
2:7 145
2:14 202
3:1 137
3:10 74, 118, 168
3:11 46

Hebrews
4:8 199
4:12 96, 188
6:12 36
6:16 238
7:12
8 222
10 222
10:25 241
10:28-29 9
11:6 81
11:7 197
11:9-10
12 174, 188
12:22 198, 203
12:27 128
13:17 252, 253